PUNS OF STEEL

Other *Argyle Sweater* Books

The Argyle Sweater: A Cartoon Collection

50% Wool, 50% Asinine

Tastes Like Chicken: An Argyle Sweater Treasury

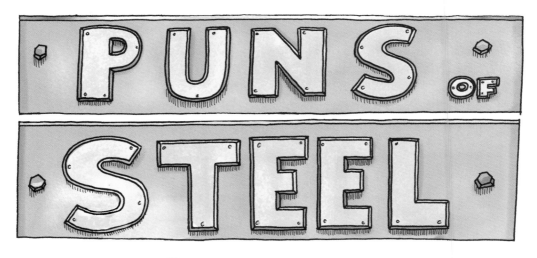

PUNS OF STEEL

An *Argyle Sweater* **Collection by Scott Hilburn**

**Andrews McMeel
Publishing, LLC**
Kansas City • Sydney • London

Andrews McMeel Publishing, LLC
an Andrews McMeel Universal company
1130 Walnut Street, Kansas City, Missouri 64106

www.andrewsmcmeel.com
www.theargylesweater.com

11 12 13 14 15 TEN 10 9 8 7 6 5 4 3 2 1

ISBN: 978-1-4494-0105-4

Library of Congress Control Number: 2010940192

─── **ATTENTION: SCHOOLS AND BUSINESSES** ───

Andrews McMeel books are available at quantity discounts with bulk purchase for educational, business, or sales promotional use. For information, please e-mail the Andrews McMeel Publishing Special Sales Department:
specialsales@amuniversal.com

To Maddie and Emma

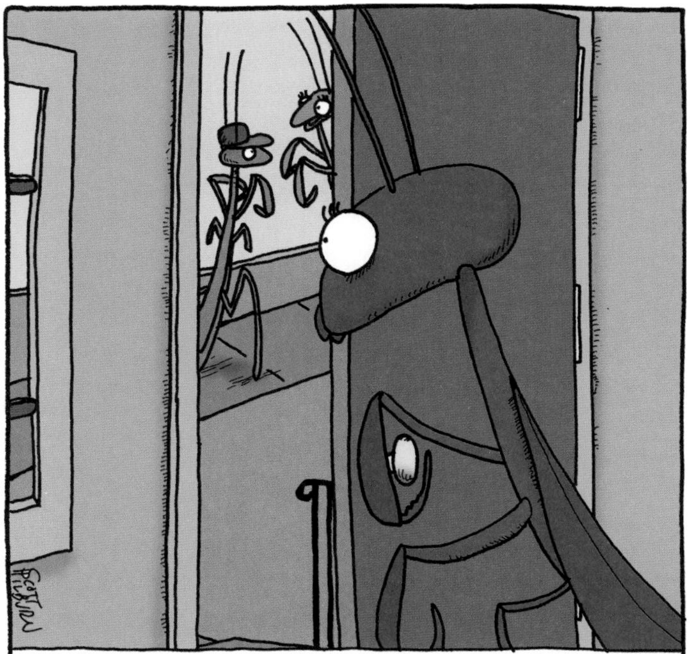
SCOTT HILBURN

BEATRICE WISHED HER HUSBAND WAS AROUND TO HAVE "THE TALK" WITH THEIR MATURING SON. THEN SHE REMEMBERED HIS ABSENCE WAS HER FAULT.

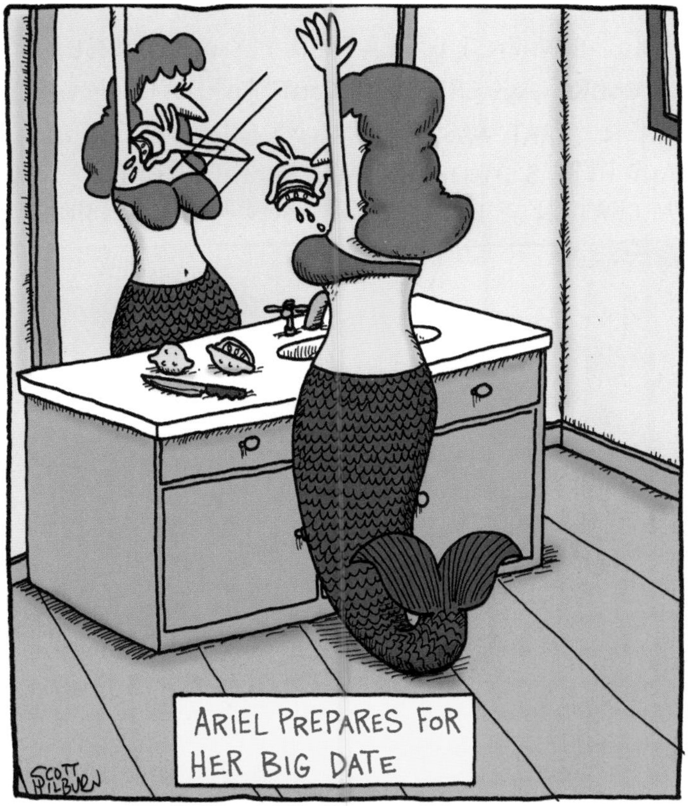
SCOTT HILBURN

ARIEL PREPARES FOR HER BIG DATE

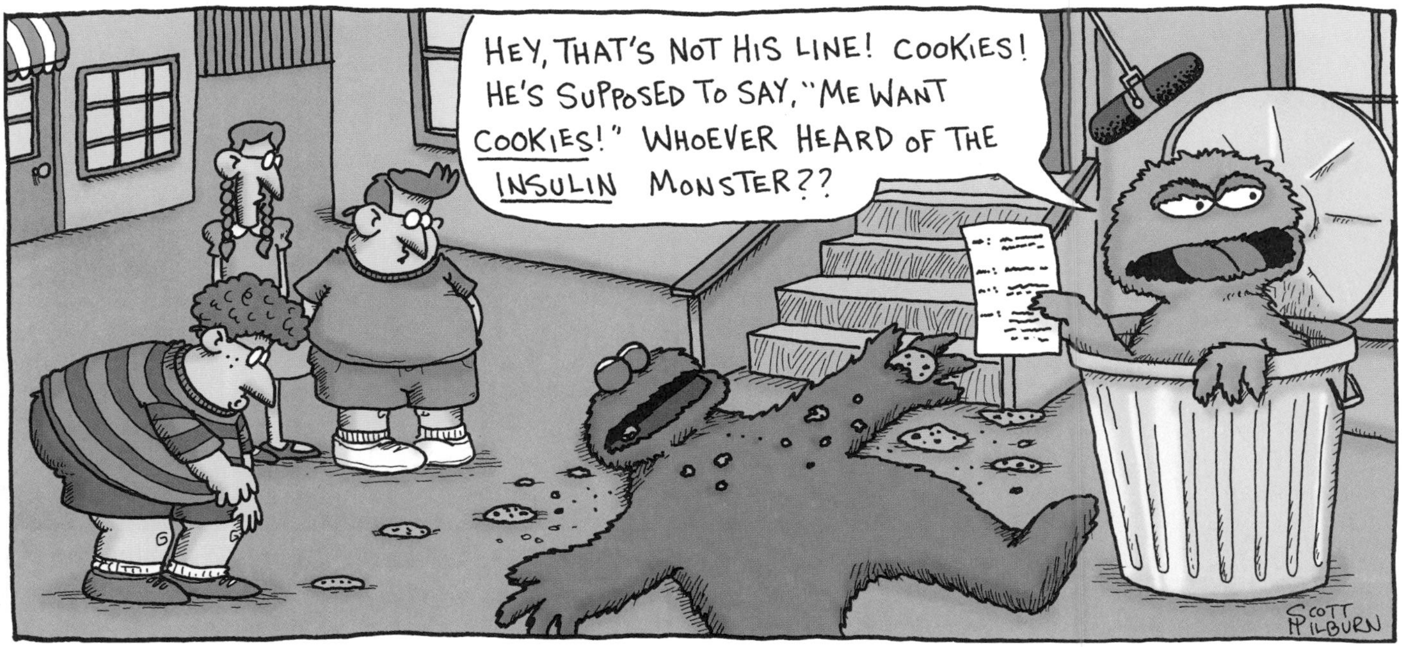
HEY, THAT'S NOT HIS LINE! COOKIES! HE'S SUPPOSED TO SAY, "ME WANT COOKIES!" WHOEVER HEARD OF THE INSULIN MONSTER??
SCOTT HILBURN

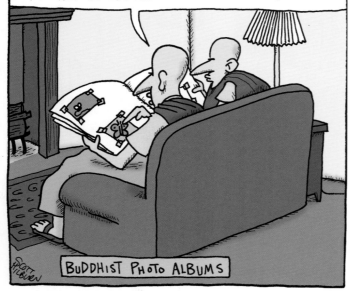

THIS IS WHEN I WAS A FRUIT FLY IN ISTANBUL – OF COURSE, WE CALLED IT CONSTANTINOPLE BACK THEN. THAT WAS, BY FAR, MY SHORTEST LIFE... AND HERE'S ME IN THE MONARCH BUTTERFLY MIGRATION OF 1884... A SPARROW ATE ME, I THINK.
SCOTT HILBURN
BUDDHIST PHOTO ALBUMS

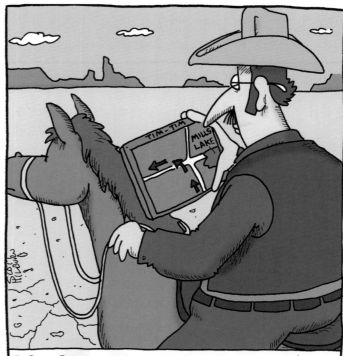

TIM-TIM
MILLS LAKE
SCOTT HILBURN
EZRA'S PURCHASE OF AN OFF-BRAND GPS DEVICE MEANT HE'D NEVER GET THE CHANCE TO MAKE HIS HORSE DRINK.

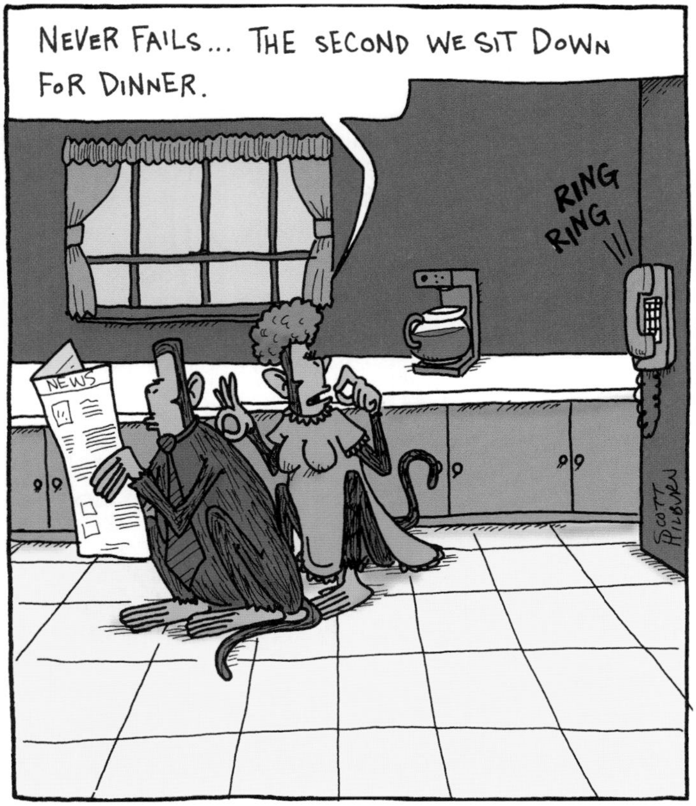
NEVER FAILS... THE SECOND WE SIT DOWN FOR DINNER.
RING RING
NEWS
SCOTT HILBURN

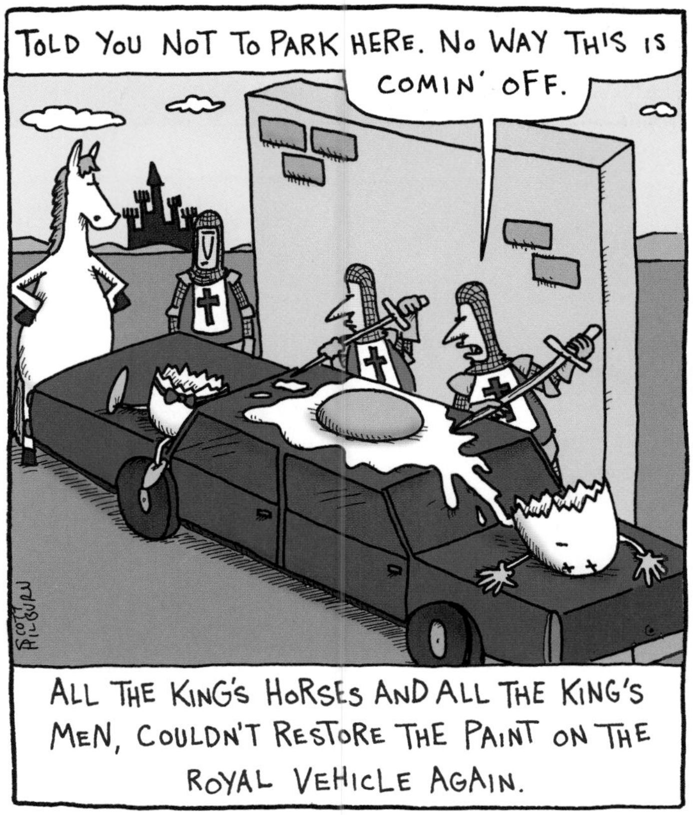
TOLD YOU NOT TO PARK HERE. NO WAY THIS IS COMIN' OFF.
SCOTT HILBURN
ALL THE KING'S HORSES AND ALL THE KING'S MEN, COULDN'T RESTORE THE PAINT ON THE ROYAL VEHICLE AGAIN.

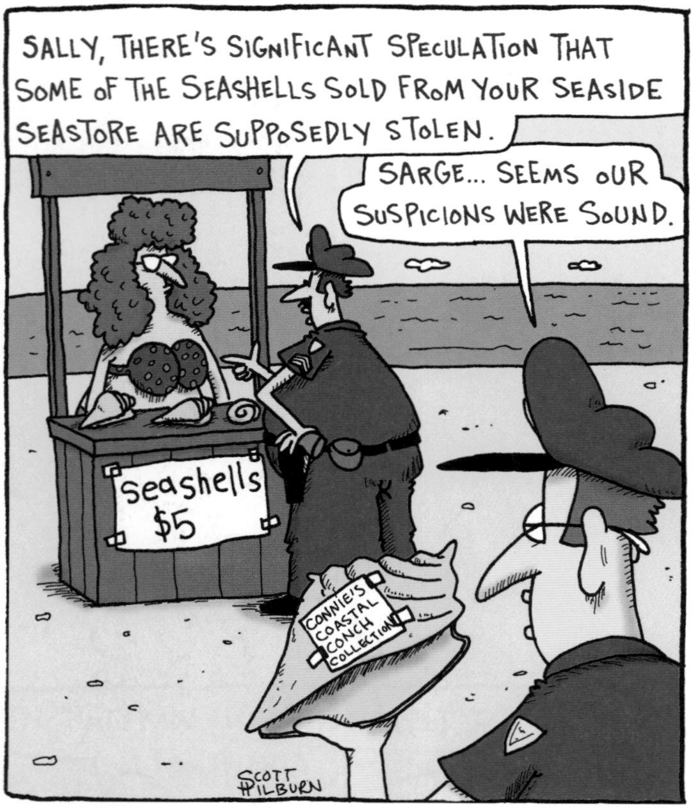
SALLY, THERE'S SIGNIFICANT SPECULATION THAT SOME OF THE SEASHELLS SOLD FROM YOUR SEASIDE SEASTORE ARE SUPPOSEDLY STOLEN.
SARGE... SEEMS OUR SUSPICIONS WERE SOUND.
Seashells $5
CONNIE'S COASTAL CONCH COLLECTION
SCOTT HILBURN

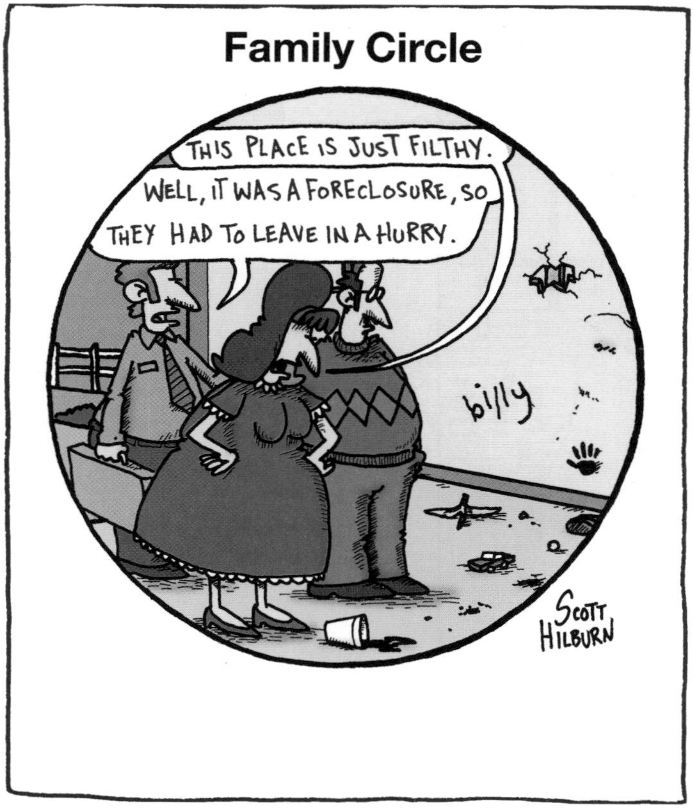
Family Circle
THIS PLACE IS JUST FILTHY.
WELL, IT WAS A FORECLOSURE, SO THEY HAD TO LEAVE IN A HURRY.
billy
SCOTT HILBURN

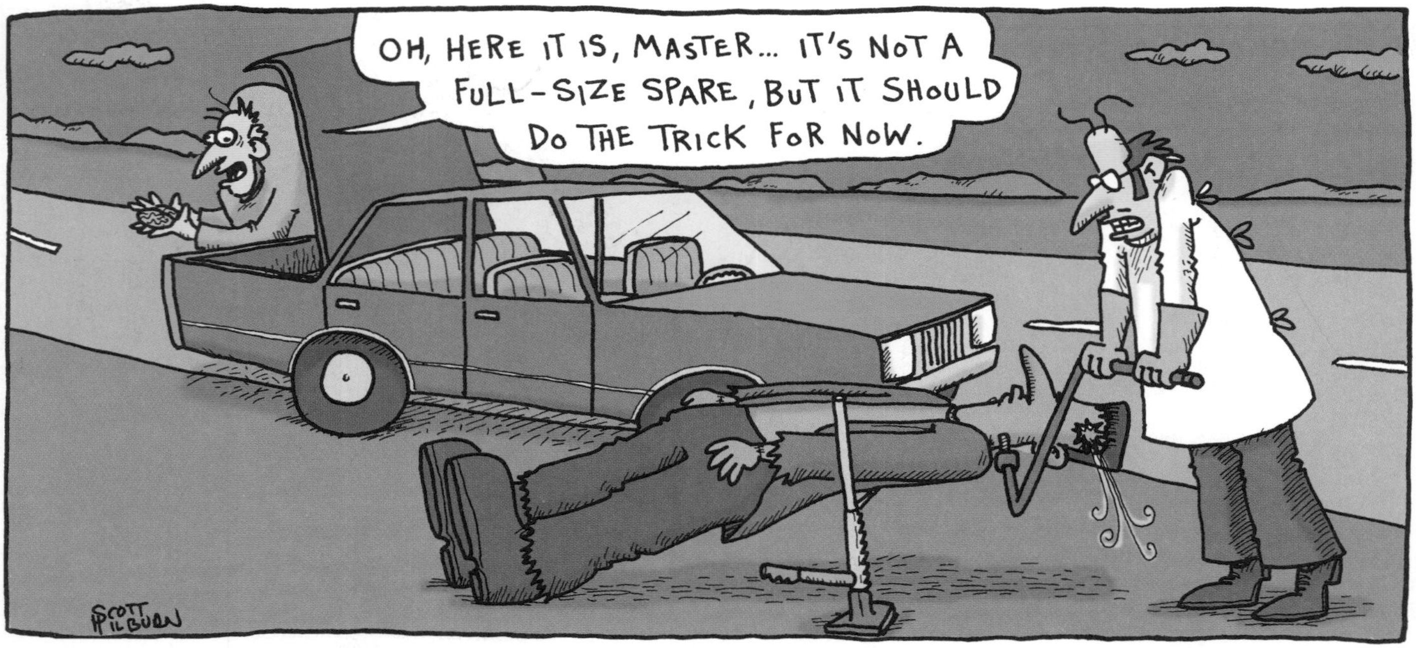
OH, HERE IT IS, MASTER... IT'S NOT A FULL-SIZE SPARE, BUT IT SHOULD DO THE TRICK FOR NOW.
SCOTT HILBURN

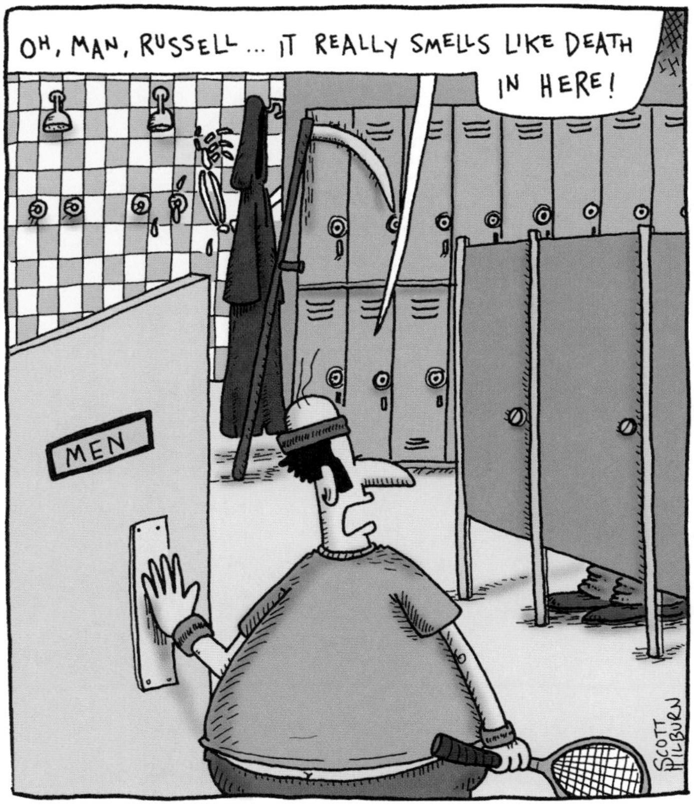
OH, MAN, RUSSELL... IT REALLY SMELLS LIKE DEATH IN HERE!
MEN
SCOTT HILBURN

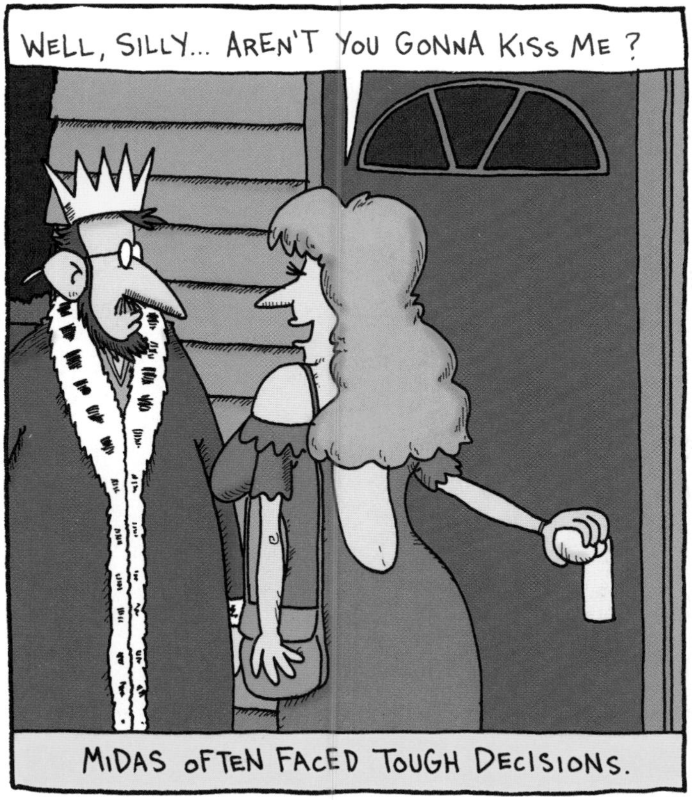
WELL, SILLY... AREN'T YOU GONNA KISS ME?
MIDAS OFTEN FACED TOUGH DECISIONS.

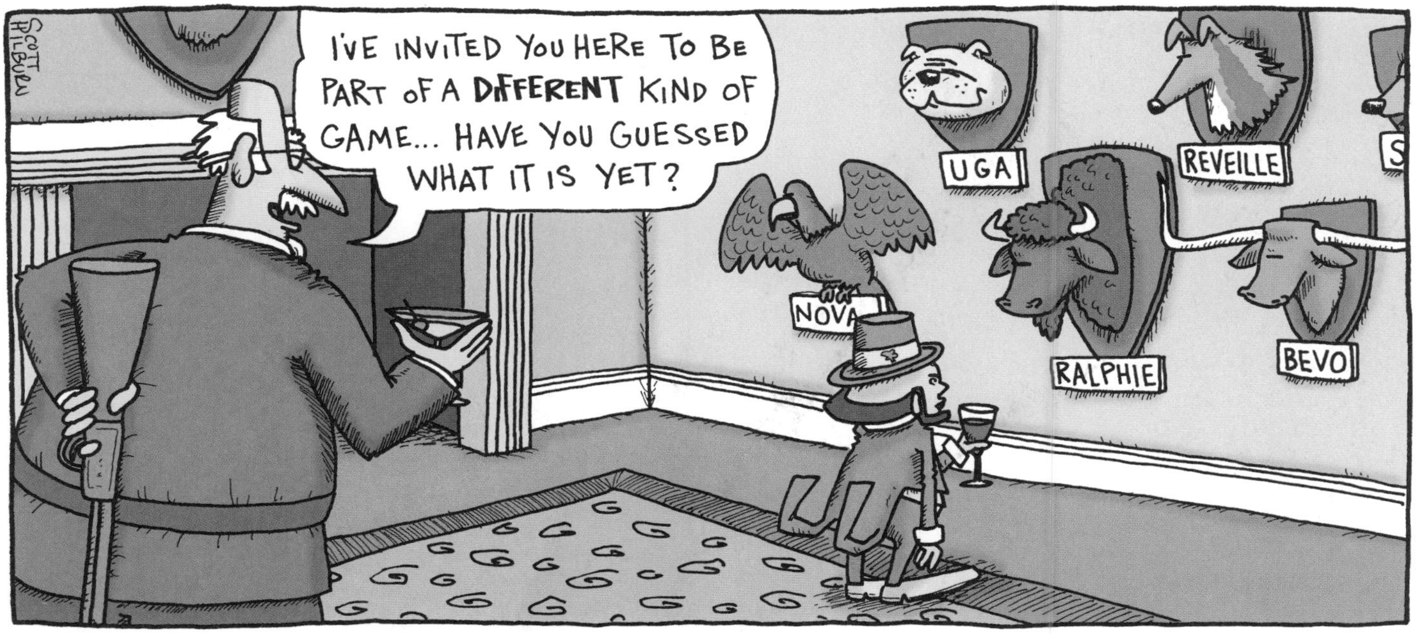
SCOTT HILBURN
I'VE INVITED YOU HERE TO BE PART OF A **DIFFERENT** KIND OF GAME... HAVE YOU GUESSED WHAT IT IS YET?
UGA
REVEILLE
NOVA
RALPHIE
BEVO

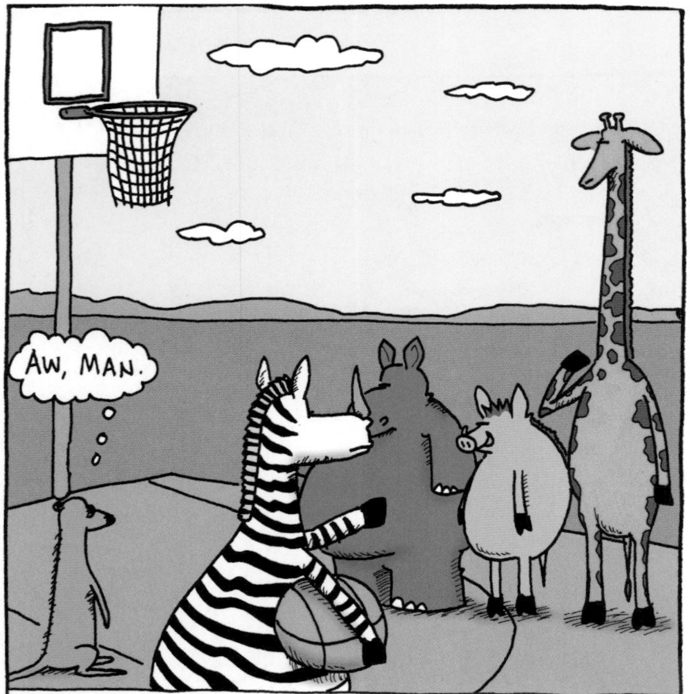
AW, MAN.

TRUTH BE TOLD, STANLEY DIDN'T EVEN LIKE BASKETBALL, DESPITE ALWAYS BEING PICKED FIRST.

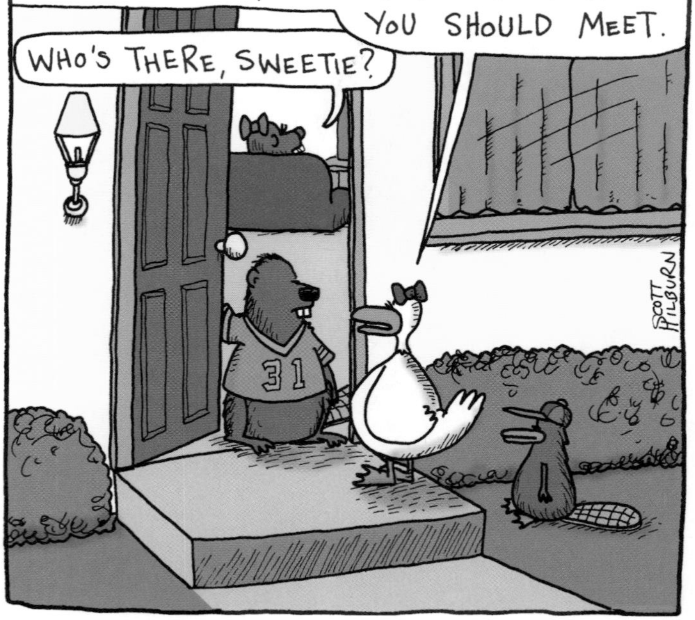
WHO'S THERE, SWEETIE?
31
SCOTT HILBURN

HI, CRAIG. IT'S TANYA. REMEMBER ME? SPRING BREAK?.. CANCUN?.. AND THAT ONE CRAZY, WONDERFUL NIGHT OF UNBRIDLED PASSION? YEAH, WELL THERE'S SOMEONE YOU SHOULD MEET.

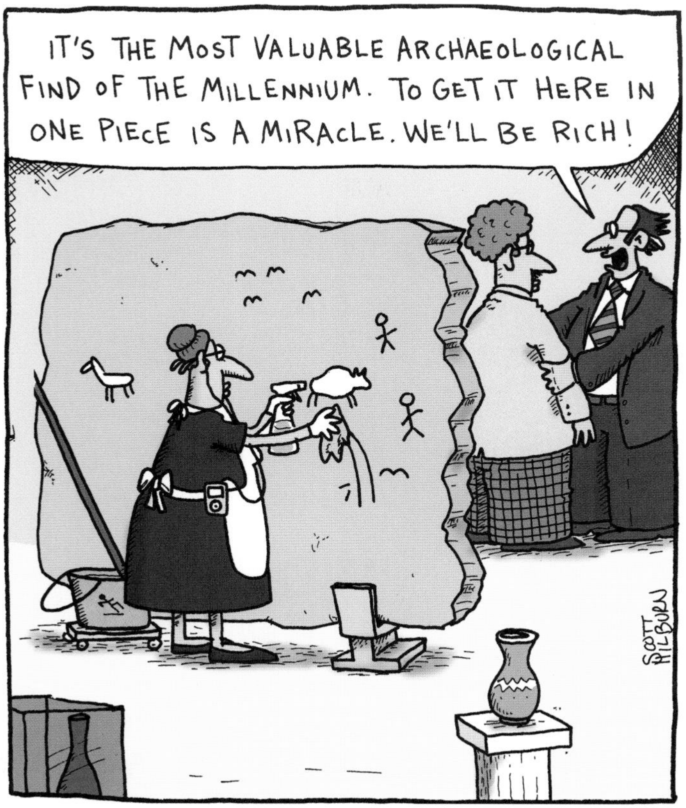
IT'S THE MOST VALUABLE ARCHAEOLOGICAL FIND OF THE MILLENNIUM. TO GET IT HERE IN ONE PIECE IS A MIRACLE. WE'LL BE RICH!
SCOTT HILBURN

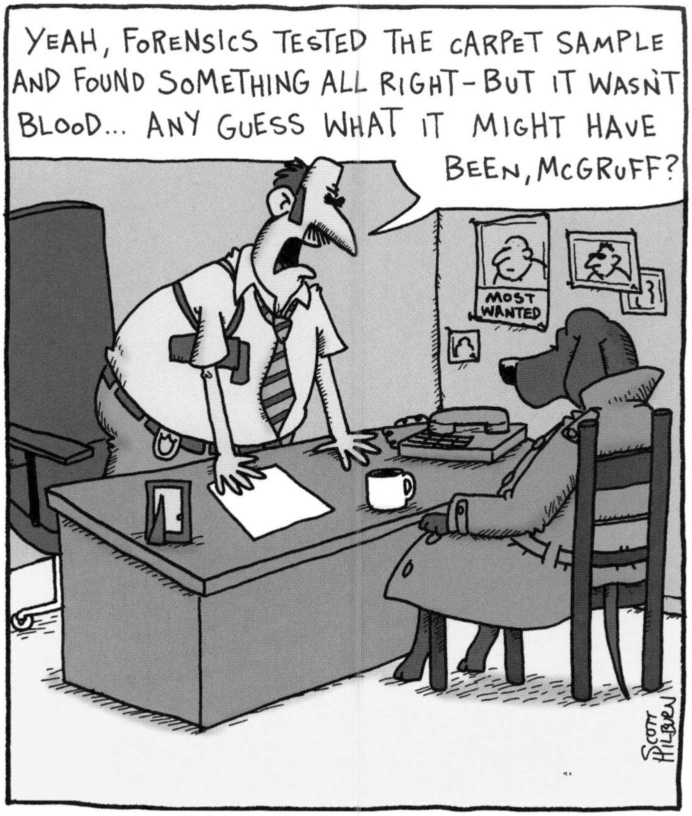
YEAH, FORENSICS TESTED THE CARPET SAMPLE AND FOUND SOMETHING ALL RIGHT – BUT IT WASN'T BLOOD... ANY GUESS WHAT IT MIGHT HAVE BEEN, MCGRUFF?
MOST WANTED
SCOTT HILBURN

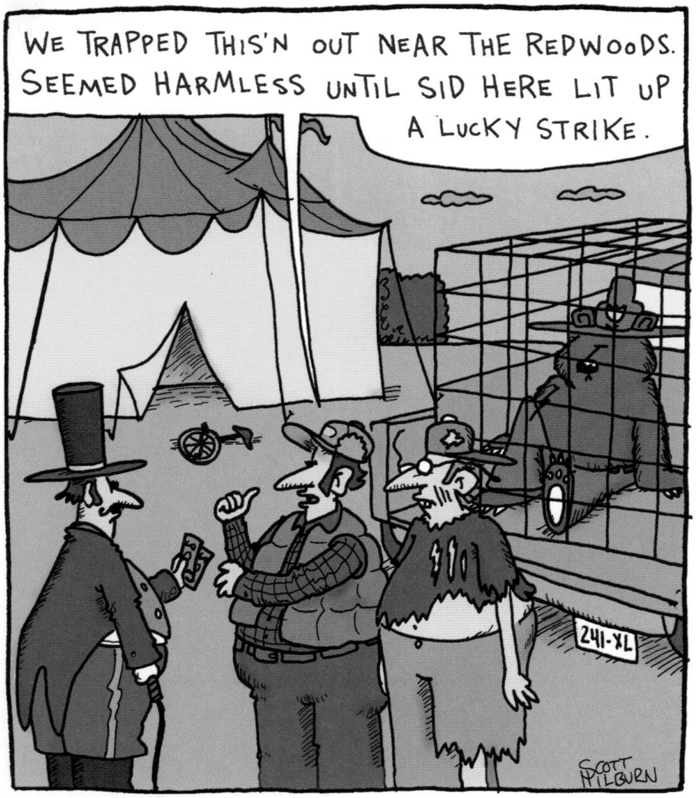
WE TRAPPED THIS'N OUT NEAR THE REDWOODS. SEEMED HARMLESS UNTIL SID HERE LIT UP A LUCKY STRIKE.
241-XL
SCOTT HILBURN

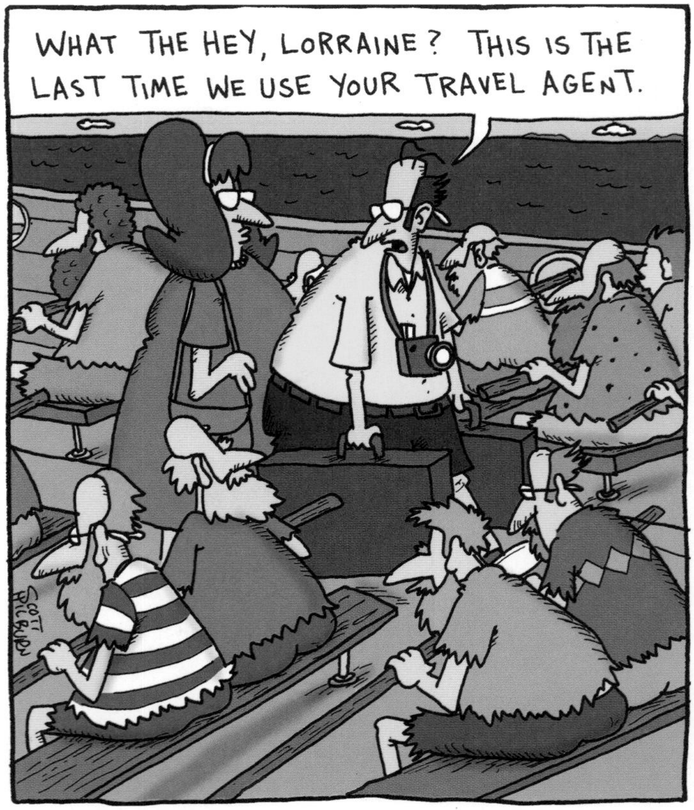
WHAT THE HEY, LORRAINE? THIS IS THE LAST TIME WE USE YOUR TRAVEL AGENT.
SCOTT HILBURN

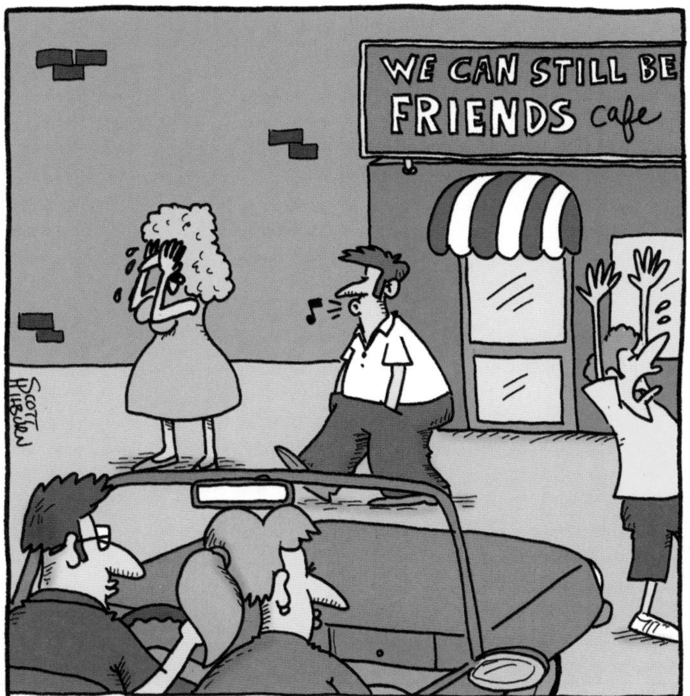
WE CAN STILL BE FRIENDS cafe
SCOTT HILBURN

AMY'S HOPES THAT KYLE MIGHT POP THE QUESTION QUICKLY FADED AS THEY ARRIVED AT THE RESTAURANT.

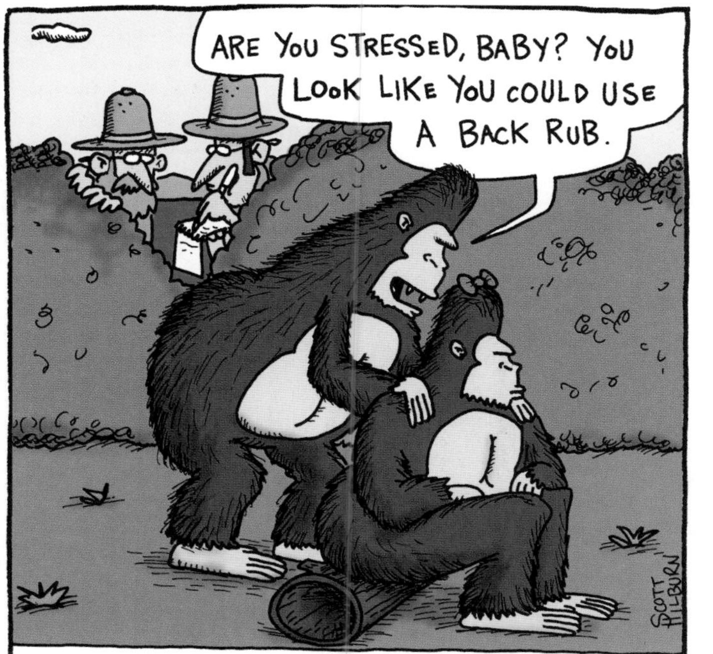
ARE YOU STRESSED, BABY? YOU LOOK LIKE YOU COULD USE A BACK RUB.
SCOTT HILBURN

AFTER MONTHS OF OBSERVATION, JEFFRIES AND CALLAHAN CONCLUDE THAT THE PRIMATES' MATING RITUALS WEREN'T UNLIKE THAT OF HUMANS.

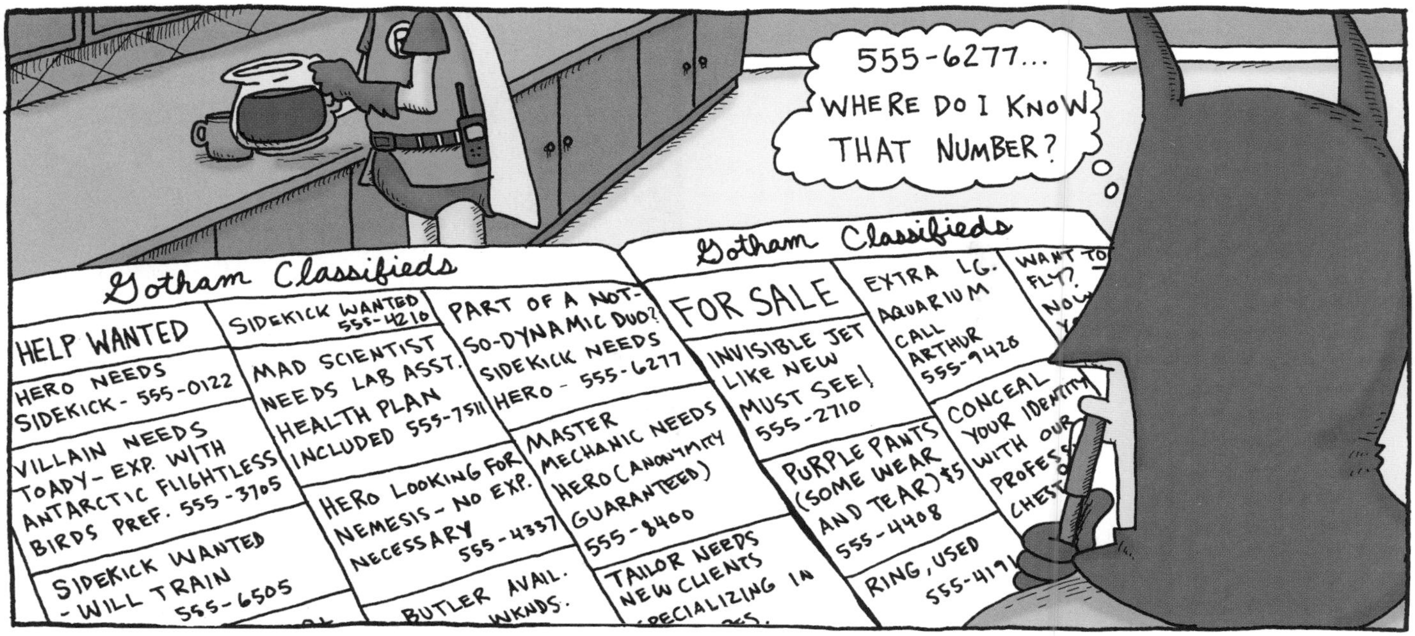
555-6277... WHERE DO I KNOW THAT NUMBER?
Gotham Classifieds
HELP WANTED
HERO NEEDS SIDEKICK - 555-0122
VILLAIN NEEDS TOADY - EXP. WITH ANTARCTIC FLIGHTLESS BIRDS PREF. 555-3705
SIDEKICK WANTED - WILL TRAIN 555-6505
SIDEKICK WANTED 555-4216
MAD SCIENTIST NEEDS LAB ASST. HEALTH PLAN INCLUDED 555-7511
HERO LOOKING FOR NEMESIS - NO EXP. NECESSARY 555-4337
BUTLER AVAIL. WKNDS.
PART OF A NOT-SO-DYNAMIC DUO? SIDEKICK NEEDS HERO - 555-6277
MASTER MECHANIC NEEDS HERO (ANONYMITY GUARANTEED) 555-8400
TAILOR NEEDS NEW CLIENTS SPECIALIZING IN
Gotham Classifieds
FOR SALE
INVISIBLE JET LIKE NEW MUST SEE! 555-2710
PURPLE PANTS (SOME WEAR AND TEAR) $5 555-4408
EXTRA LG. AQUARIUM CALL ARTHUR 555-9428
RING, USED

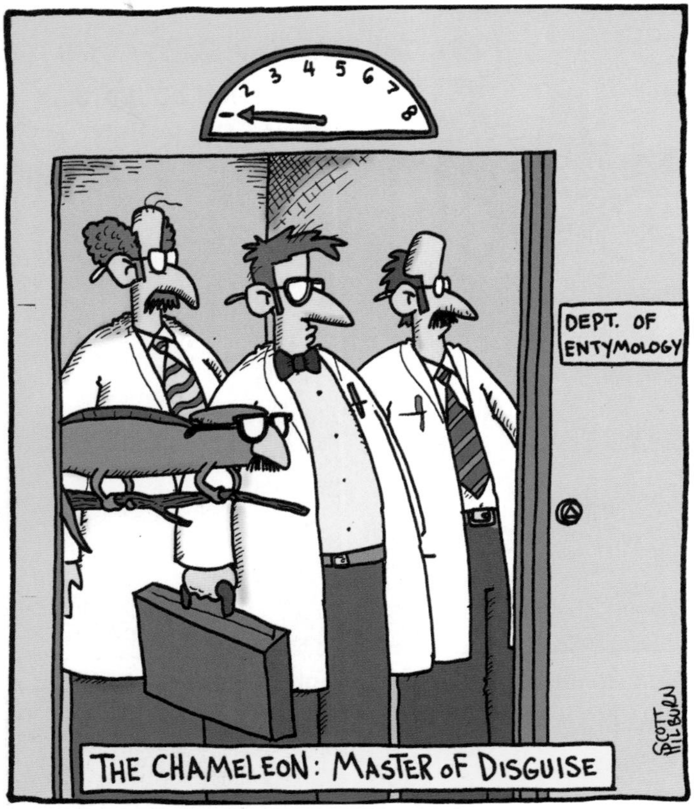
2 3 4 5 6 7 8
DEPT. OF ENTYMOLOGY
SCOTT HILBURN
THE CHAMELEON: MASTER OF DISGUISE

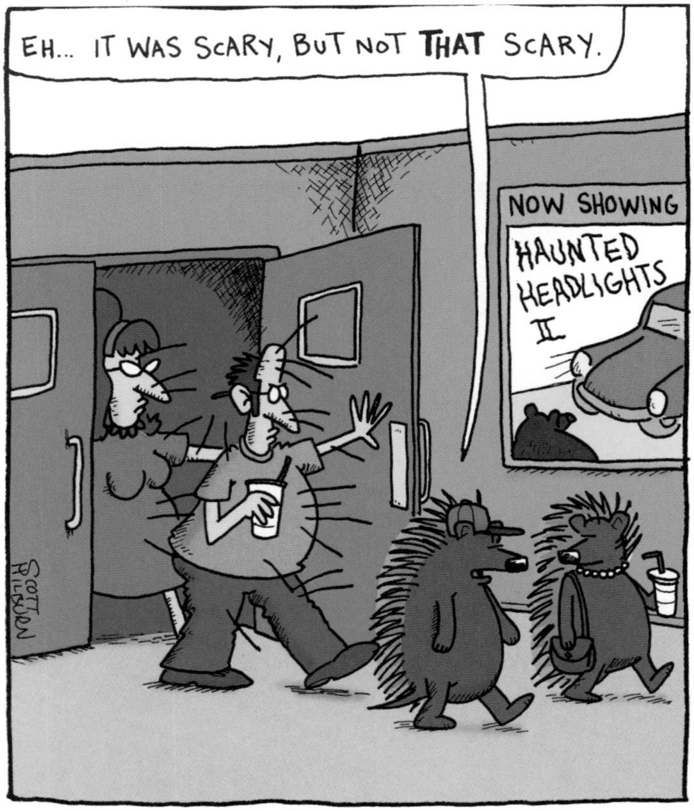
EH... IT WAS SCARY, BUT NOT THAT SCARY.
NOW SHOWING
HAUNTED HEADLIGHTS II
SCOTT HILBURN

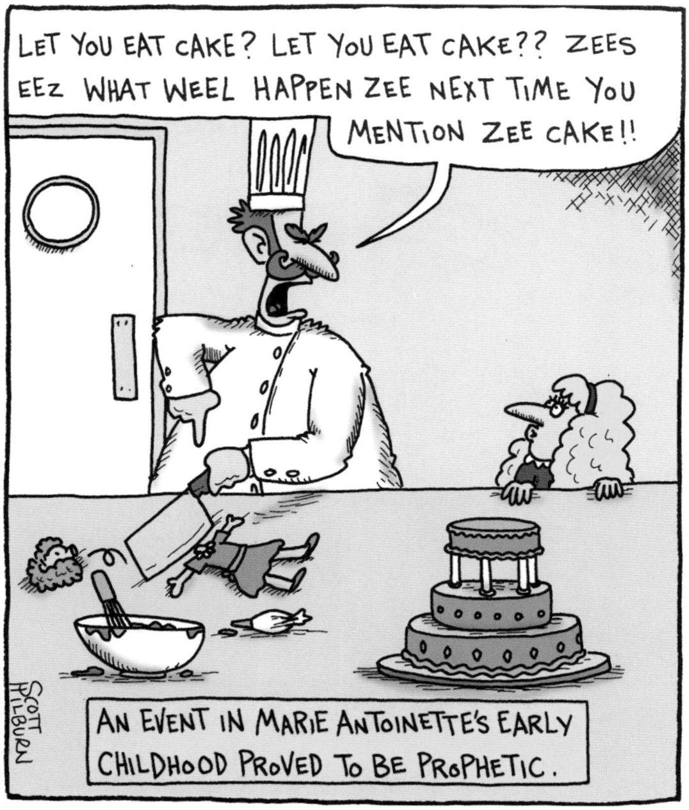
LET YOU EAT CAKE? LET YOU EAT CAKE?? ZEES EEZ WHAT WEEL HAPPEN ZEE NEXT TIME YOU MENTION ZEE CAKE!!
SCOTT HILBURN

AN EVENT IN MARIE ANTOINETTE'S EARLY CHILDHOOD PROVED TO BE PROPHETIC.

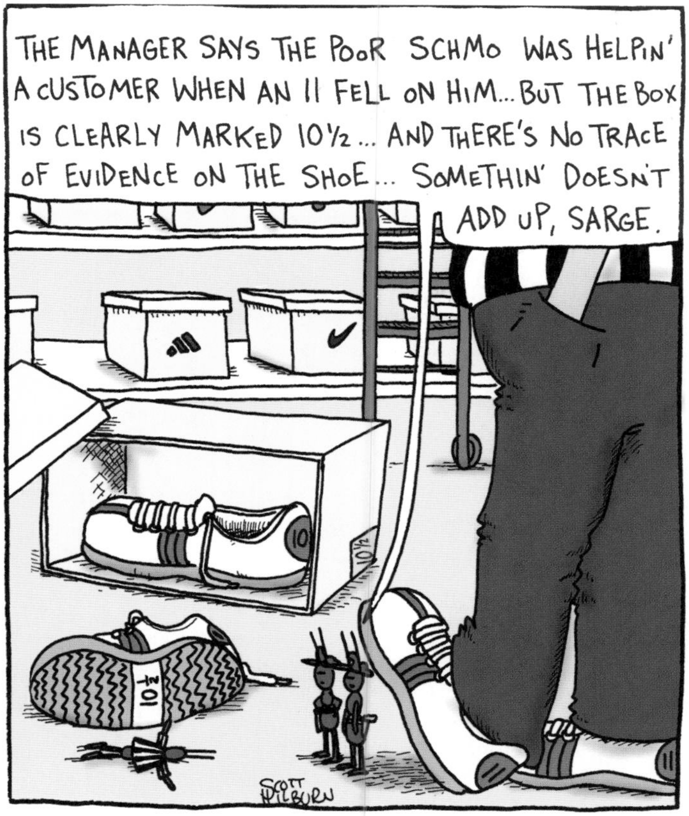
THE MANAGER SAYS THE POOR SCHMO WAS HELPIN' A CUSTOMER WHEN AN 11 FELL ON HIM... BUT THE BOX IS CLEARLY MARKED 10½ ... AND THERE'S NO TRACE OF EVIDENCE ON THE SHOE... SOMETHIN' DOESN'T ADD UP, SARGE.
SCOTT HILBURN

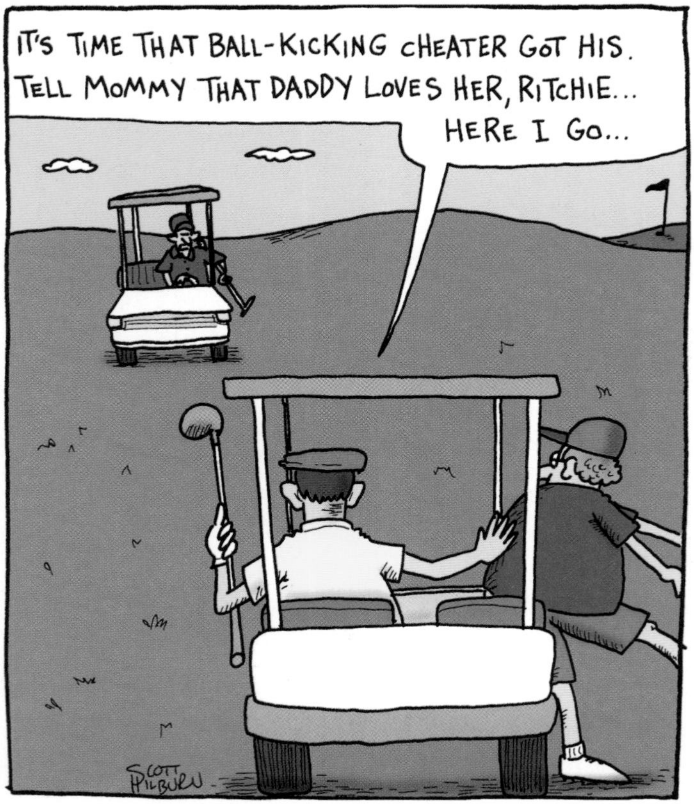
IT'S TIME THAT BALL-KICKING CHEATER GOT HIS. TELL MOMMY THAT DADDY LOVES HER, RITCHIE... HERE I GO...
SCOTT HILBURN

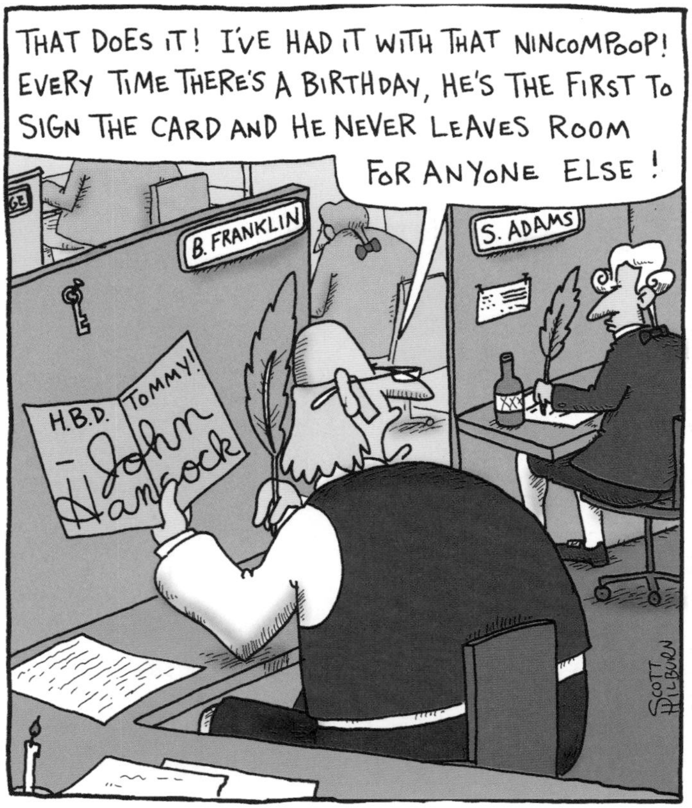
THAT DOES IT! I'VE HAD IT WITH THAT NINCOMPOOP! EVERY TIME THERE'S A BIRTHDAY, HE'S THE FIRST TO SIGN THE CARD AND HE NEVER LEAVES ROOM FOR ANYONE ELSE!
B. FRANKLIN
S. ADAMS
H.B.D. TOMMY!
— John Hancock
SCOTT HILBURN

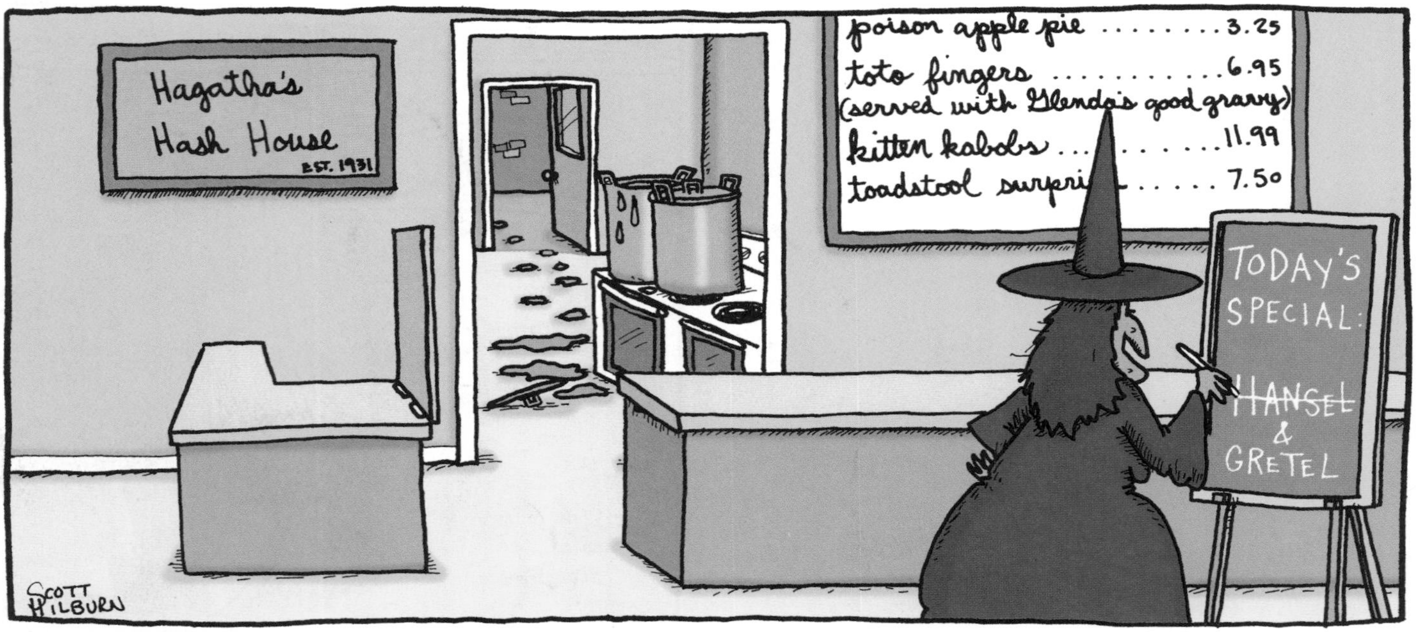
Hagatha's Hash House
EST. 1931
poison apple pie 3.25
toto fingers 6.95
(served with Glenda's good gravy)
kitten kabobs 11.99
toadstool surpri 7.50
TODAY'S SPECIAL:
HANSEL & GRETEL
SCOTT HILBURN

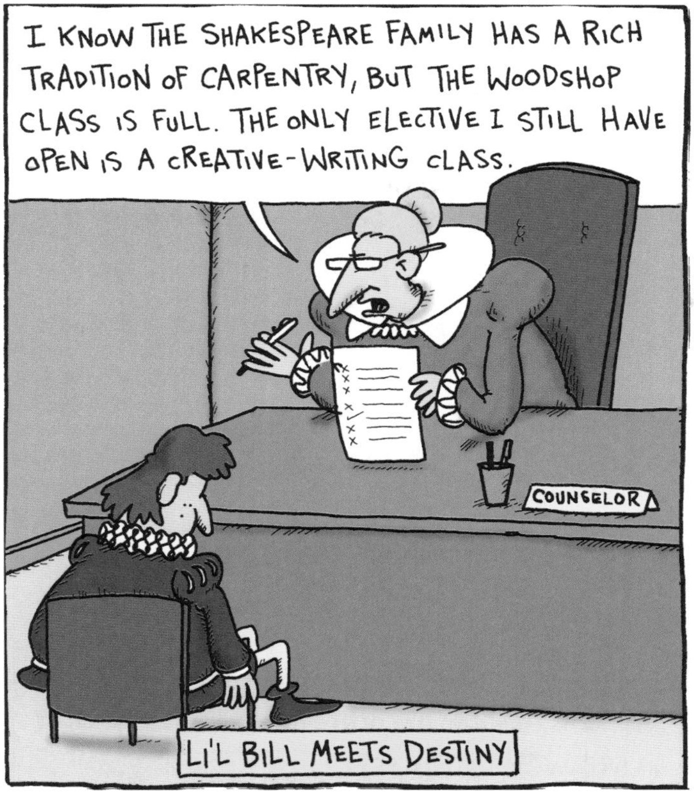
I KNOW THE SHAKESPEARE FAMILY HAS A RICH TRADITION OF CARPENTRY, BUT THE WOODSHOP CLASS IS FULL. THE ONLY ELECTIVE I STILL HAVE OPEN IS A CREATIVE-WRITING CLASS.
COUNSELOR
LI'L BILL MEETS DESTINY

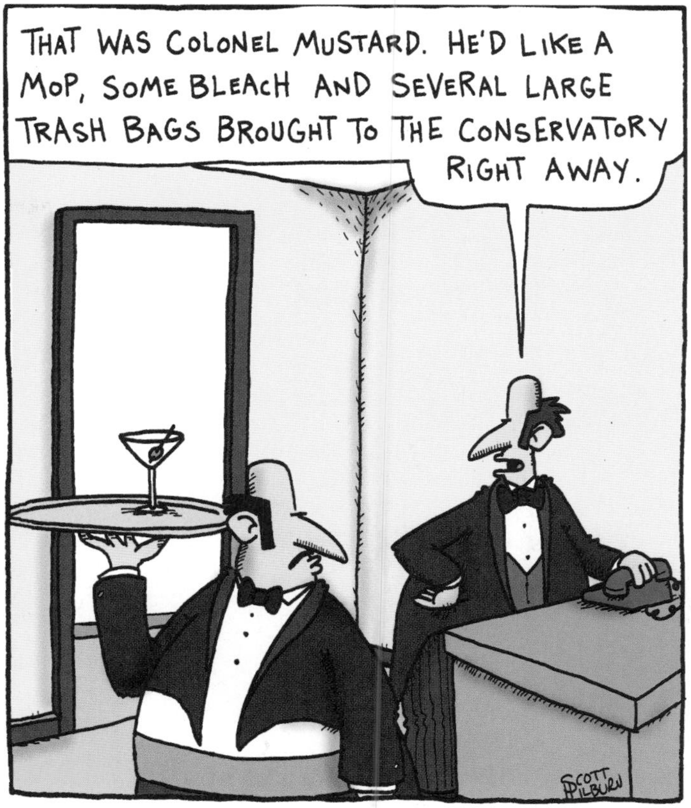
THAT WAS COLONEL MUSTARD. HE'D LIKE A MOP, SOME BLEACH AND SEVERAL LARGE TRASH BAGS BROUGHT TO THE CONSERVATORY RIGHT AWAY.
SCOTT HILBURN

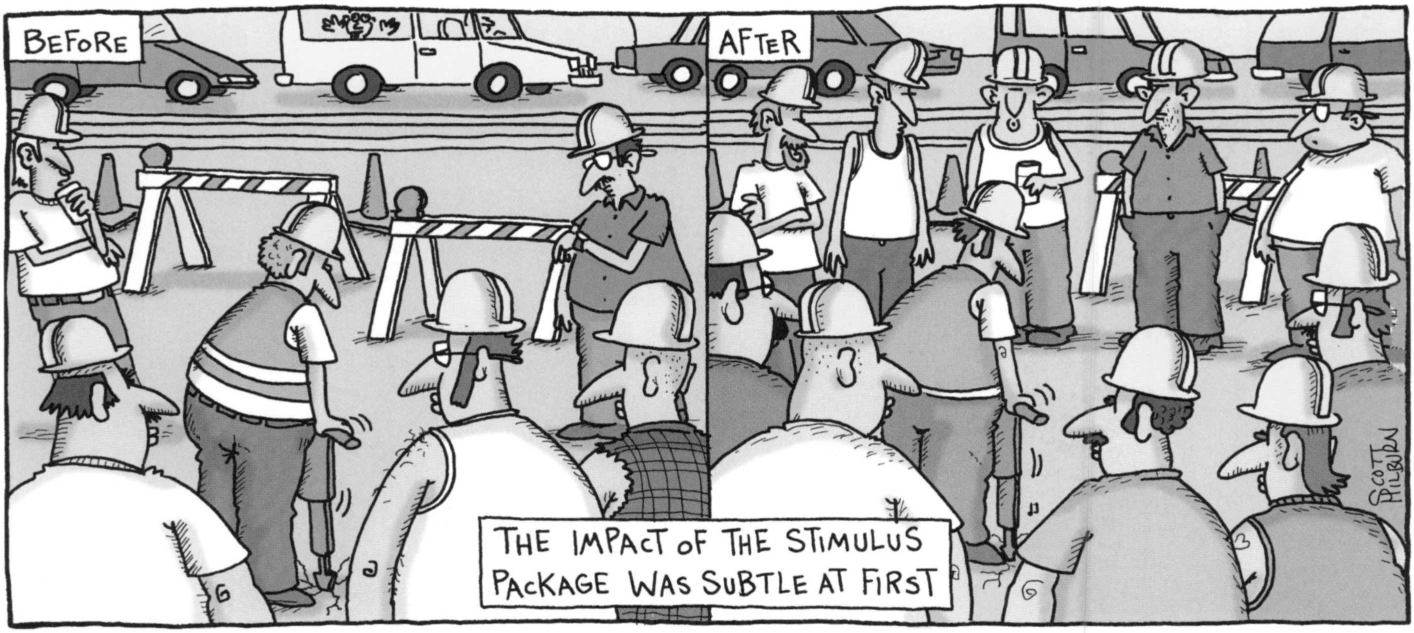
BEFORE
AFTER
SCOTT HILBURN
THE IMPACT OF THE STIMULUS PACKAGE WAS SUBTLE AT FIRST

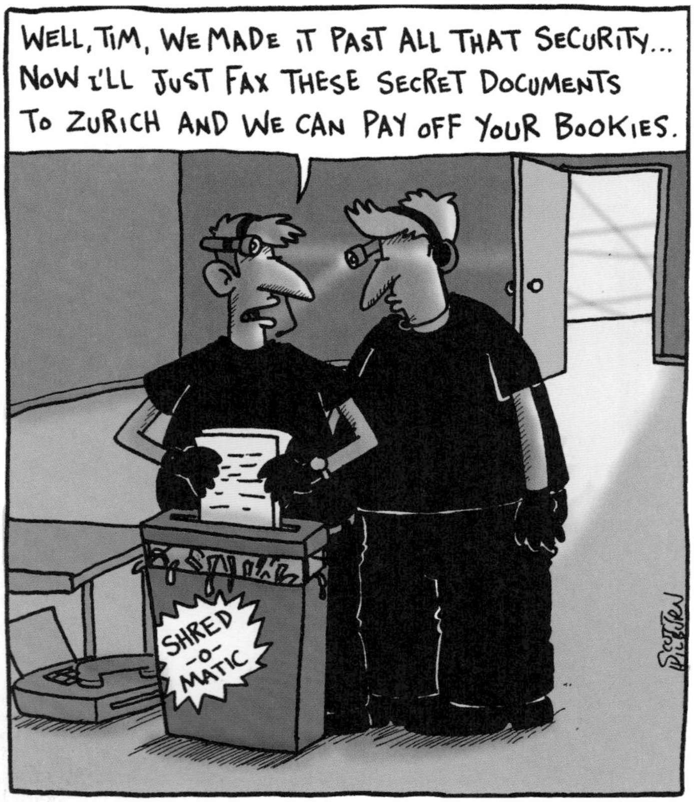
WELL, TIM, WE MADE IT PAST ALL THAT SECURITY... NOW I'LL JUST FAX THESE SECRET DOCUMENTS TO ZURICH AND WE CAN PAY OFF YOUR BOOKIES.
SHRED-O-MATIC

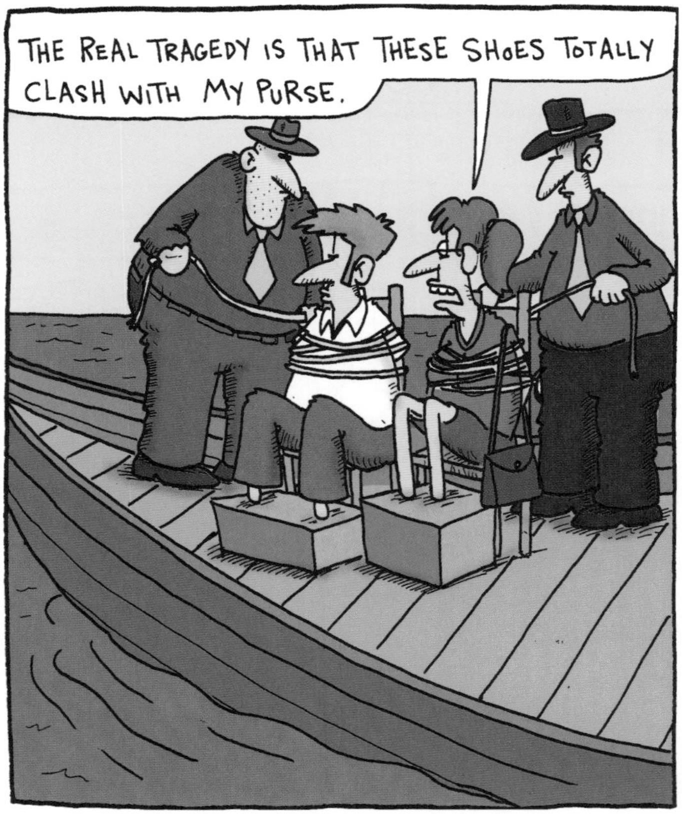
THE REAL TRAGEDY IS THAT THESE SHOES TOTALLY CLASH WITH MY PURSE.

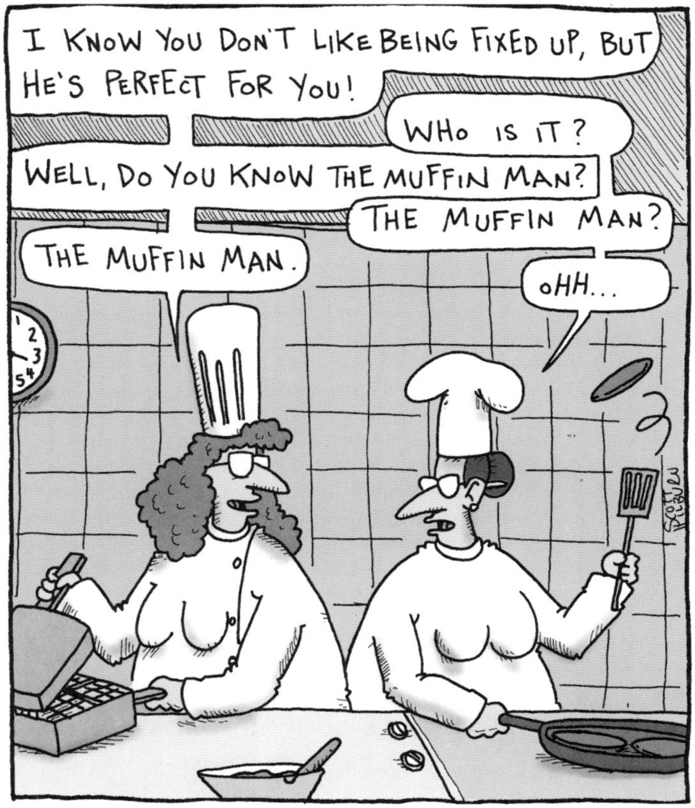
I KNOW YOU DON'T LIKE BEING FIXED UP, BUT HE'S PERFECT FOR YOU!
WHO IS IT?
WELL, DO YOU KNOW THE MUFFIN MAN?
THE MUFFIN MAN?
THE MUFFIN MAN.
OHH...
SCOTT HILBURN

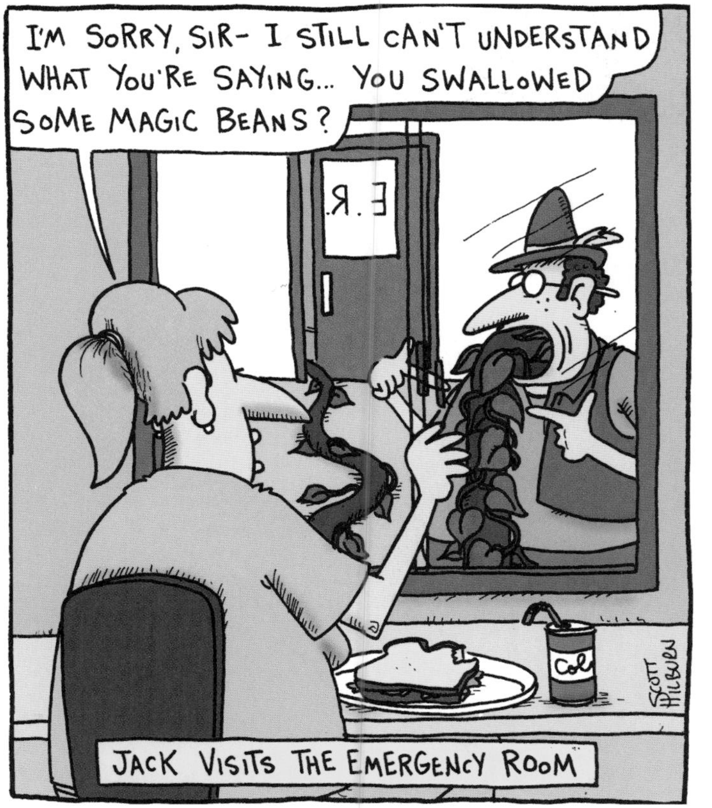
I'M SORRY, SIR- I STILL CAN'T UNDERSTAND WHAT YOU'RE SAYING... YOU SWALLOWED SOME MAGIC BEANS?
E.R.
SCOTT HILBURN
JACK VISITS THE EMERGENCY ROOM

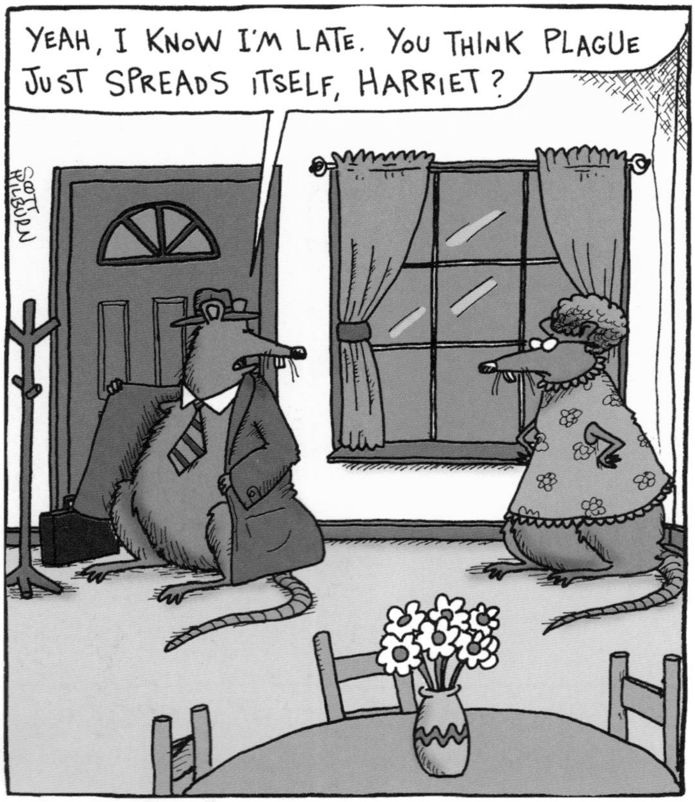
YEAH, I KNOW I'M LATE. YOU THINK PLAGUE JUST SPREADS ITSELF, HARRIET?
SCOTT HILBURN

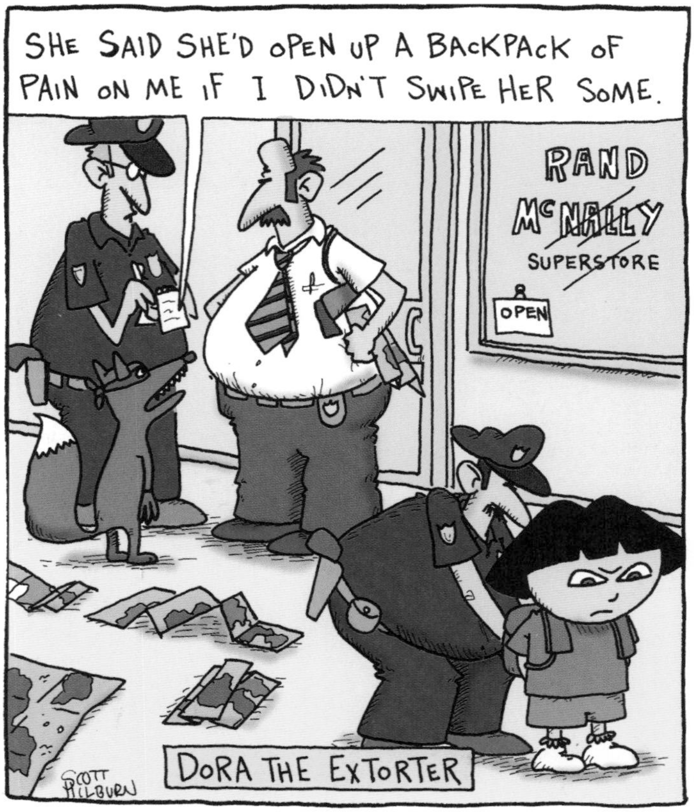
SHE SAID SHE'D OPEN UP A BACKPACK OF PAIN ON ME IF I DIDN'T SWIPE HER SOME.
RAND McNALLY
SUPERSTORE
OPEN
DORA THE EXTORTER
SCOTT HILBURN

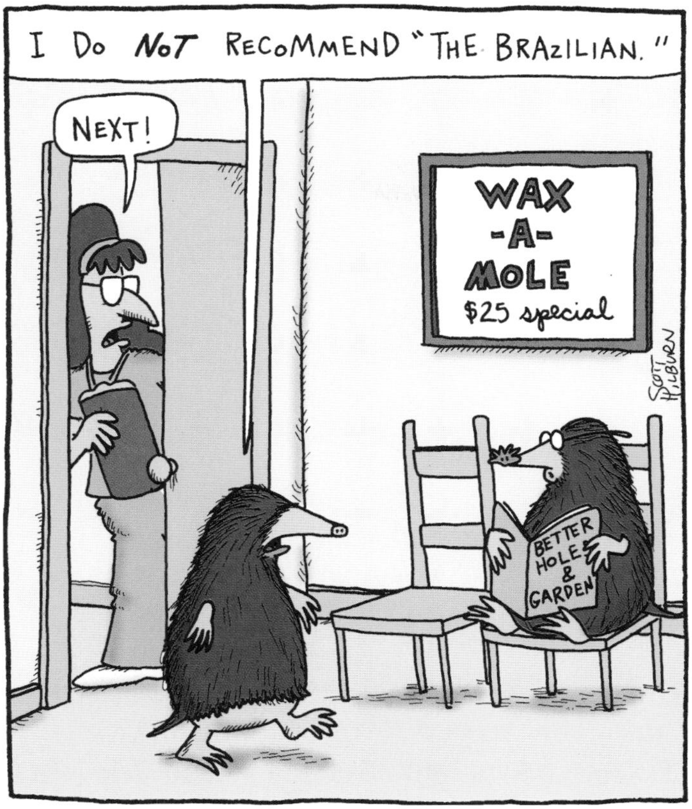
NEXT!
WAX -A- MOLE $25 special
BETTER HOLES & GARDEN
SCOTT HILBURN
I DO **NOT** RECOMMEND "THE BRAZILIAN."

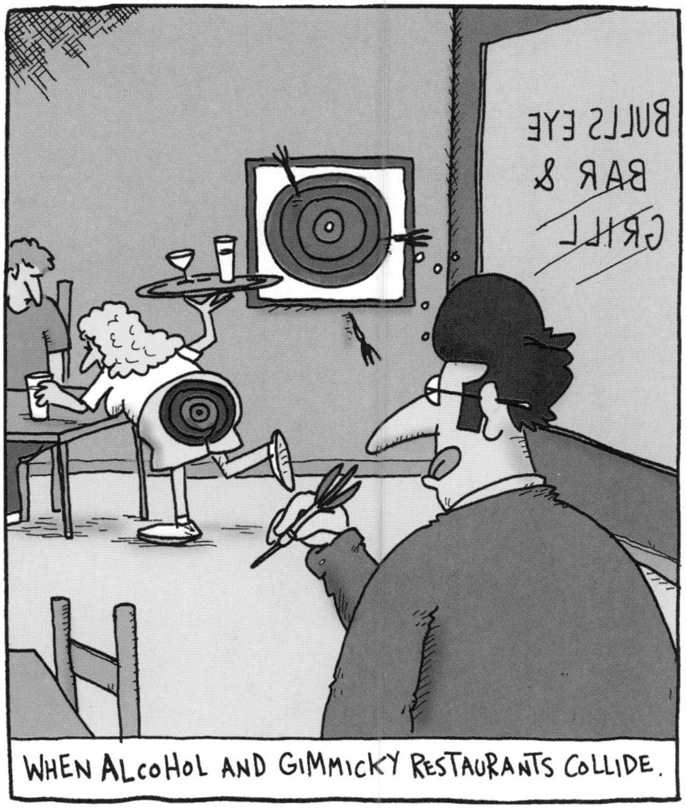
BULLS EYE BAR & GRILL
WHEN ALCOHOL AND GIMMICKY RESTAURANTS COLLIDE.

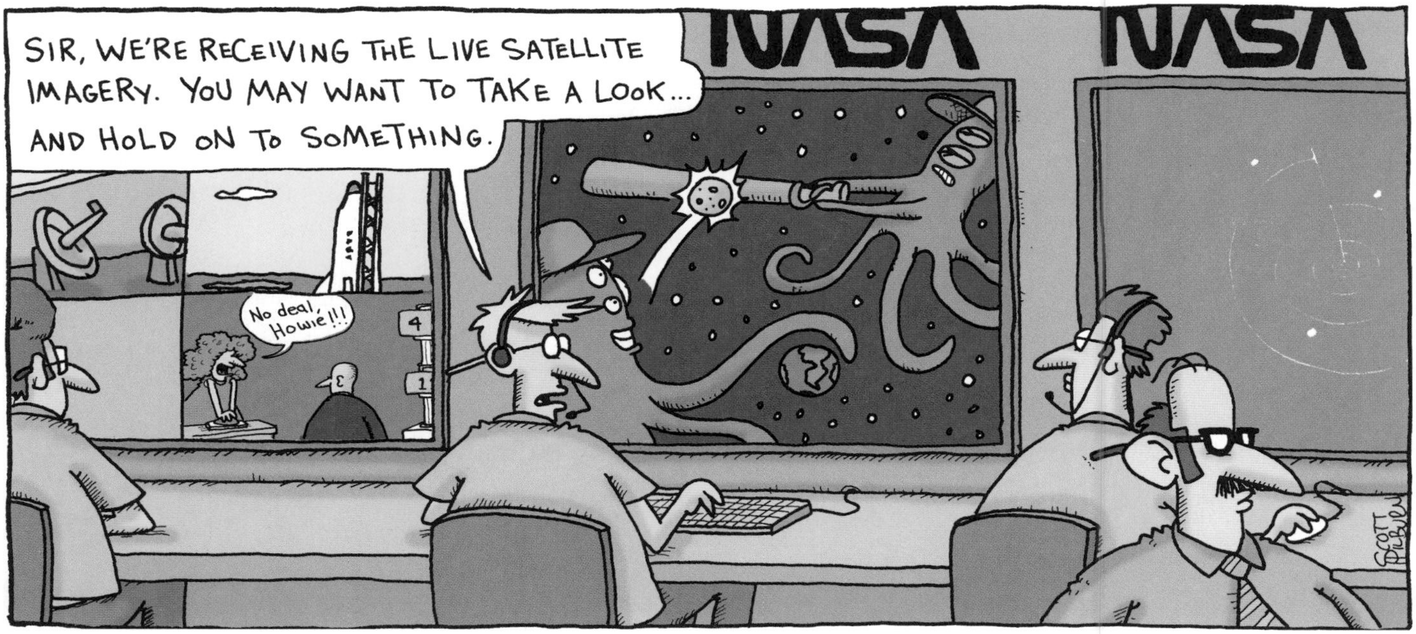
SIR, WE'RE RECEIVING THE LIVE SATELLITE IMAGERY. YOU MAY WANT TO TAKE A LOOK... AND HOLD ON TO SOMETHING.
NASA
NASA
No deal, Howie!!!
SCOTT HILBURN

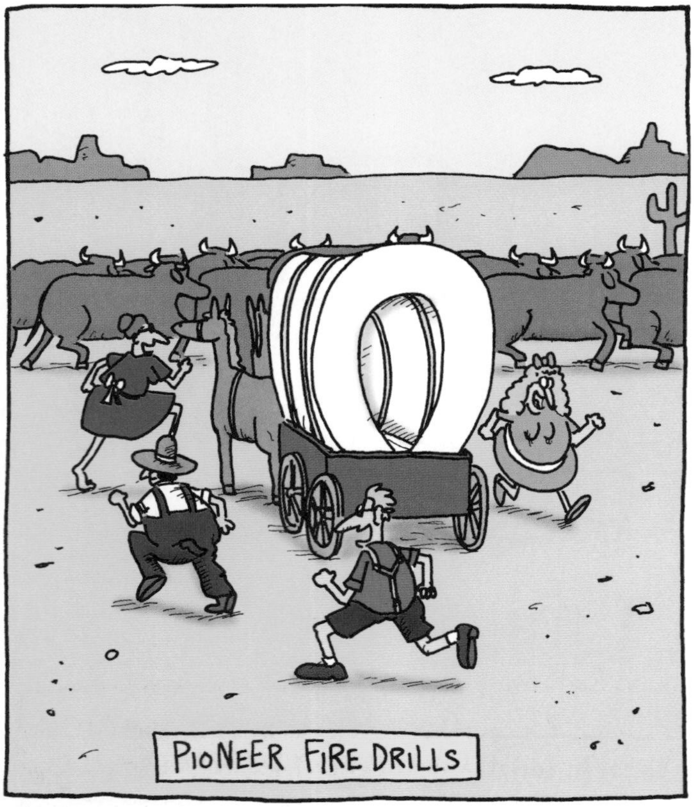
PIONEER FIRE DRILLS

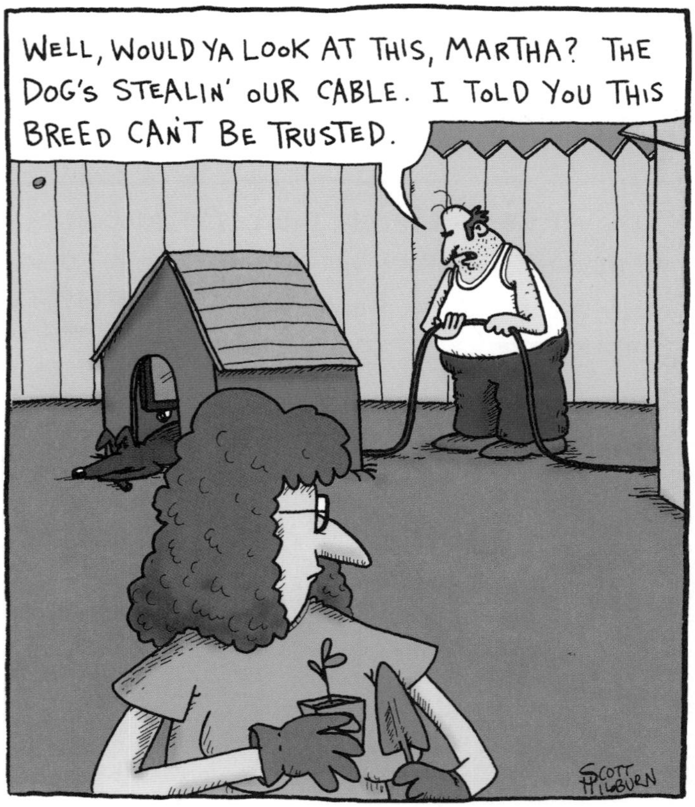
WELL, WOULD YA LOOK AT THIS, MARTHA? THE DOG'S STEALIN' OUR CABLE. I TOLD YOU THIS BREED CAN'T BE TRUSTED.
SCOTT HILBURN

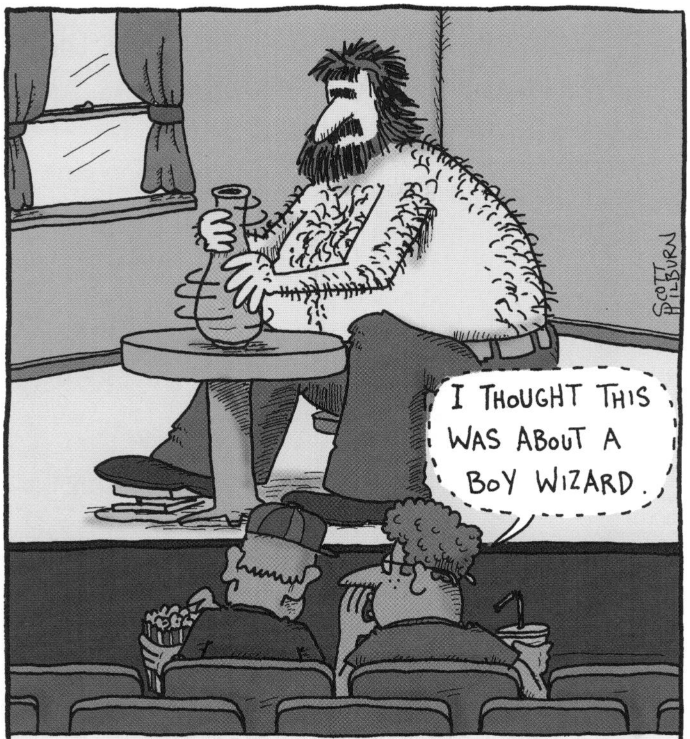
I THOUGHT THIS WAS ABOUT A BOY WIZARD.
SCOTT HILBURN
BLOCKBUSTER BOOK ADAPTATIONS GONE WRONG

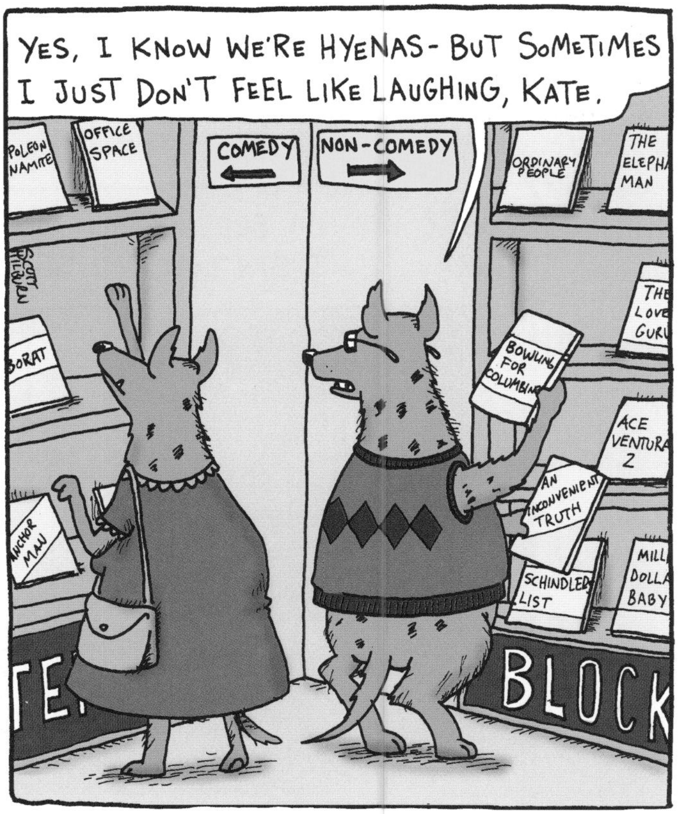
YES, I KNOW WE'RE HYENAS - BUT SOMETIMES I JUST DON'T FEEL LIKE LAUGHING, KATE.
COMEDY
NON-COMEDY
OFFICE SPACE
ORDINARY PEOPLE
BORAT
ANCHOR MAN
AN INCONVENIENT TRUTH
SCHINDLER'S LIST
ACE VENTURA 2
SCOTT HILBURN

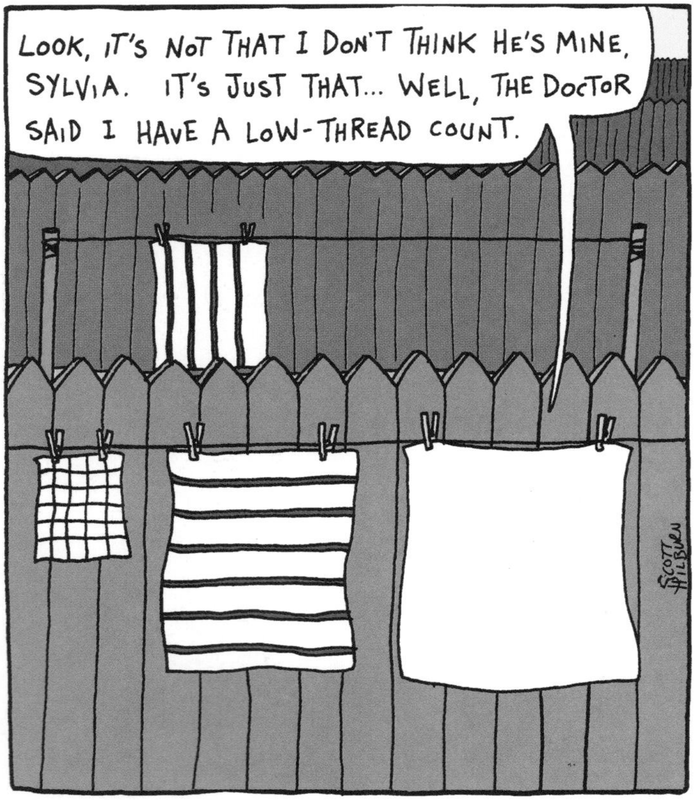
LOOK, IT'S NOT THAT I DON'T THINK HE'S MINE, SYLVIA. IT'S JUST THAT... WELL, THE DOCTOR SAID I HAVE A LOW-THREAD COUNT.
SCOTT HILBURN

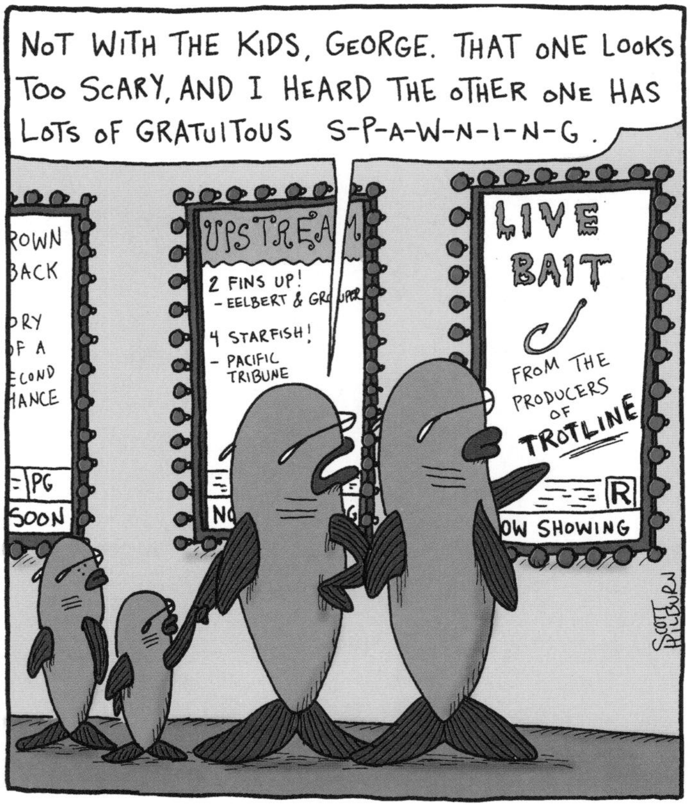
NOT WITH THE KIDS, GEORGE. THAT ONE LOOKS TOO SCARY, AND I HEARD THE OTHER ONE HAS LOTS OF GRATUITOUS S-P-A-W-N-I-N-G.
PG
SOON
UPSTREAM
2 FINS UP!
4 STARFISH!
- PACIFIC TRIBUNE
LIVE BAIT
FROM THE PRODUCERS OF TROTLINE
R
OW SHOWING
SCOTT HILBURN

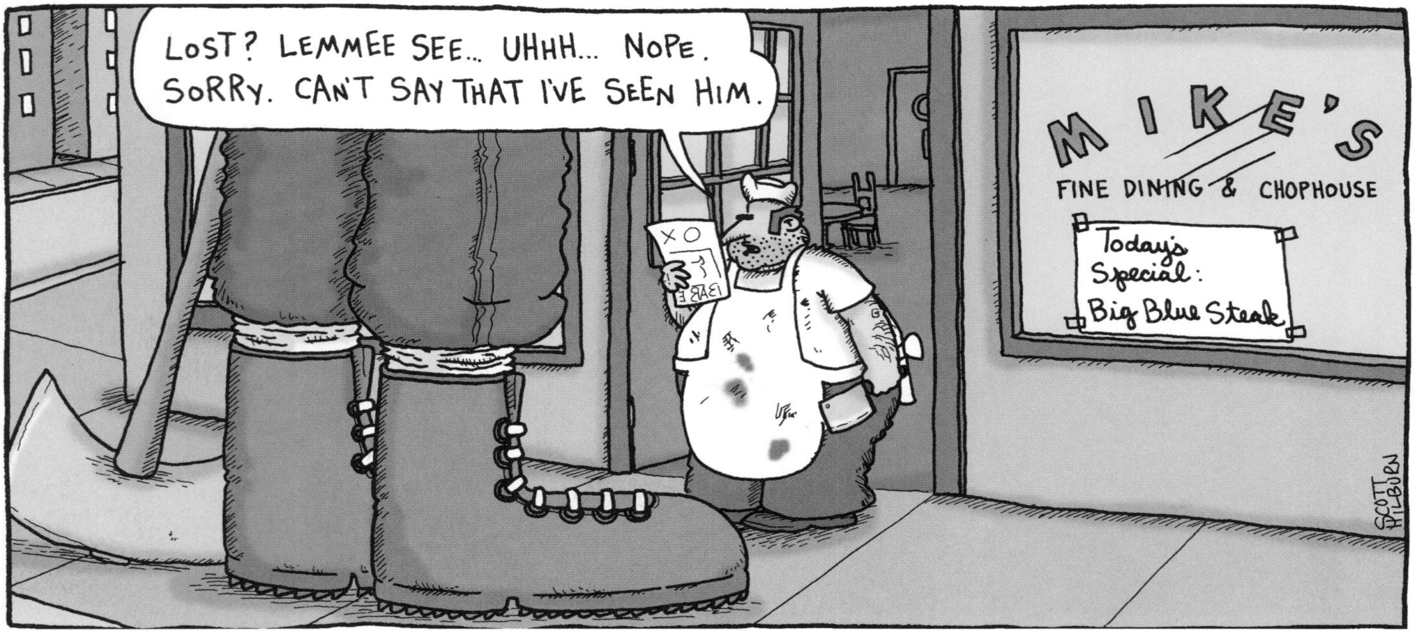
LOST? LEMMEE SEE... UHHH... NOPE. SORRY. CAN'T SAY THAT I'VE SEEN HIM.
MIKE'S
FINE DINING & CHOPHOUSE
Today's Special: Big Blue Steak
SCOTT HILBURN

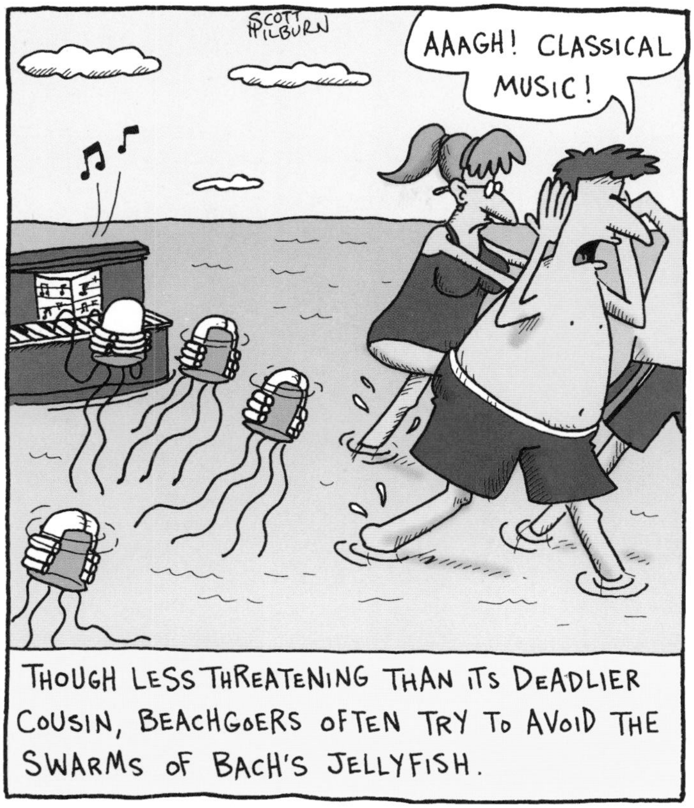
SCOTT HILBURN
AAAGH! CLASSICAL MUSIC!
THOUGH LESS THREATENING THAN ITS DEADLIER COUSIN, BEACHGOERS OFTEN TRY TO AVOID THE SWARMS OF BACH'S JELLYFISH.

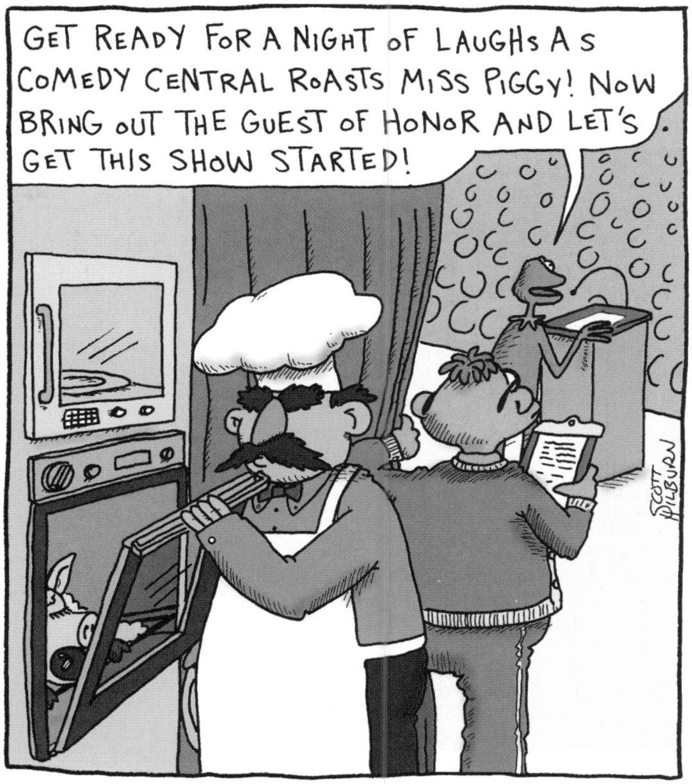
GET READY FOR A NIGHT OF LAUGHS AS COMEDY CENTRAL ROASTS MISS PIGGY! NOW BRING OUT THE GUEST OF HONOR AND LET'S GET THIS SHOW STARTED!
SCOTT HILBURN

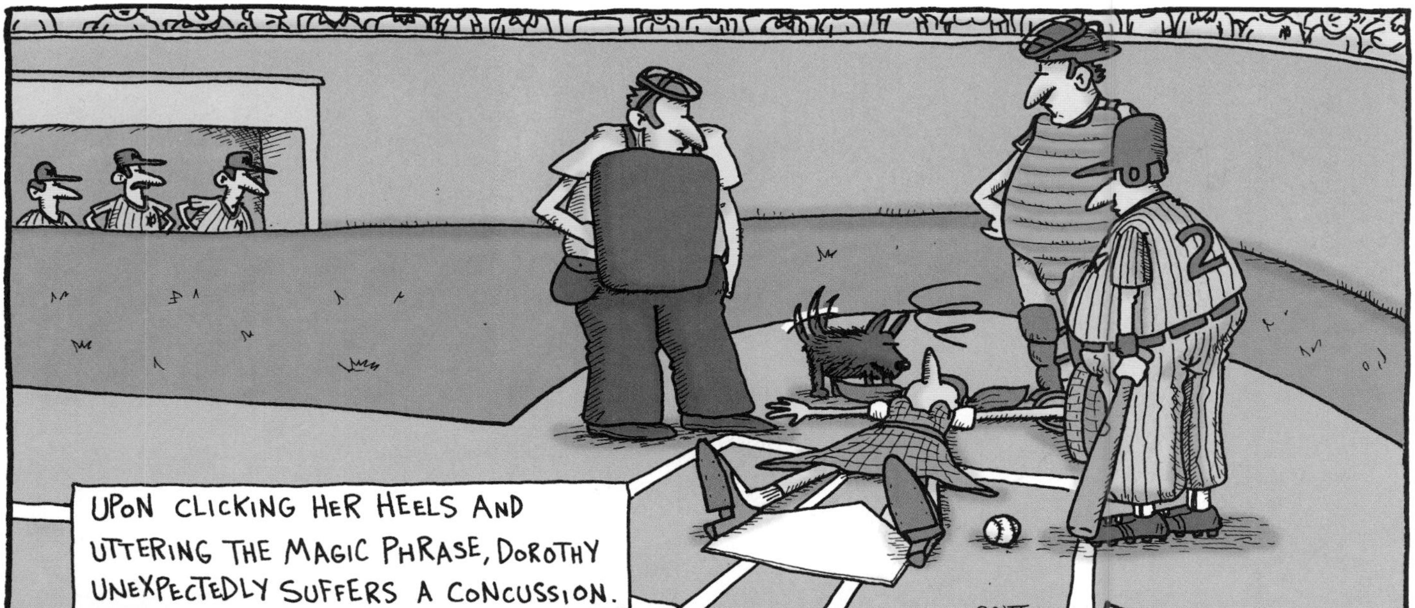
UPON CLICKING HER HEELS AND UTTERING THE MAGIC PHRASE, DOROTHY UNEXPECTEDLY SUFFERS A CONCUSSION.
SCOTT HILBURN

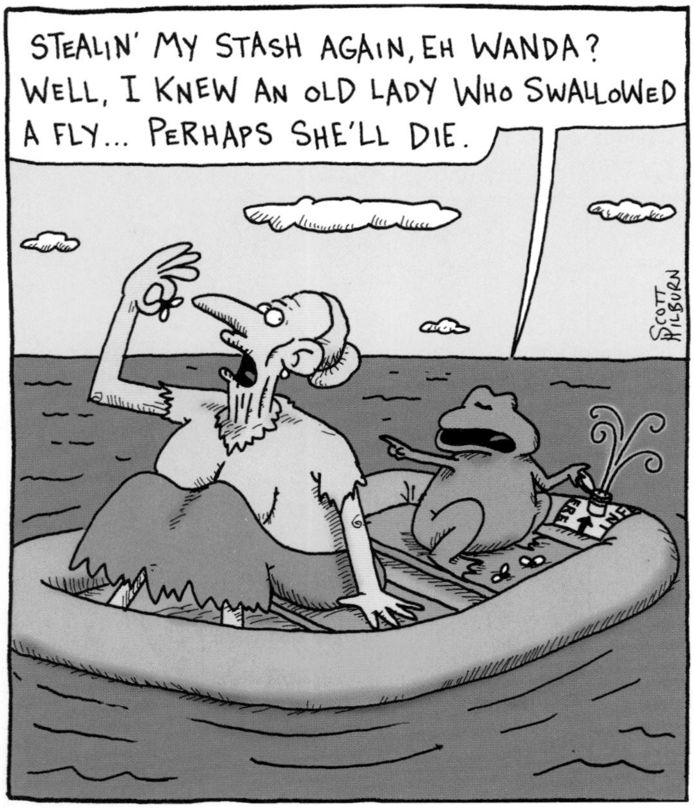
STEALIN' MY STASH AGAIN, EH WANDA? WELL, I KNEW AN OLD LADY WHO SWALLOWED A FLY... PERHAPS SHE'LL DIE.
SCOTT HILBURN

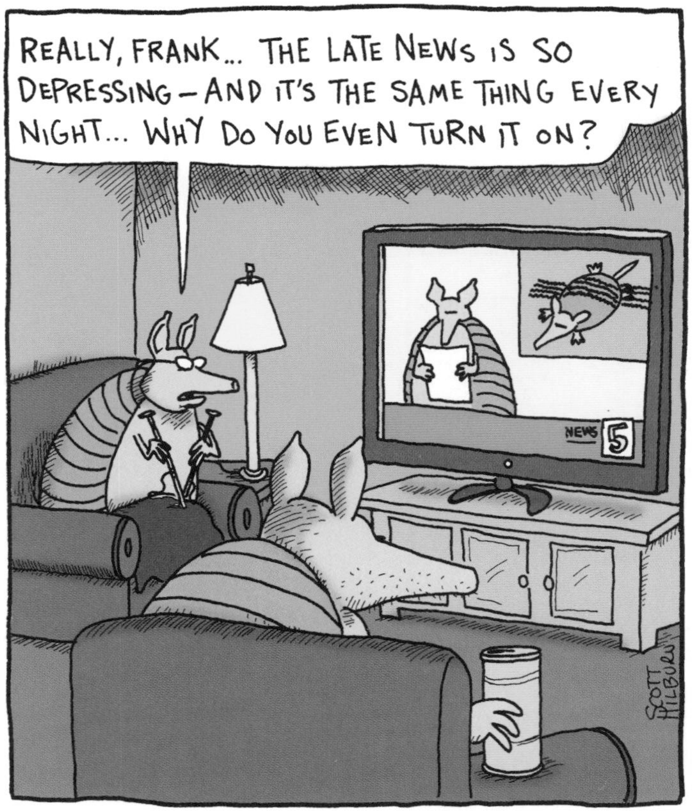
REALLY, FRANK... THE LATE NEWS IS SO DEPRESSING – AND IT'S THE SAME THING EVERY NIGHT... WHY DO YOU EVEN TURN IT ON?
NEWS 5
SCOTT HILBURN

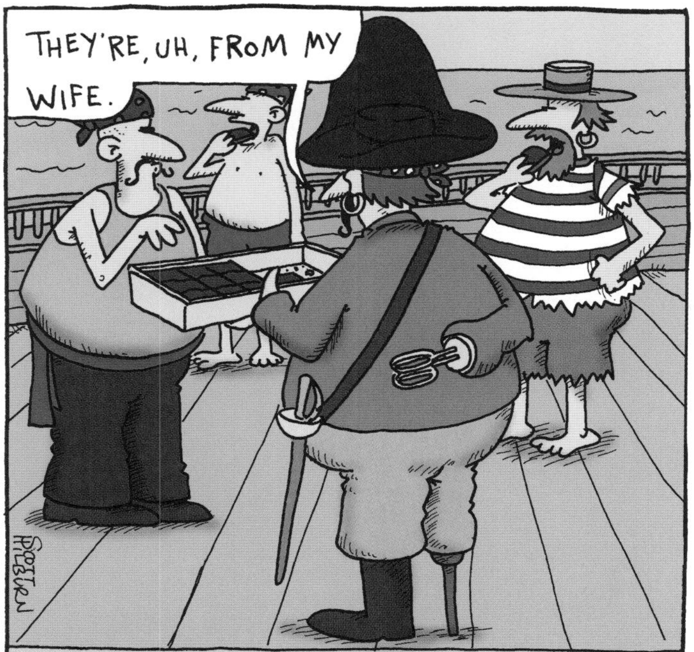
THEY'RE, UH, FROM MY WIFE.

IT BECAME INCREASINGLY DIFFICULT FOR THE CAPTAIN TO REWARD HIS CREW AND STILL MAINTAIN HIS FEROCIOUS REPUTATION.

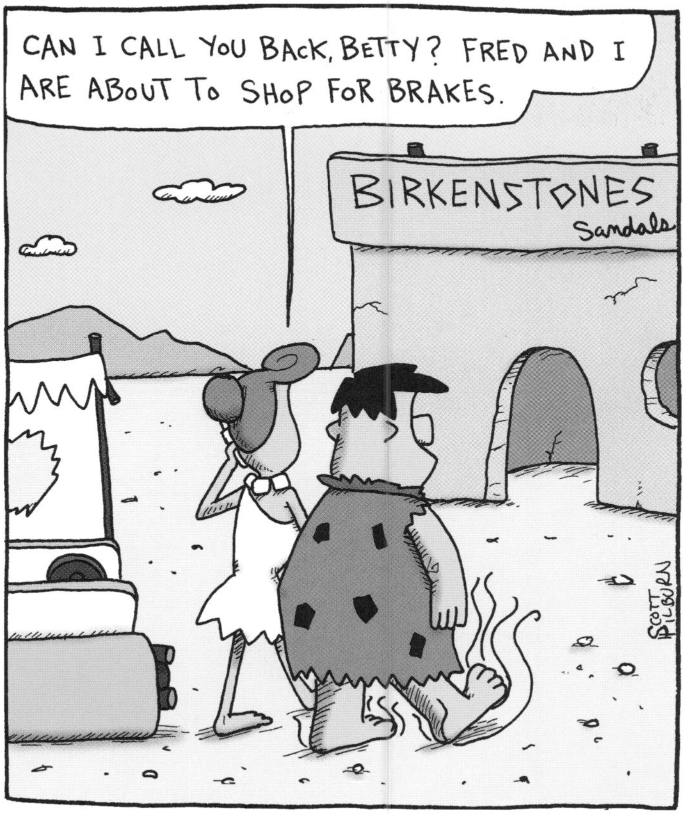
CAN I CALL YOU BACK, BETTY? FRED AND I ARE ABOUT TO SHOP FOR BRAKES.
BIRKENSTONES
Sandals

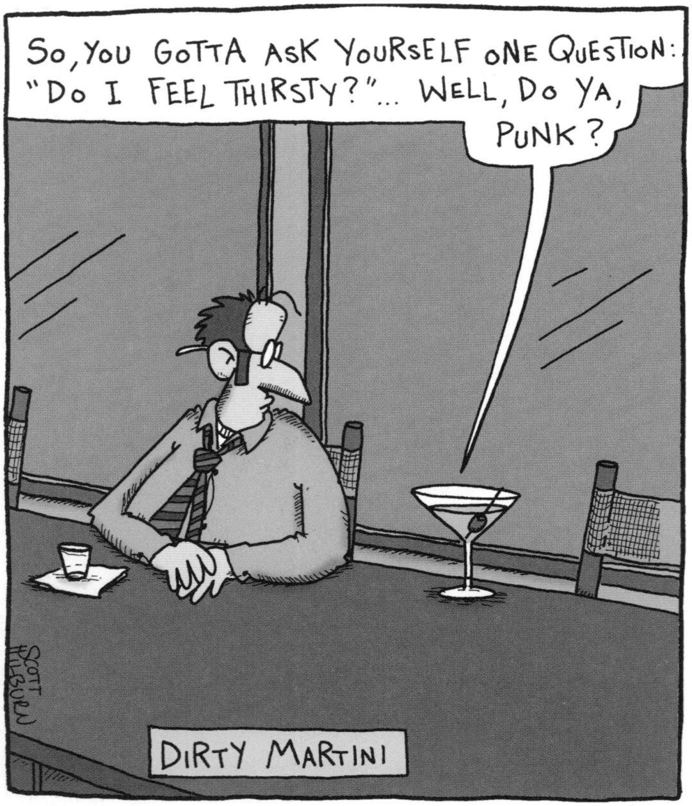
So, You GOTTA ASK YOURSELF ONE QUESTION: "Do I FEEL THIRSTY?"... WELL, Do YA, PUNK?
SCOTT HILBURN

DIRTY MARTINI

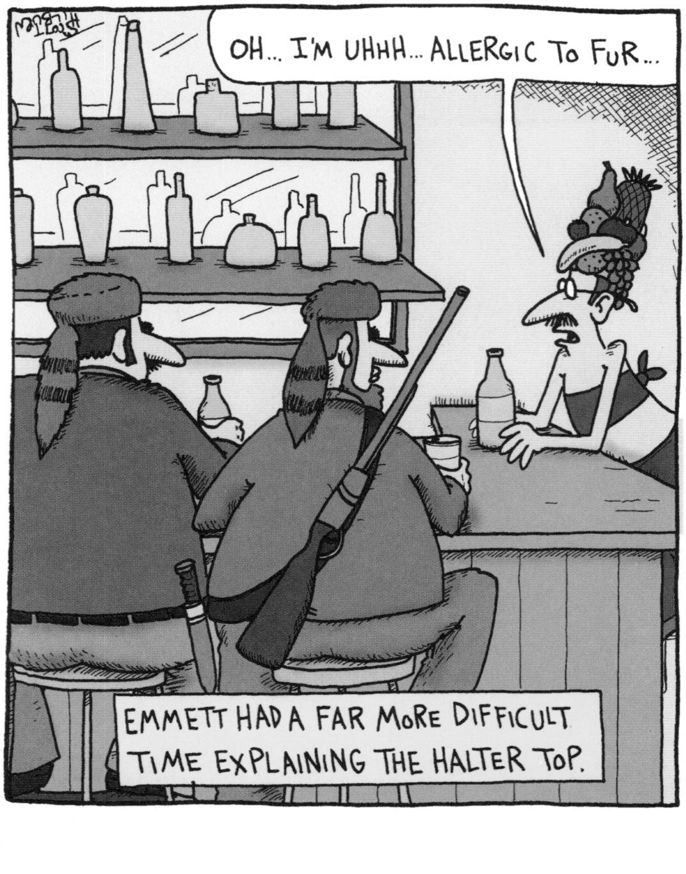
OH... I'M UHHH... ALLERGIC To FUR...

EMMETT HAD A FAR MORE DIFFICULT TIME EXPLAINING THE HALTER TOP.

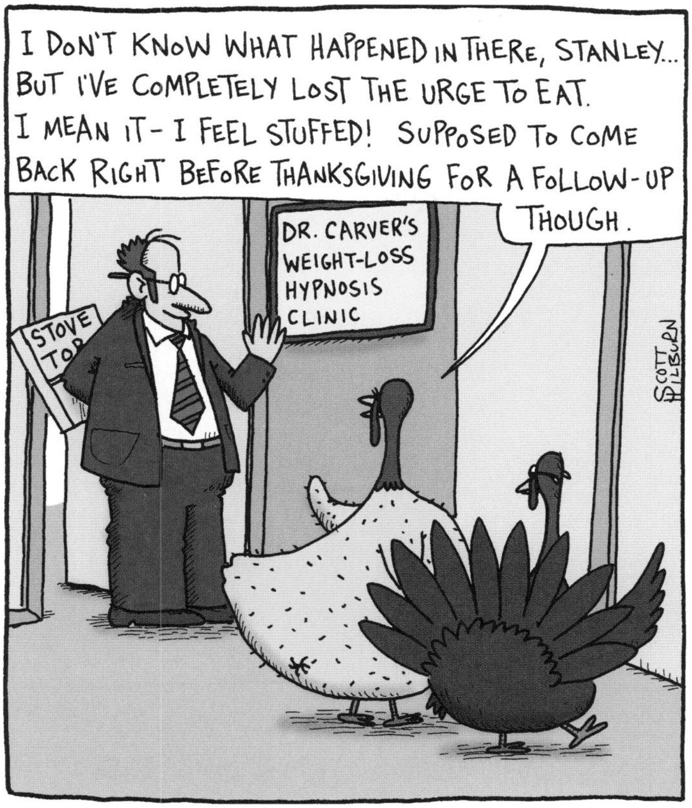
I DON'T KNOW WHAT HAPPENED IN THERE, STANLEY... BUT I'VE COMPLETELY LOST THE URGE TO EAT. I MEAN IT- I FEEL STUFFED! SUPPOSED TO COME BACK RIGHT BEFORE THANKSGIVING FOR A FOLLOW-UP THOUGH.
DR. CARVER'S WEIGHT-LOSS HYPNOSIS CLINIC
STOVE TOP
SCOTT HILBURN

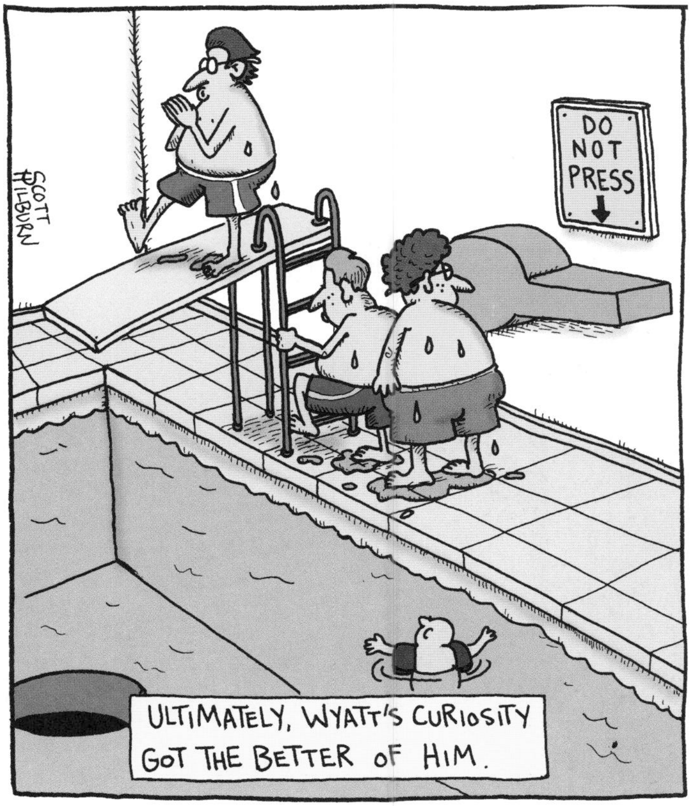
DO NOT PRESS
SCOTT HILBURN
ULTIMATELY, WYATT'S CURIOSITY GOT THE BETTER OF HIM.

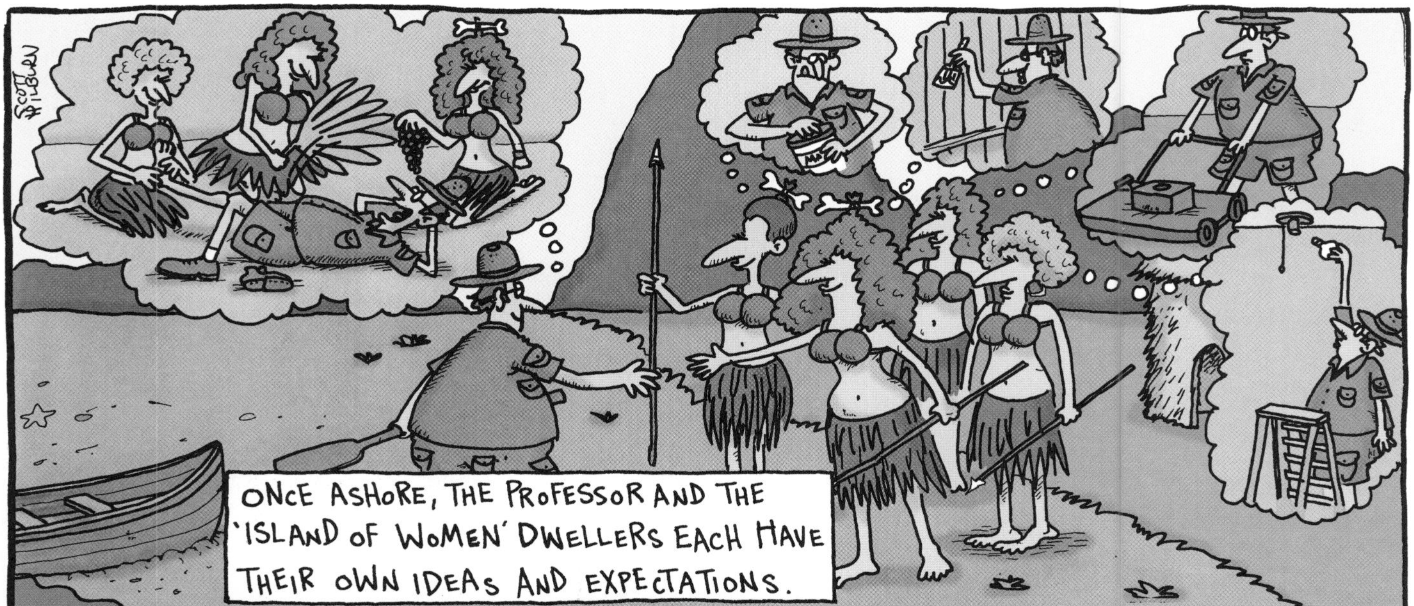
SCOTT HILBURN
ONCE ASHORE, THE PROFESSOR AND THE 'ISLAND OF WOMEN' DWELLERS EACH HAVE THEIR OWN IDEAS AND EXPECTATIONS.

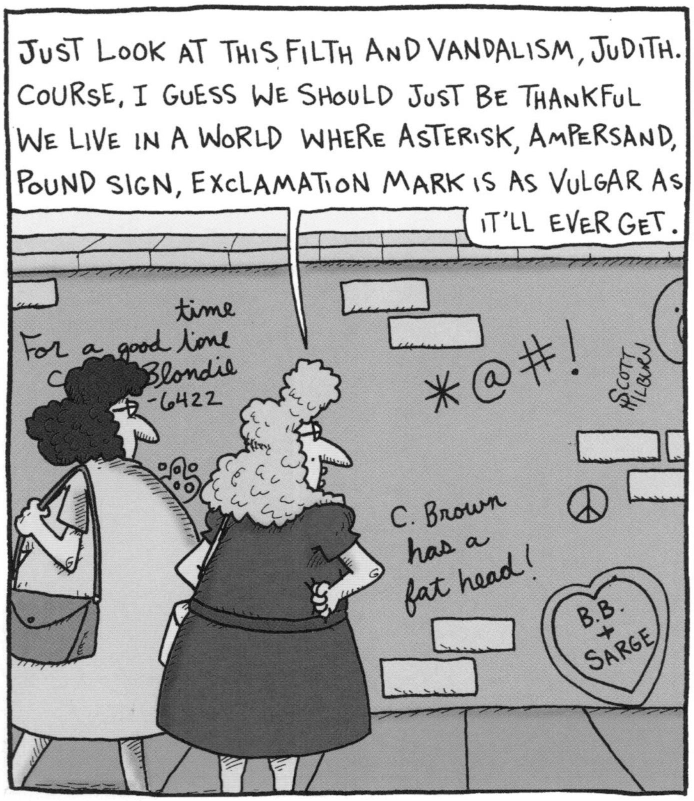
JUST LOOK AT THIS FILTH AND VANDALISM, JUDITH. COURSE, I GUESS WE SHOULD JUST BE THANKFUL WE LIVE IN A WORLD WHERE ASTERISK, AMPERSAND, POUND SIGN, EXCLAMATION MARK IS AS VULGAR AS IT'LL EVER GET.
time
For a good
Blondie
-6422
*@#!
C. Brown has a fat head!
B.B. + SARGE
SCOTT HILBURN

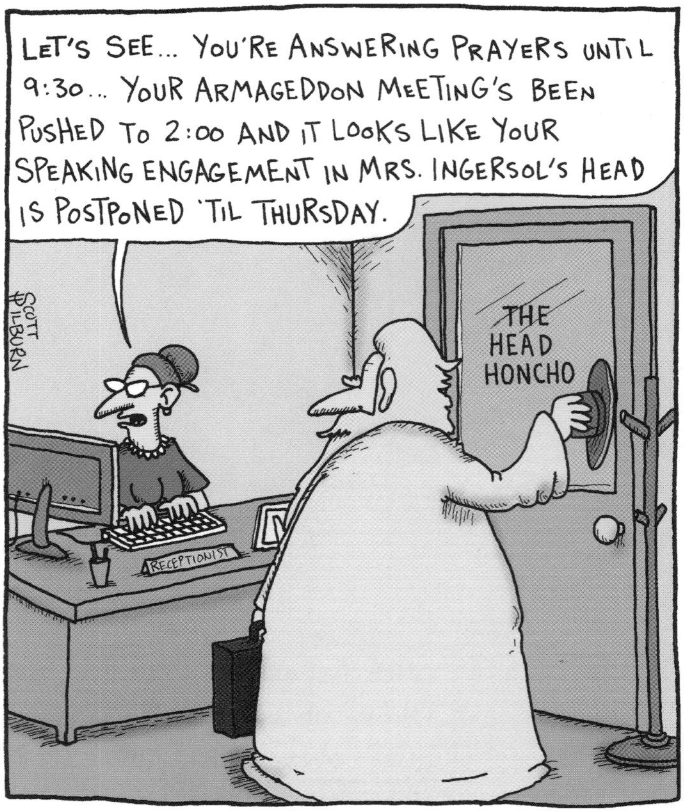
LET'S SEE... YOU'RE ANSWERING PRAYERS UNTIL 9:30... YOUR ARMAGEDDON MEETING'S BEEN PUSHED TO 2:00 AND IT LOOKS LIKE YOUR SPEAKING ENGAGEMENT IN MRS. INGERSOL'S HEAD IS POSTPONED 'TIL THURSDAY.
THE HEAD HONCHO
RECEPTIONIST
SCOTT HILBURN

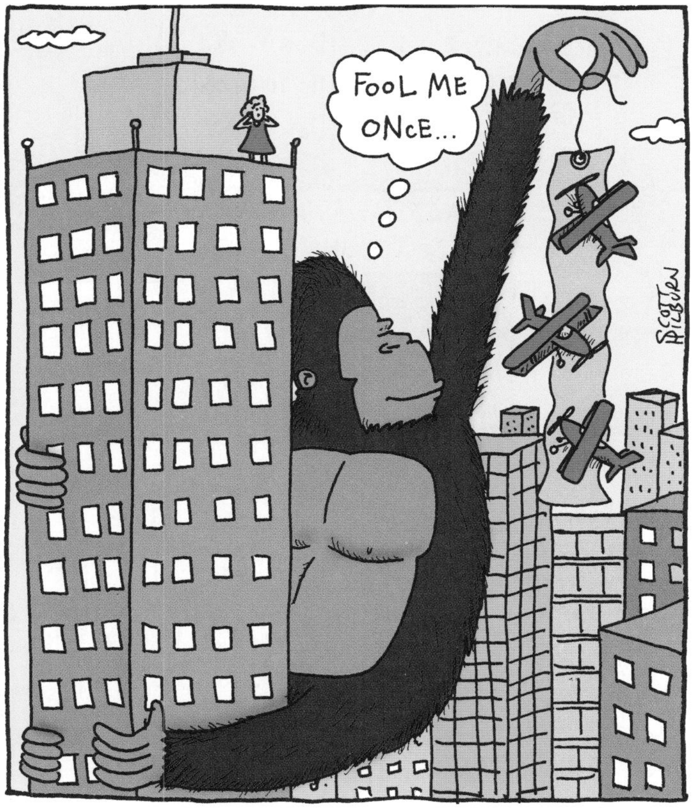
FOOL ME ONCE...
SCOTT HILBURN

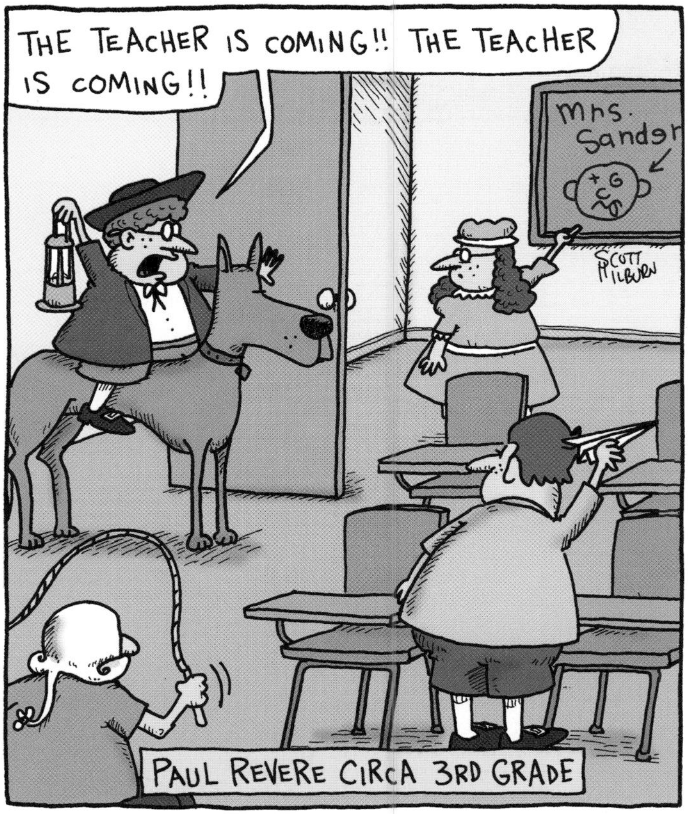
THE TEACHER IS COMING!! THE TEACHER IS COMING!!
Mrs. Sander
SCOTT HILBURN
PAUL REVERE CIRCA 3RD GRADE

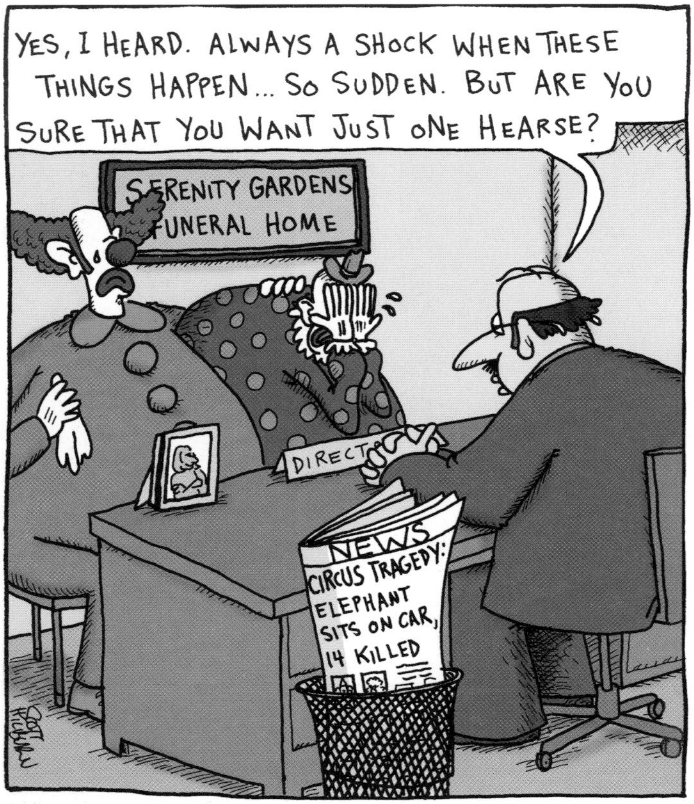
YES, I HEARD. ALWAYS A SHOCK WHEN THESE THINGS HAPPEN... SO SUDDEN. BUT ARE YOU SURE THAT YOU WANT JUST ONE HEARSE?
SERENITY GARDENS FUNERAL HOME
DIRECT
NEWS
CIRCUS TRAGEDY: ELEPHANT SITS ON CAR, 14 KILLED
SCOTT HILBURN

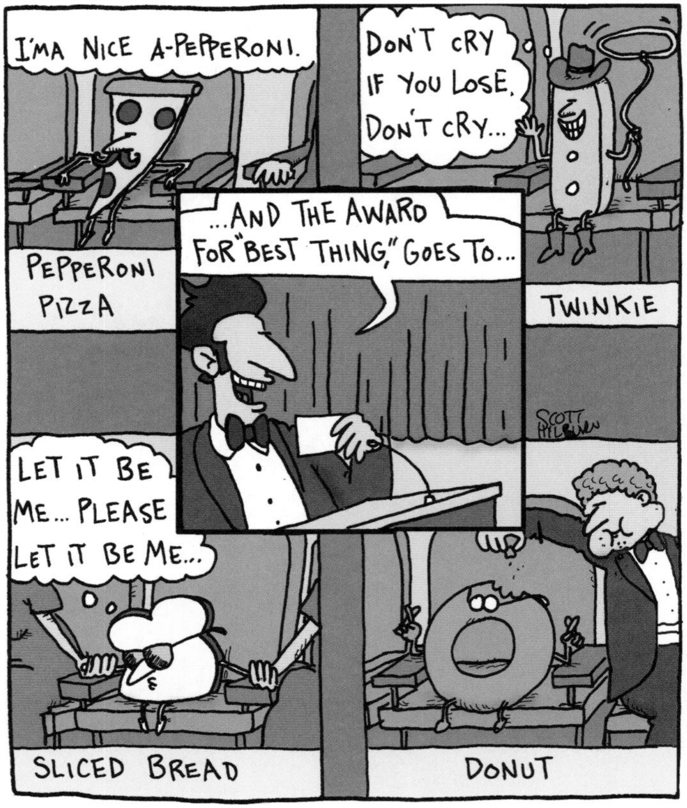
I'MA NICE A-PEPPERONI.
PEPPERONI PIZZA
DON'T CRY IF YOU LOSE. DON'T CRY...
TWINKIE
...AND THE AWARD FOR "BEST THING," GOES TO...
SCOTT HILBURN
LET IT BE ME... PLEASE LET IT BE ME...
SLICED BREAD
DONUT

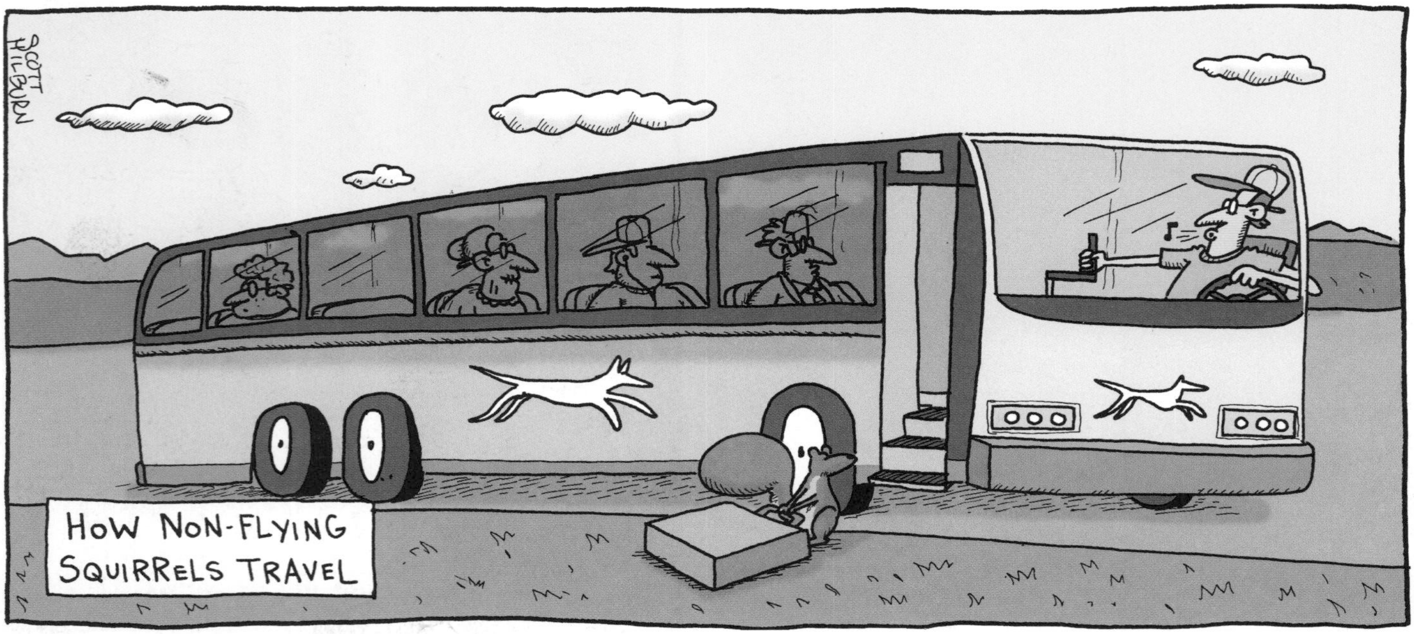
SCOTT HILBURN

HOW NON-FLYING SQUIRRELS TRAVEL

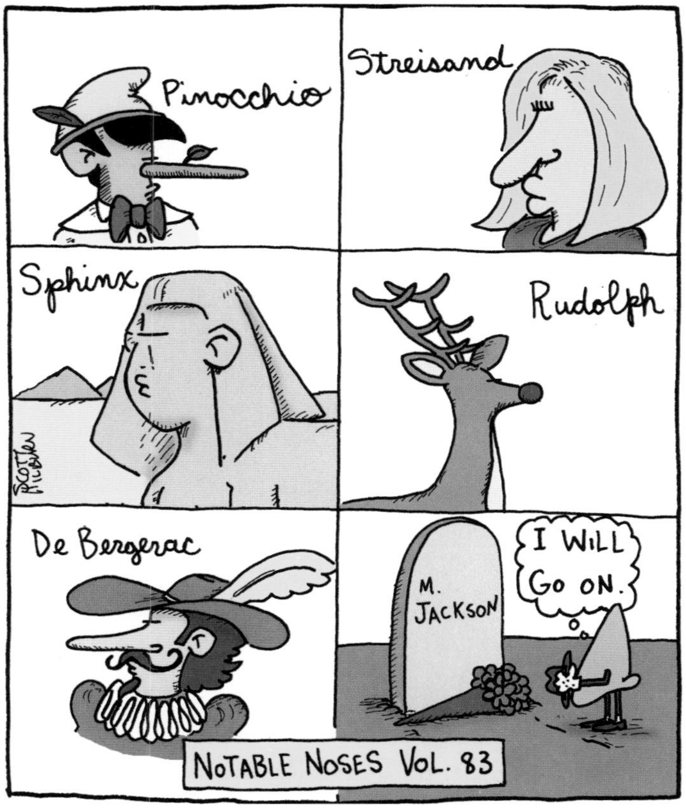
Pinocchio
Streisand
Sphinx
Rudolph
SCOTT HILBURN
De Bergerac
M. JACKSON
I WILL GO ON.
NOTABLE NOSES VOL. 83

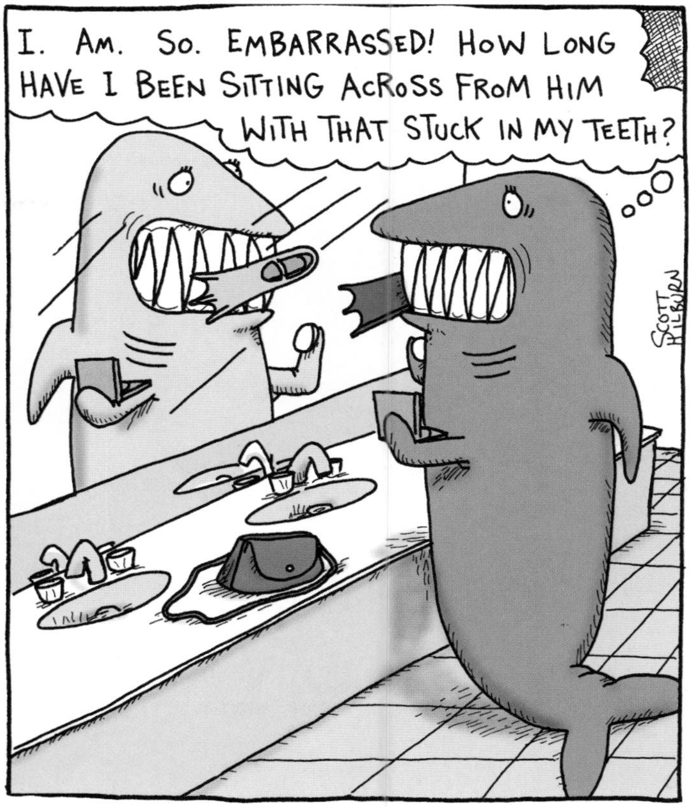
I. AM. SO. EMBARRASSED! HOW LONG HAVE I BEEN SITTING ACROSS FROM HIM WITH THAT STUCK IN MY TEETH?
SCOTT HILBURN

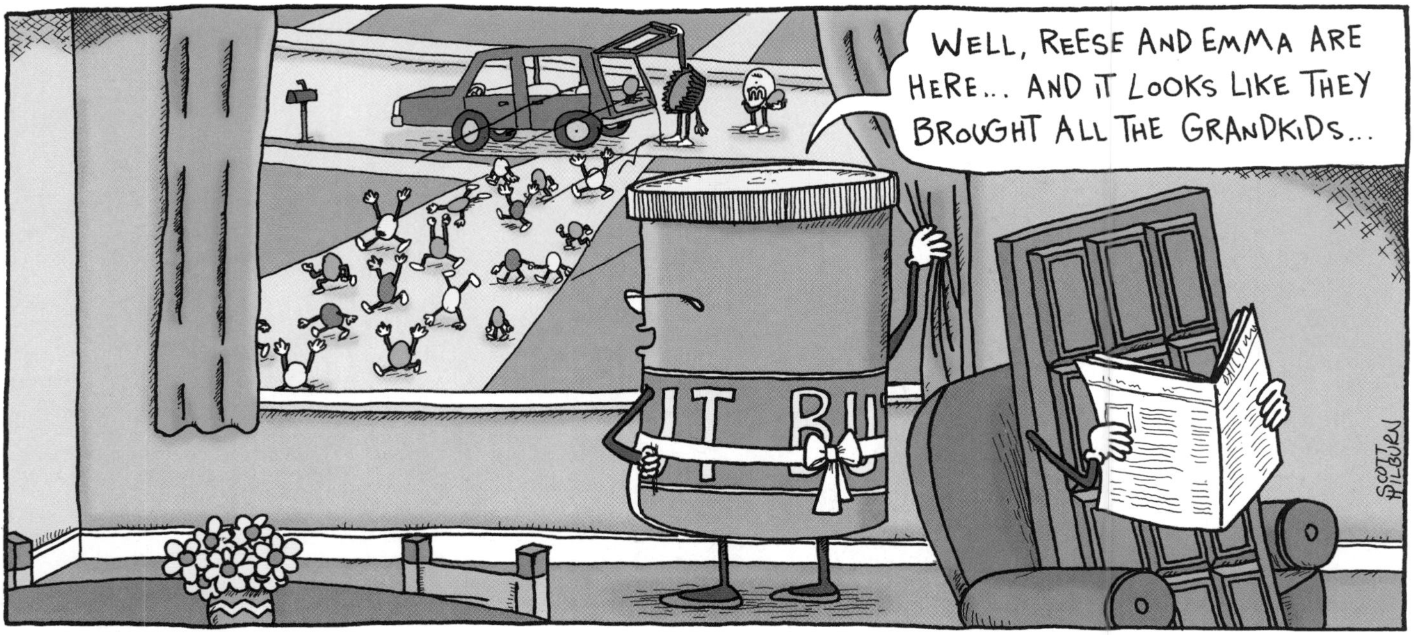
WELL, REESE AND EMMA ARE HERE... AND IT LOOKS LIKE THEY BROUGHT ALL THE GRANDKIDS...
SCOTT HILBURN

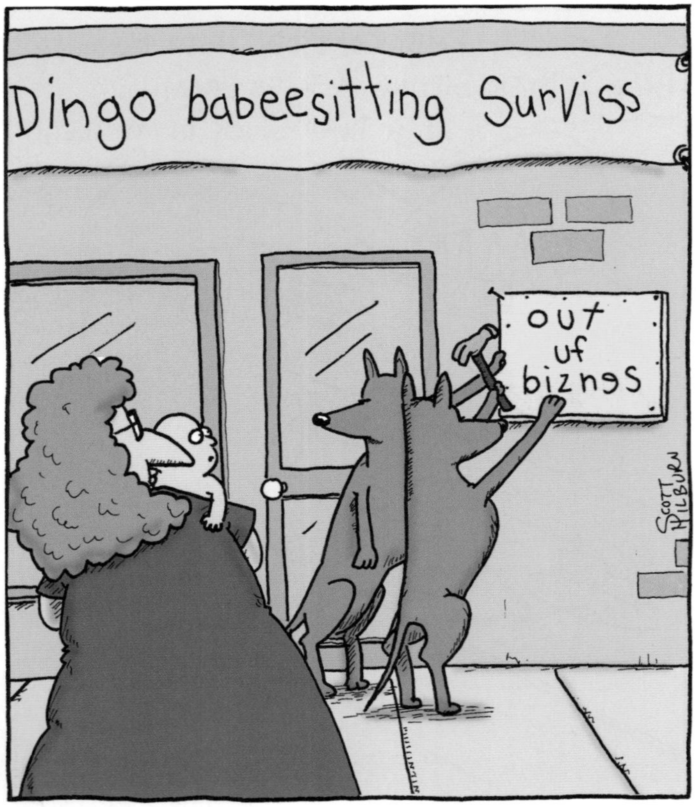
Dingo babeesitting Surviss
out uf biznes
SCOTT HILBURN

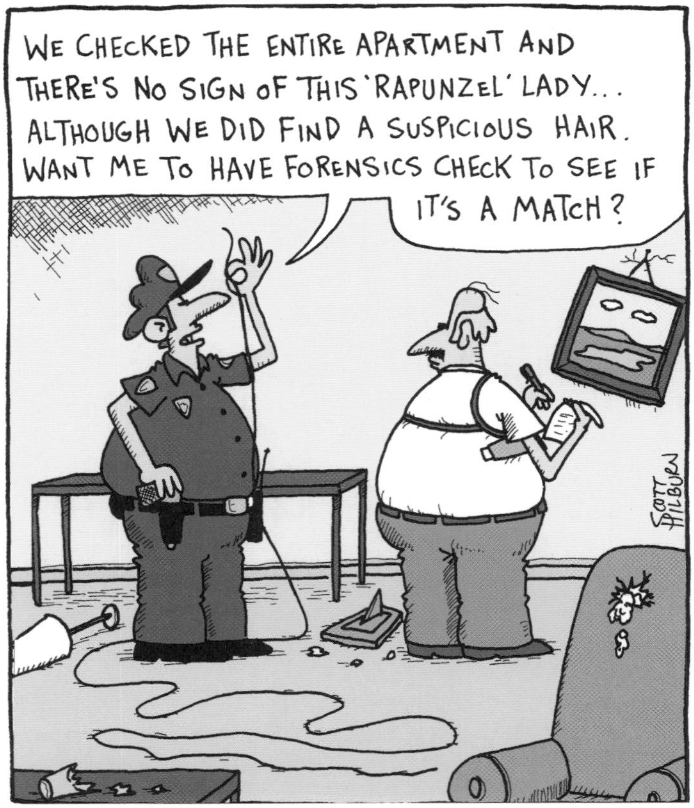
WE CHECKED THE ENTIRE APARTMENT AND THERE'S NO SIGN OF THIS 'RAPUNZEL' LADY... ALTHOUGH WE DID FIND A SUSPICIOUS HAIR. WANT ME TO HAVE FORENSICS CHECK TO SEE IF IT'S A MATCH?
SCOTT HILBURN

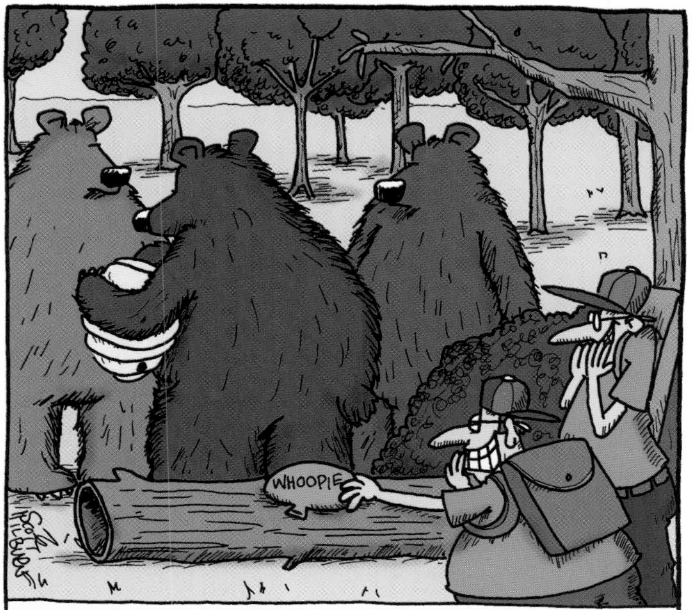
WHOOPIE
SCOTT HILBURN

FRANK AND BYRON WERE ABOUT TO LEARN THAT THE ONE THING THESE ANIMALS DISLIKED MORE THAN BEING SURPRISED BY HUMANS WAS BEING HUMILIATED BY THEM.

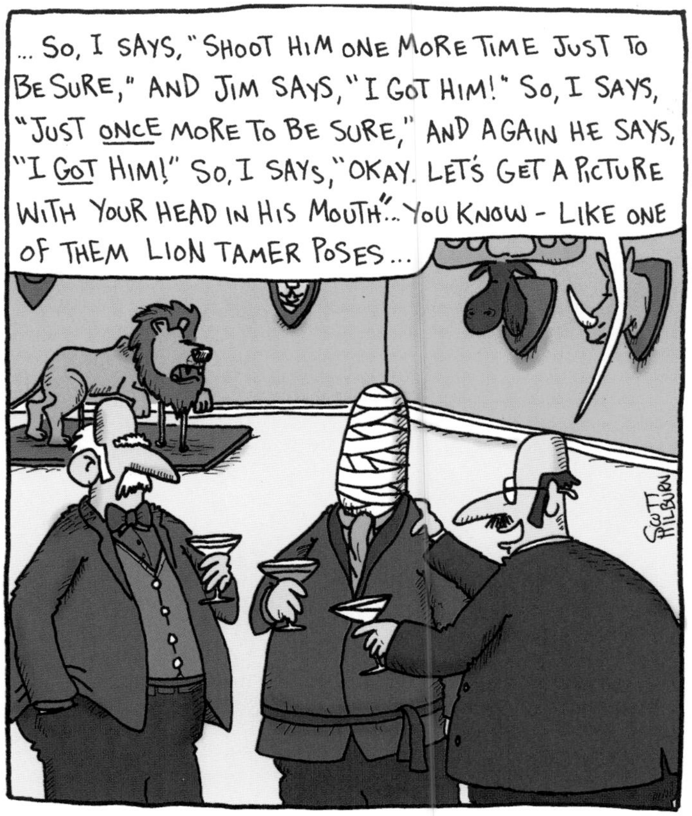
... SO, I SAYS, "SHOOT HIM ONE MORE TIME JUST TO BE SURE," AND JIM SAYS, "I GOT HIM!" SO, I SAYS, "JUST ONCE MORE TO BE SURE," AND AGAIN HE SAYS, "I GOT HIM!" SO, I SAYS, "OKAY. LET'S GET A PICTURE WITH YOUR HEAD IN HIS MOUTH."... YOU KNOW - LIKE ONE OF THEM LION TAMER POSES...
SCOTT HILBURN

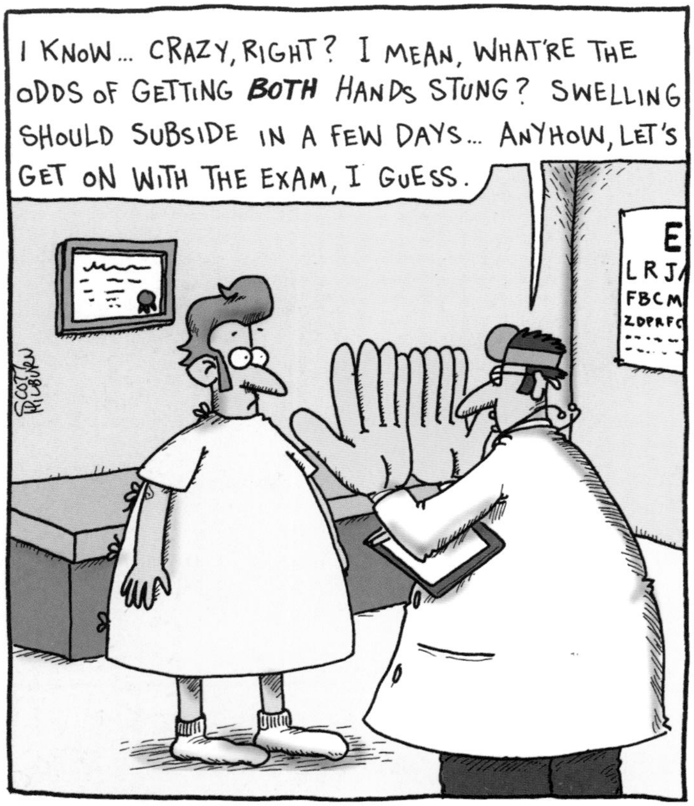
I KNOW... CRAZY, RIGHT? I MEAN, WHAT'RE THE ODDS OF GETTING **BOTH** HANDS STUNG? SWELLING SHOULD SUBSIDE IN A FEW DAYS... ANYHOW, LET'S GET ON WITH THE EXAM, I GUESS.
SCOTT HILBURN

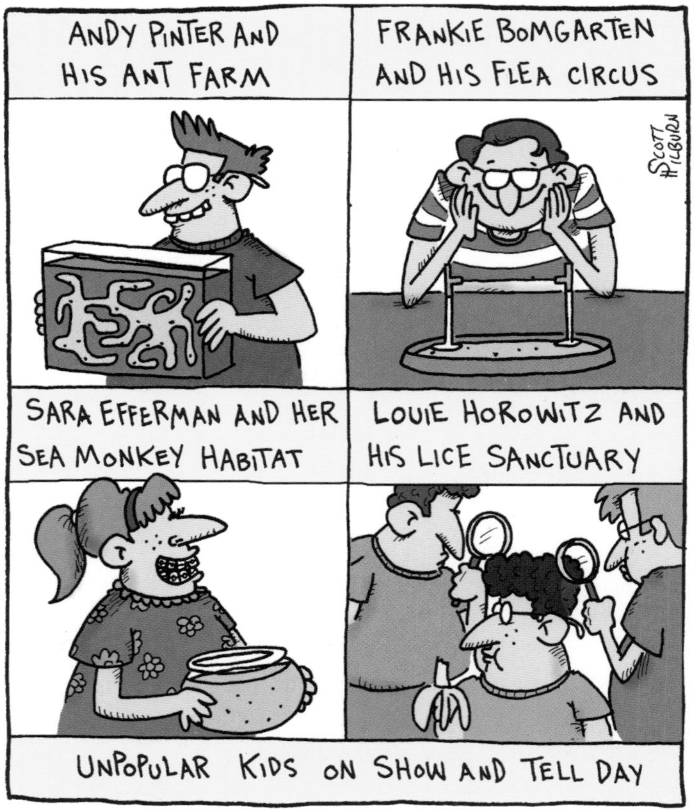
ANDY PINTER AND HIS ANT FARM
FRANKIE BOMGARTEN AND HIS FLEA CIRCUS
SCOTT HILBURN
SARA EFFERMAN AND HER SEA MONKEY HABITAT
LOUIE HOROWITZ AND HIS LICE SANCTUARY
UNPOPULAR KIDS ON SHOW AND TELL DAY

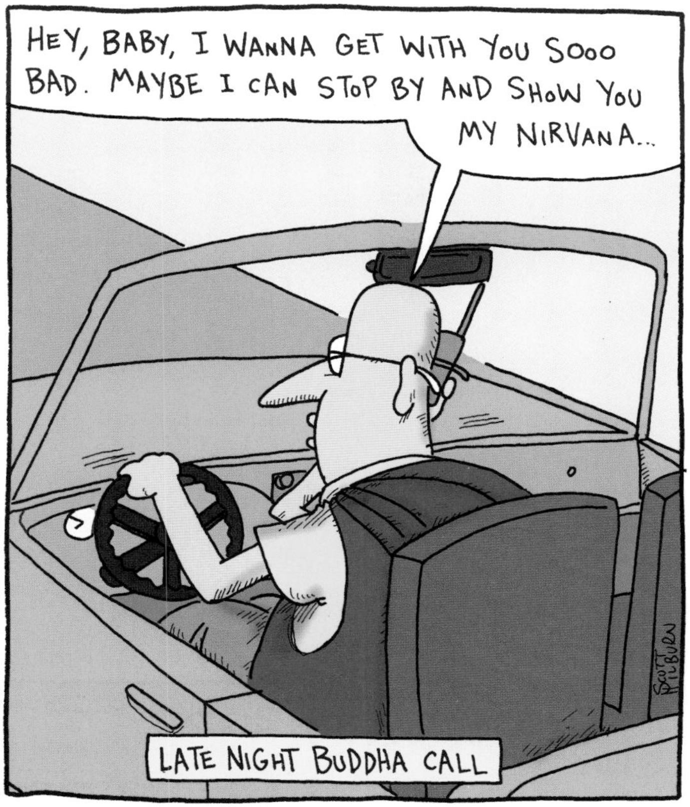
HEY, BABY, I WANNA GET WITH YOU SOOO BAD. MAYBE I CAN STOP BY AND SHOW YOU MY NIRVANA...
LATE NIGHT BUDDHA CALL
SCOTT HILBURN

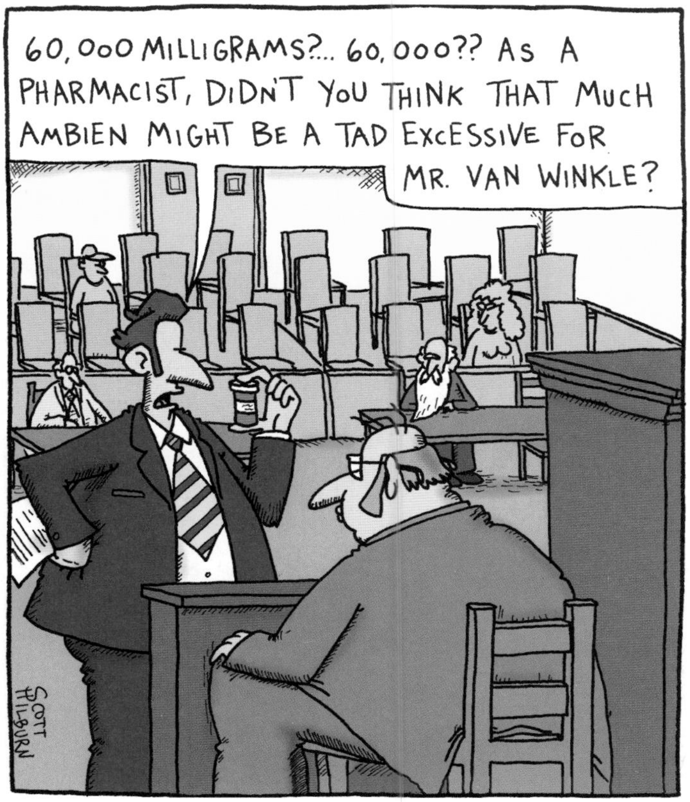
60,000 MILLIGRAMS?... 60,000?? AS A PHARMACIST, DIDN'T YOU THINK THAT MUCH AMBIEN MIGHT BE A TAD EXCESSIVE FOR MR. VAN WINKLE?
SCOTT HILBURN

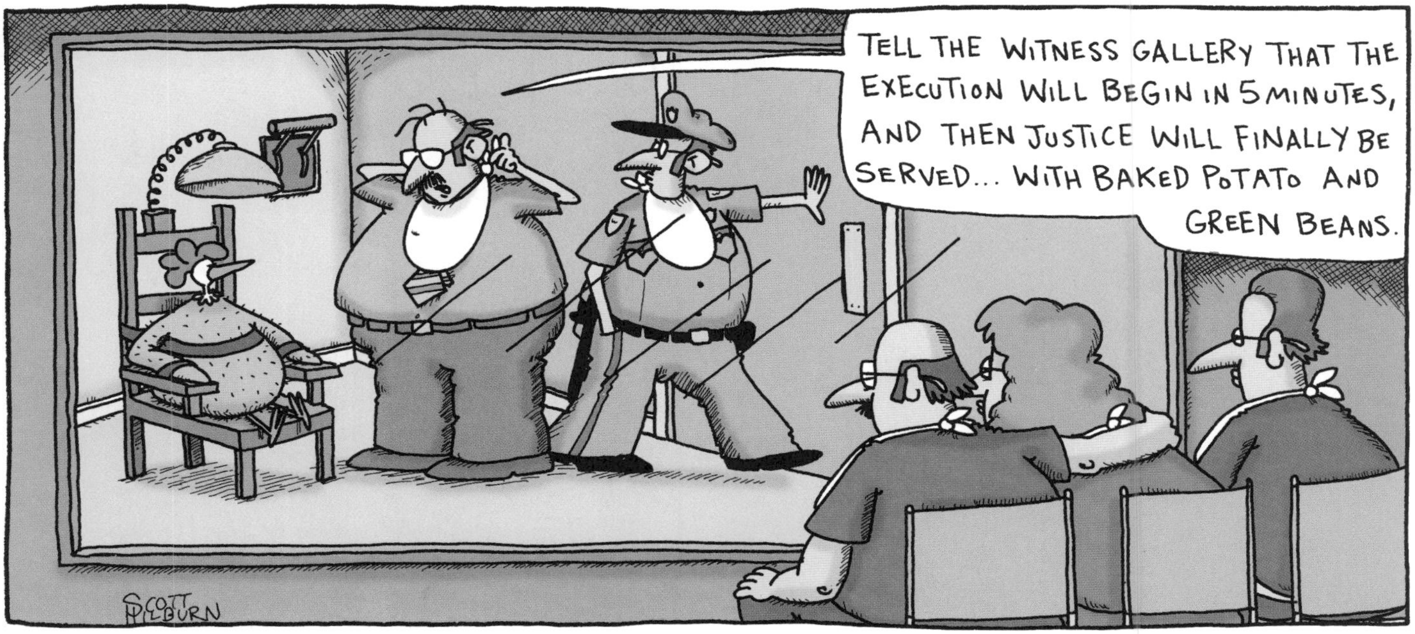
TELL THE WITNESS GALLERY THAT THE EXECUTION WILL BEGIN IN 5 MINUTES, AND THEN JUSTICE WILL FINALLY BE SERVED... WITH BAKED POTATO AND GREEN BEANS.
SCOTT HILBURN

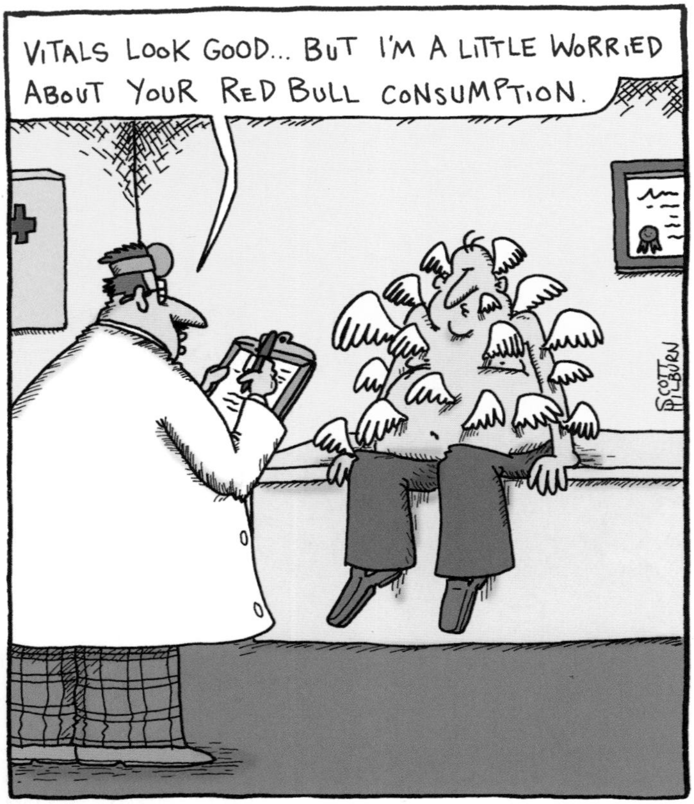
VITALS LOOK GOOD... BUT I'M A LITTLE WORRIED ABOUT YOUR RED BULL CONSUMPTION.
SCOTT HILBURN

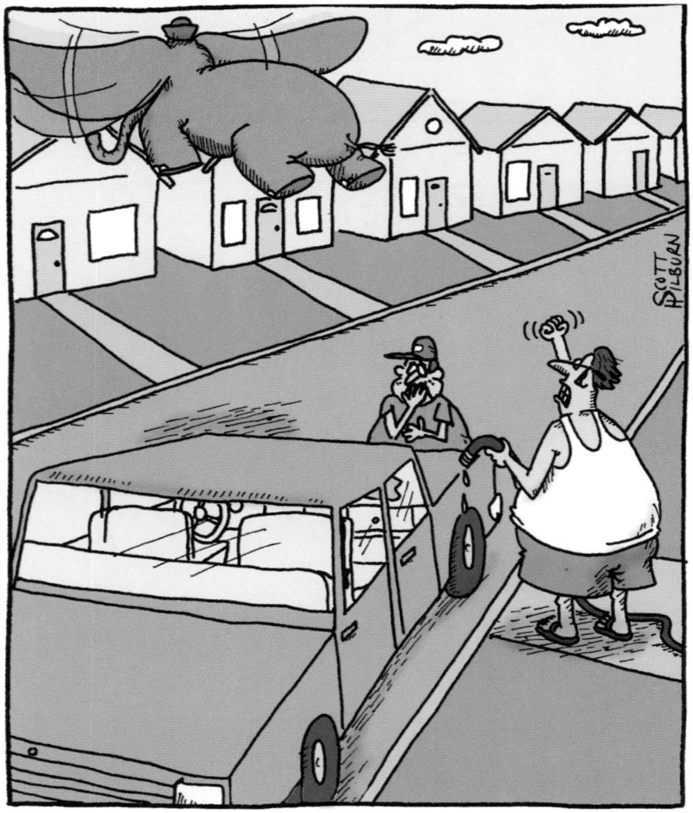
SCOTT HILBURN

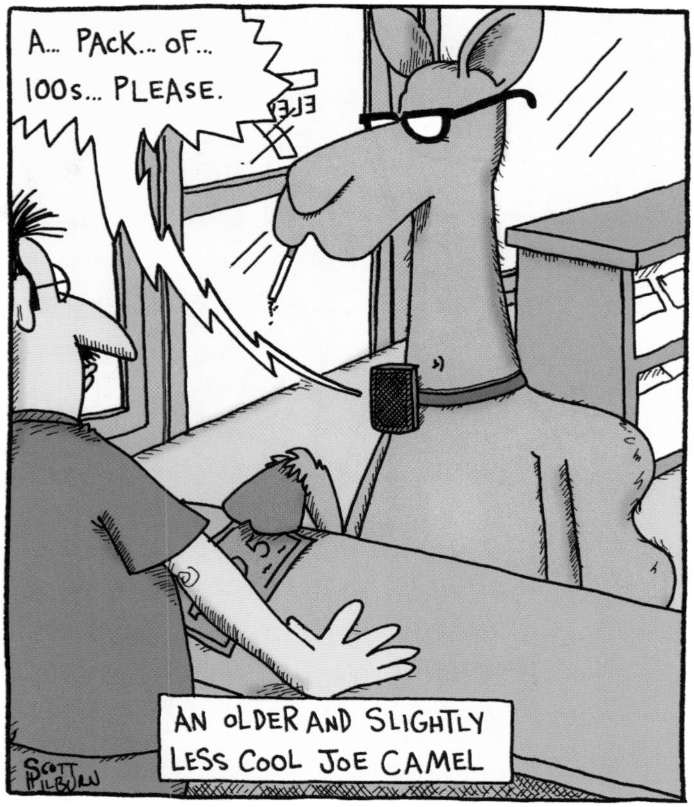
A... PACK... OF...
100s... PLEASE.
AN OLDER AND SLIGHTLY
LESS COOL JOE CAMEL
SCOTT HILBURN

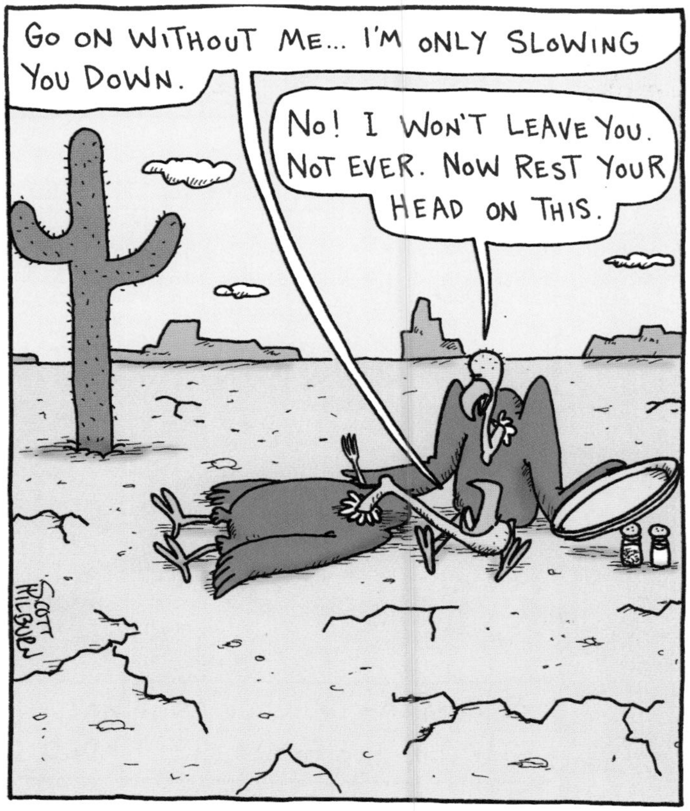
GO ON WITHOUT ME... I'M ONLY SLOWING YOU DOWN.
NO! I WON'T LEAVE YOU. NOT EVER. NOW REST YOUR HEAD ON THIS.
SCOTT HILBURN

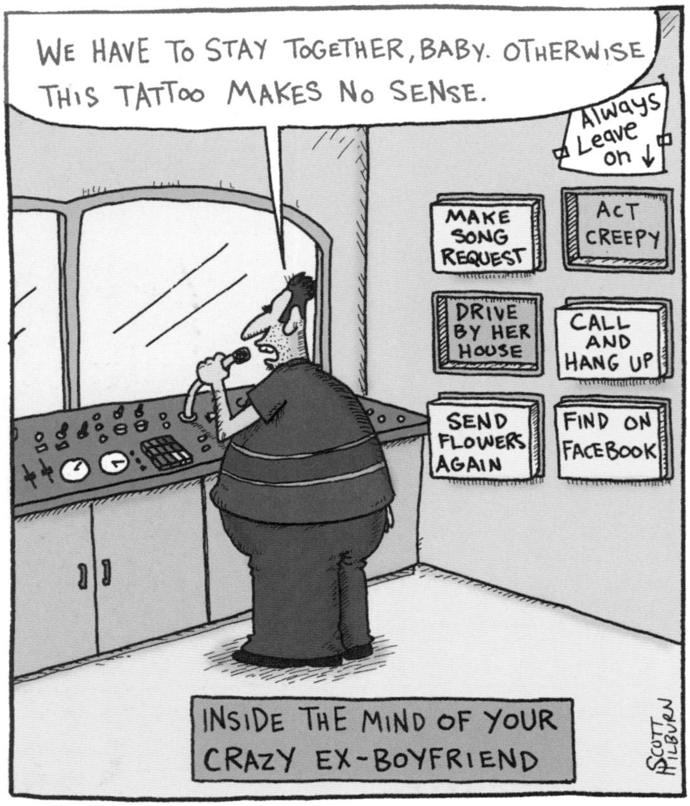
WE HAVE TO STAY TOGETHER, BABY. OTHERWISE THIS TATTOO MAKES NO SENSE.
Always Leave on ↓
MAKE SONG REQUEST
ACT CREEPY
DRIVE BY HER HOUSE
CALL AND HANG UP
SEND FLOWERS AGAIN
FIND ON FACEBOOK
INSIDE THE MIND OF YOUR CRAZY EX-BOYFRIEND
SCOTT HILBURN

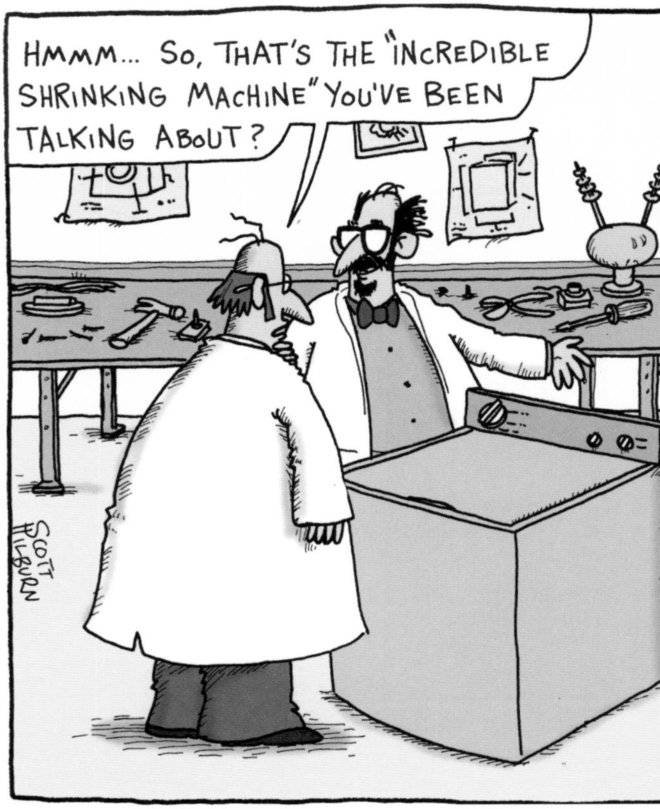
HMMM... SO, THAT'S THE "INCREDIBLE SHRINKING MACHINE" YOU'VE BEEN TALKING ABOUT?
SCOTT HILBURN

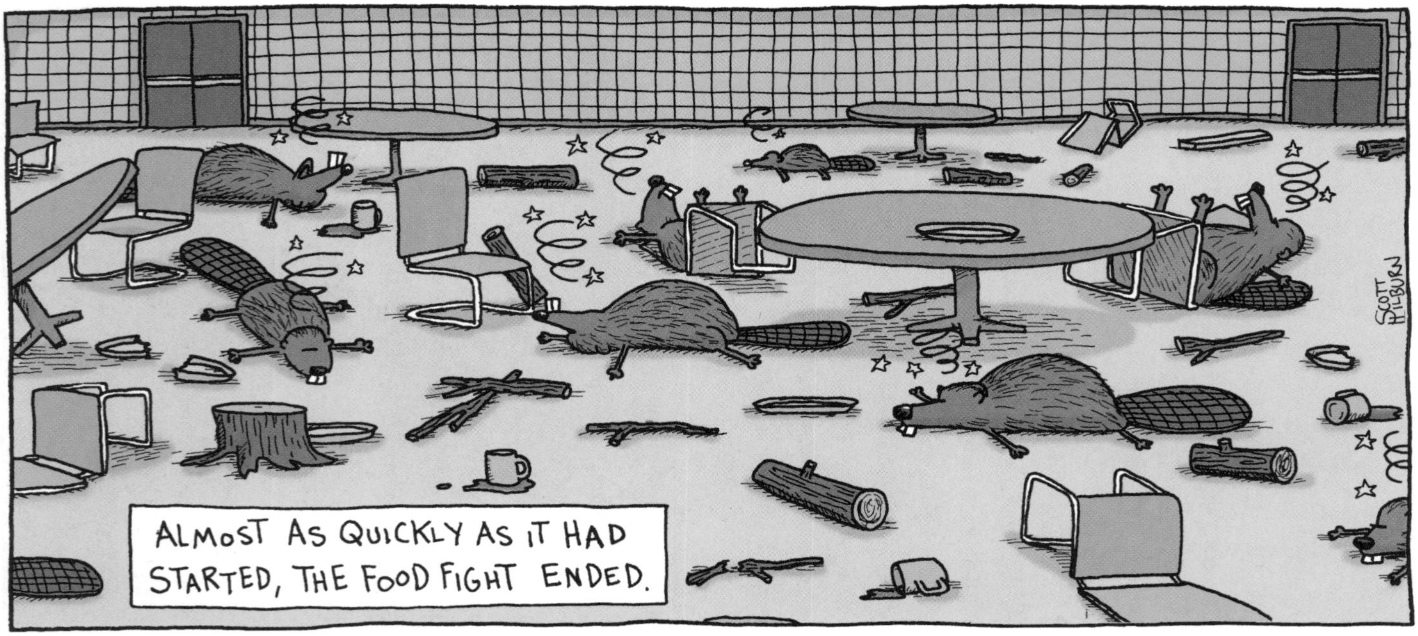
ALMOST AS QUICKLY AS IT HAD STARTED, THE FOOD FIGHT ENDED.
SCOTT HILBURN

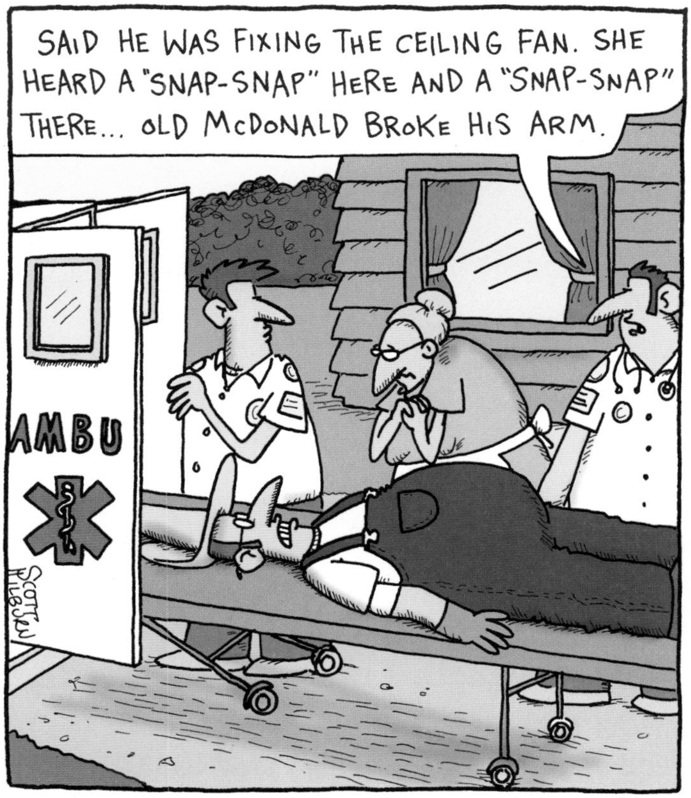
SAID HE WAS FIXING THE CEILING FAN. SHE HEARD A "SNAP-SNAP" HERE AND A "SNAP-SNAP" THERE... OLD McDONALD BROKE HIS ARM.
AMBU
SCOTT HILBURN

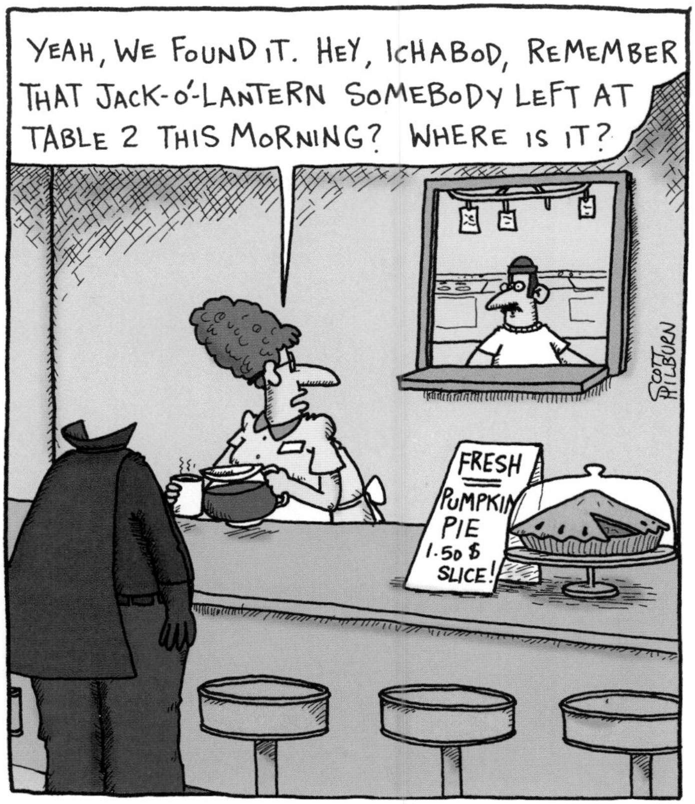
YEAH, WE FOUND IT. HEY, ICHABOD, REMEMBER THAT JACK-O'-LANTERN SOMEBODY LEFT AT TABLE 2 THIS MORNING? WHERE IS IT?
FRESH
PUMPKI
PIE
1.50 $
SLICE!
SCOTT HILBURN

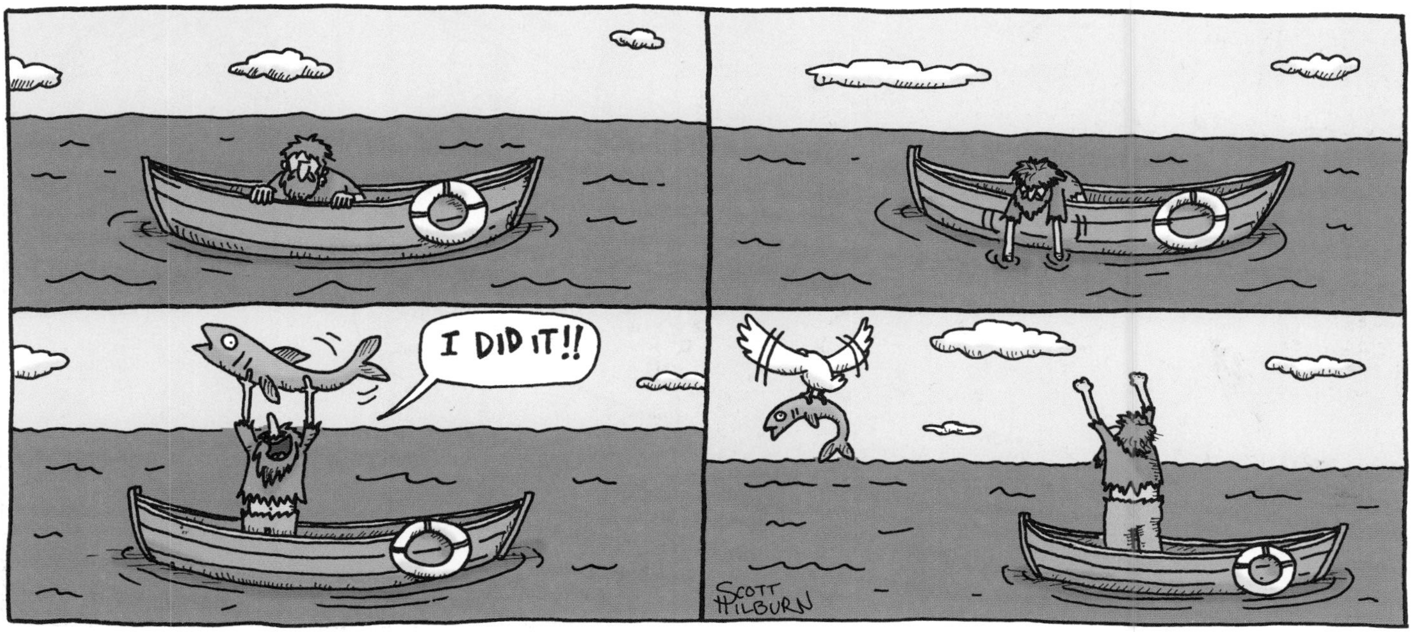
I DID IT!!
SCOTT HILBURN

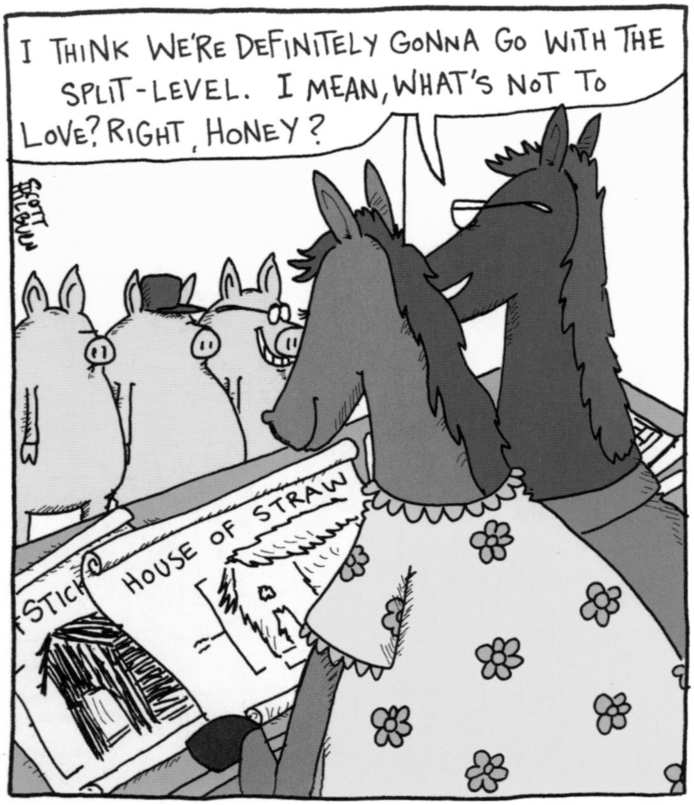
I THINK WE'RE DEFINITELY GONNA GO WITH THE SPLIT-LEVEL. I MEAN, WHAT'S NOT TO LOVE? RIGHT, HONEY?
HOUSE OF STRAW
STICK
SCOTT HILBURN

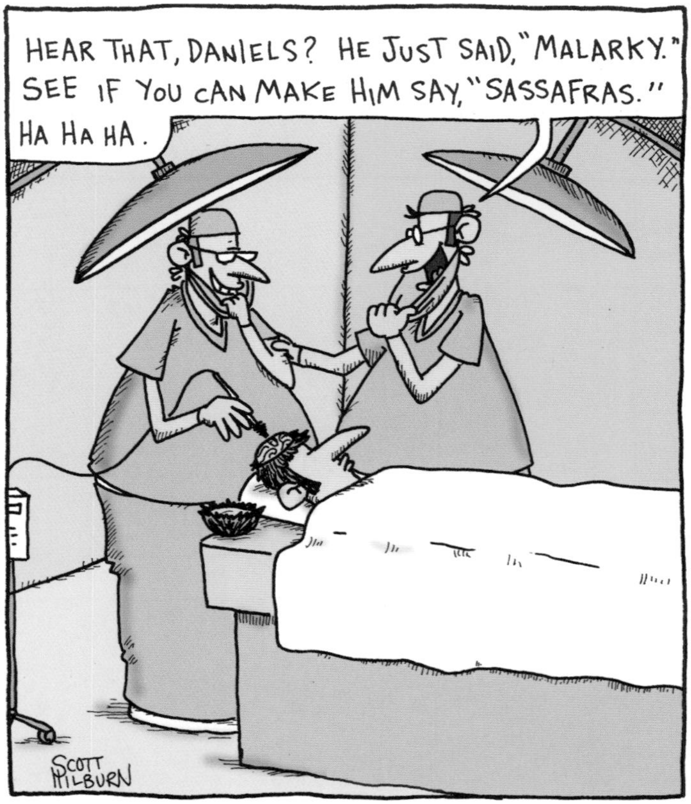
HEAR THAT, DANIELS? HE JUST SAID, "MALARKY." SEE IF YOU CAN MAKE HIM SAY, "SASSAFRAS." HA HA HA.
SCOTT HILBURN

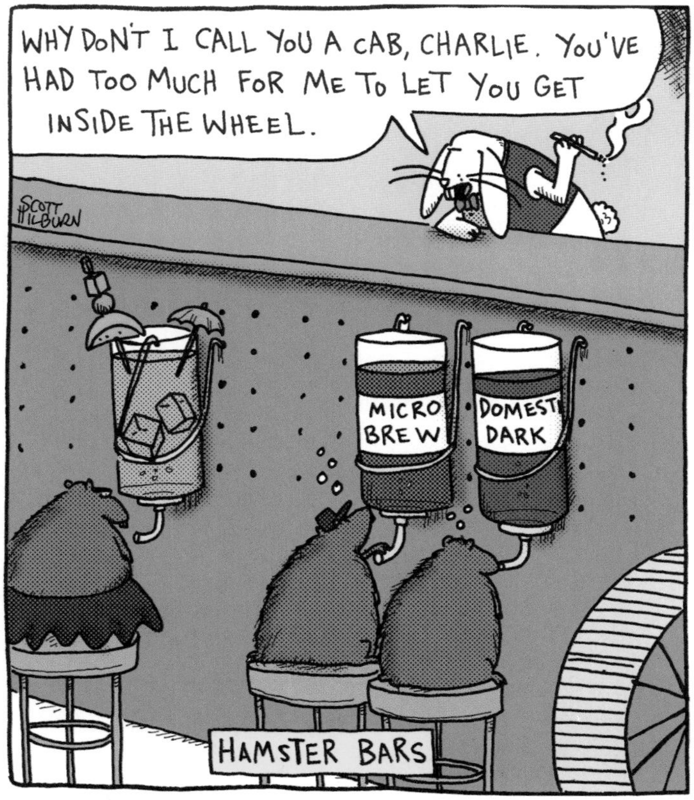
WHY DON'T I CALL YOU A CAB, CHARLIE. YOU'VE HAD TOO MUCH FOR ME TO LET YOU GET INSIDE THE WHEEL.
SCOTT HILBURN
MICRO BREW
DOMESTI DARK
HAMSTER BARS

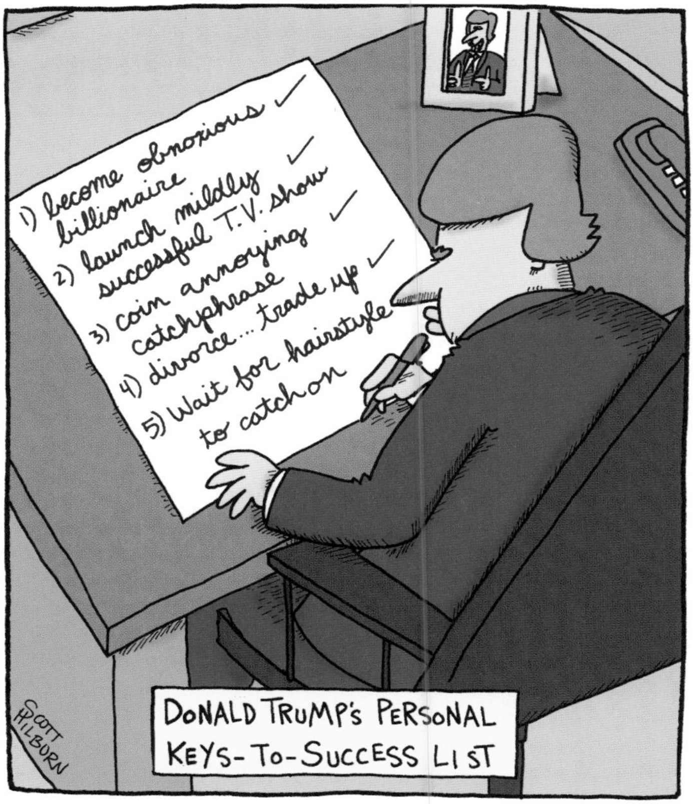
1) become obnoxious billionaire
2) launch mildly successful T.V. show
3) coin annoying catchphrase
4) divorce... trade up
5) Wait for hairstyle to catch on
SCOTT HILBURN
DONALD TRUMP'S PERSONAL KEYS-TO-SUCCESS LIST

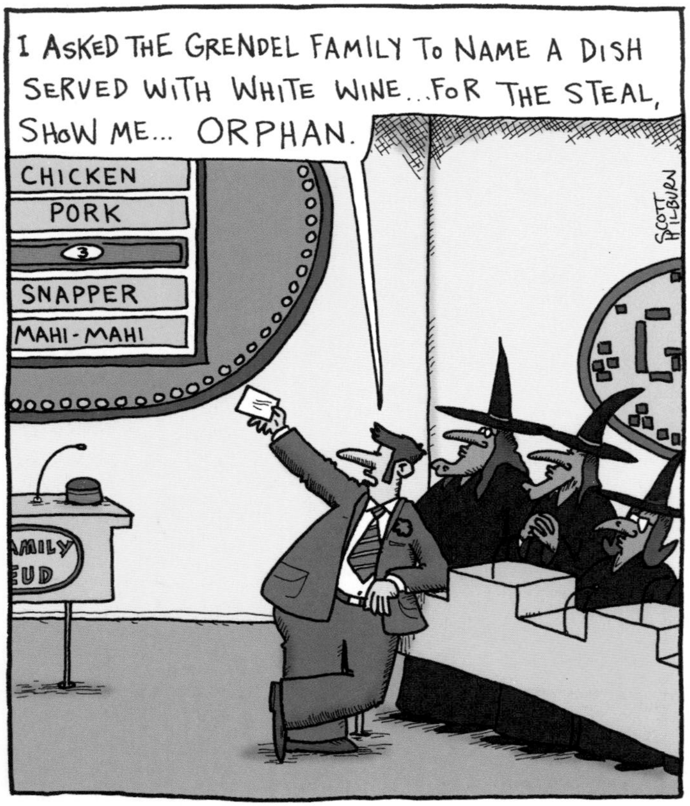
I ASKED THE GRENDEL FAMILY TO NAME A DISH SERVED WITH WHITE WINE...FOR THE STEAL, SHOW ME... ORPHAN.
CHICKEN
PORK
3
SNAPPER
MAHI-MAHI
SCOTT HILBURN

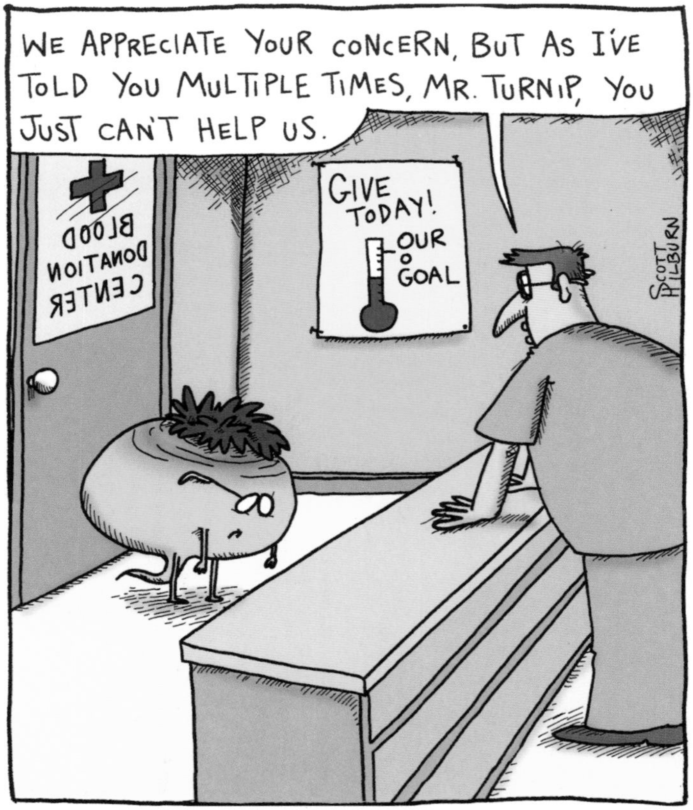
WE APPRECIATE YOUR CONCERN, BUT AS I'VE TOLD YOU MULTIPLE TIMES, MR. TURNIP, YOU JUST CAN'T HELP US.
BLOOD DONATION CENTER
GIVE TODAY!
OUR GOAL
SCOTT HILBURN

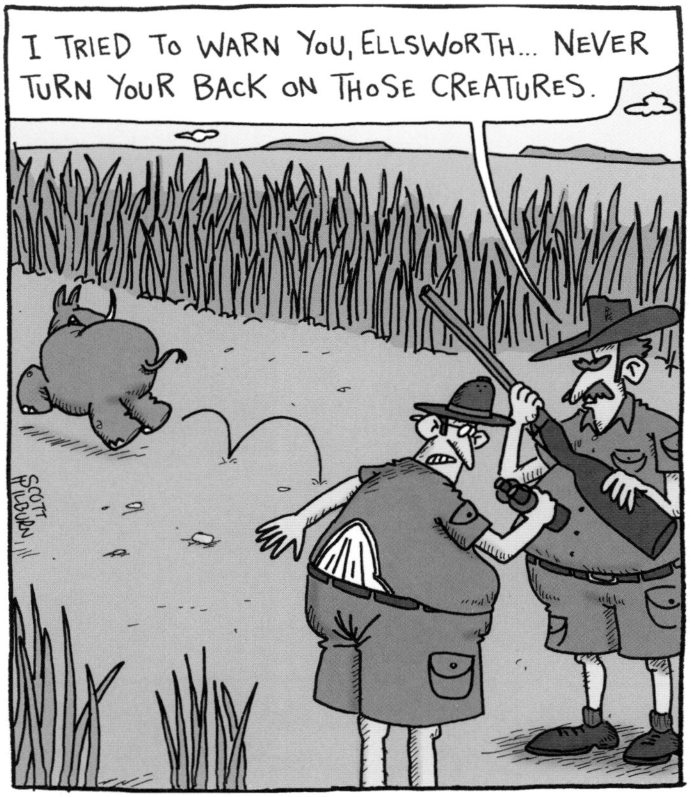
I TRIED TO WARN YOU, ELLSWORTH... NEVER TURN YOUR BACK ON THOSE CREATURES.
SCOTT HILBURN

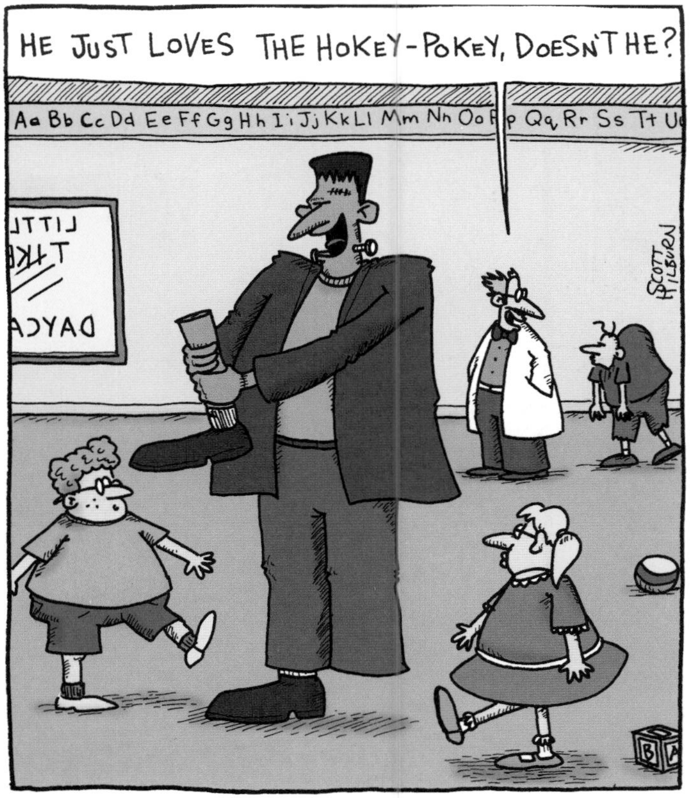
HE JUST LOVES THE HOKEY-POKEY, DOESN'T HE?
SCOTT HILBURN

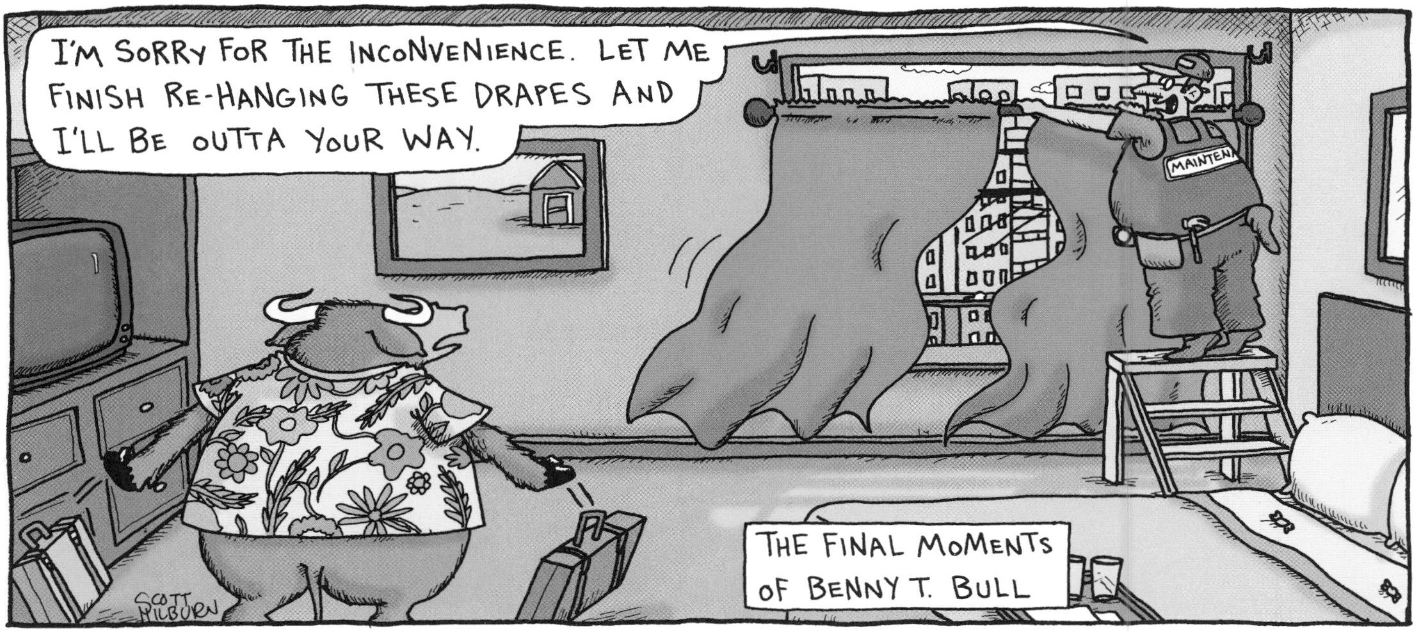
I'M SORRY FOR THE INCONVENIENCE. LET ME FINISH RE-HANGING THESE DRAPES AND I'LL BE OUTTA YOUR WAY.
MAINTEN
SCOTT HILBURN

THE FINAL MOMENTS OF BENNY T. BULL

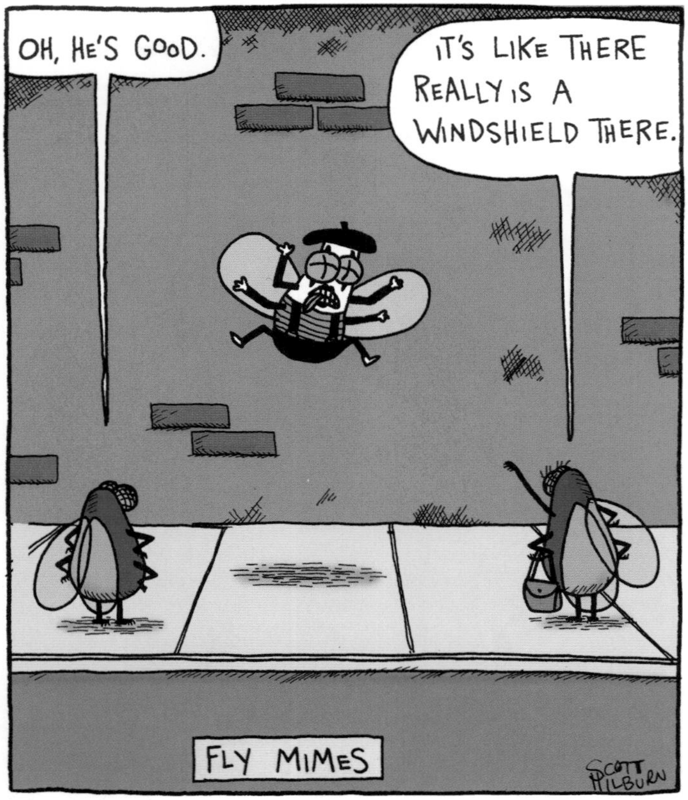
OH, HE'S GOOD.
IT'S LIKE THERE REALLY IS A WINDSHIELD THERE.
FLY MIMES
SCOTT HILBURN

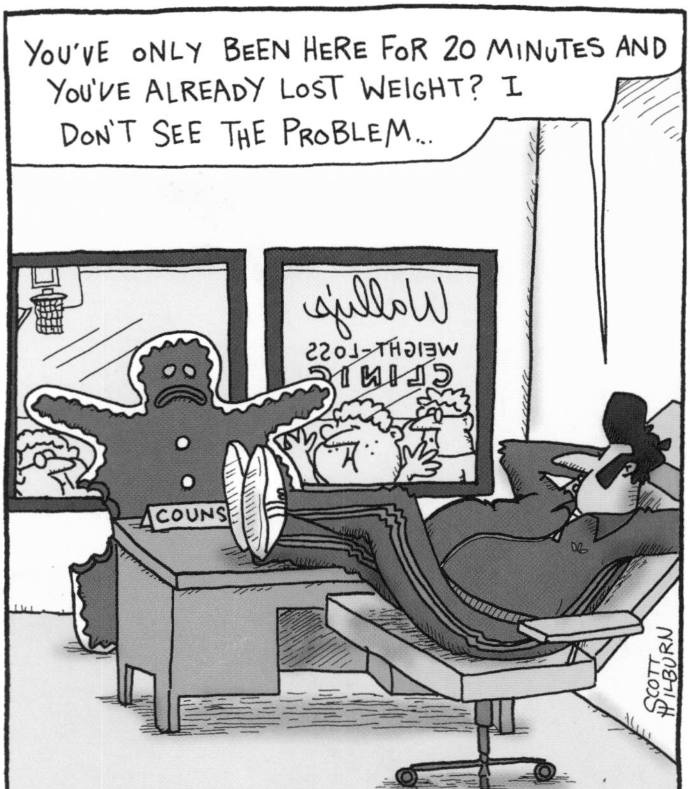
YOU'VE ONLY BEEN HERE FOR 20 MINUTES AND YOU'VE ALREADY LOST WEIGHT? I DON'T SEE THE PROBLEM...
WEIGHT-LOSS
COUNS
SCOTT HILBURN

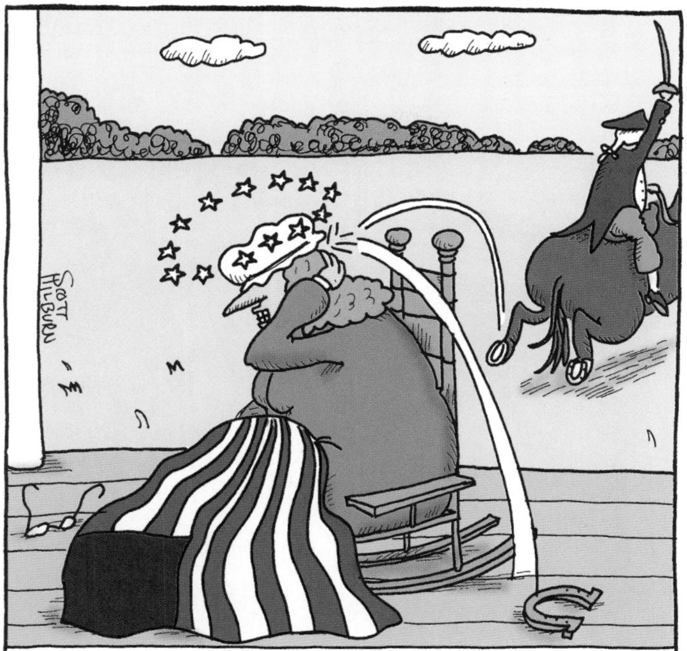
SCOTT HILBURN

HER FLAG PROJECT NEAR COMPLETION, BETSY ROSS PONDERS A PATRIOTIC WAY TO REPRESENT THE COLONIES WHEN INSPIRATION SUDDENLY STRIKES HER.

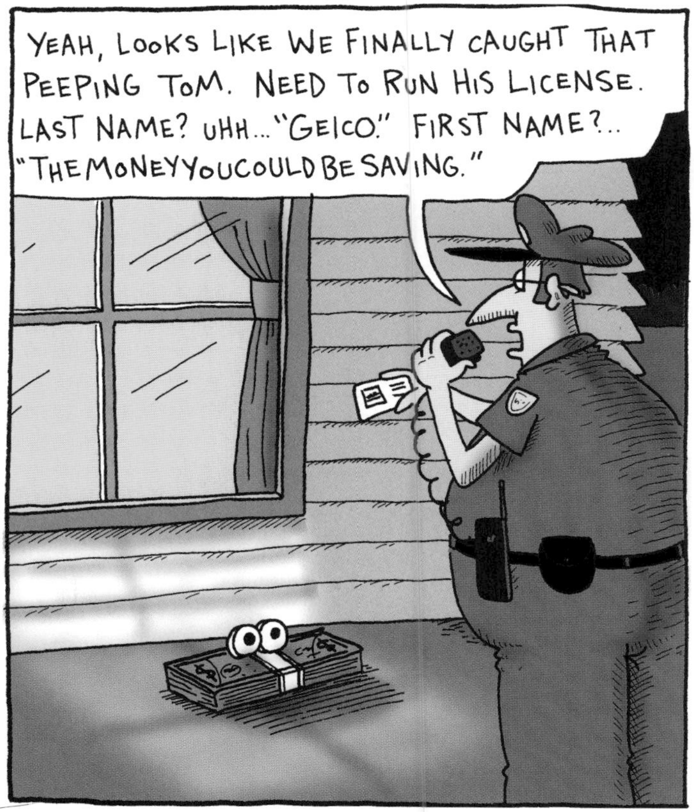
YEAH, LOOKS LIKE WE FINALLY CAUGHT THAT PEEPING TOM. NEED TO RUN HIS LICENSE. LAST NAME? UHH... "GEICO." FIRST NAME?.. "THE MONEY YOU COULD BE SAVING."

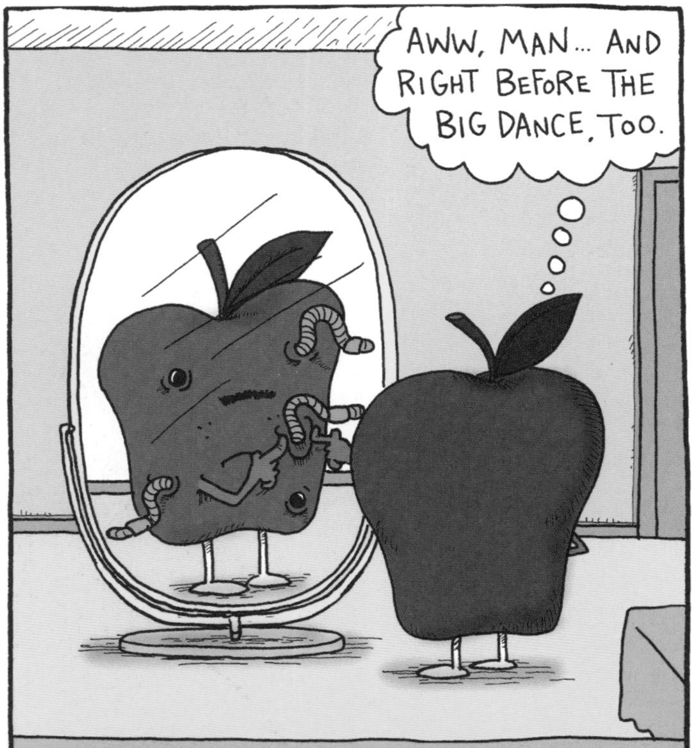
AWW, MAN... AND RIGHT BEFORE THE BIG DANCE, TOO.

THE TEEN YEARS OF A RED DELICIOUS.

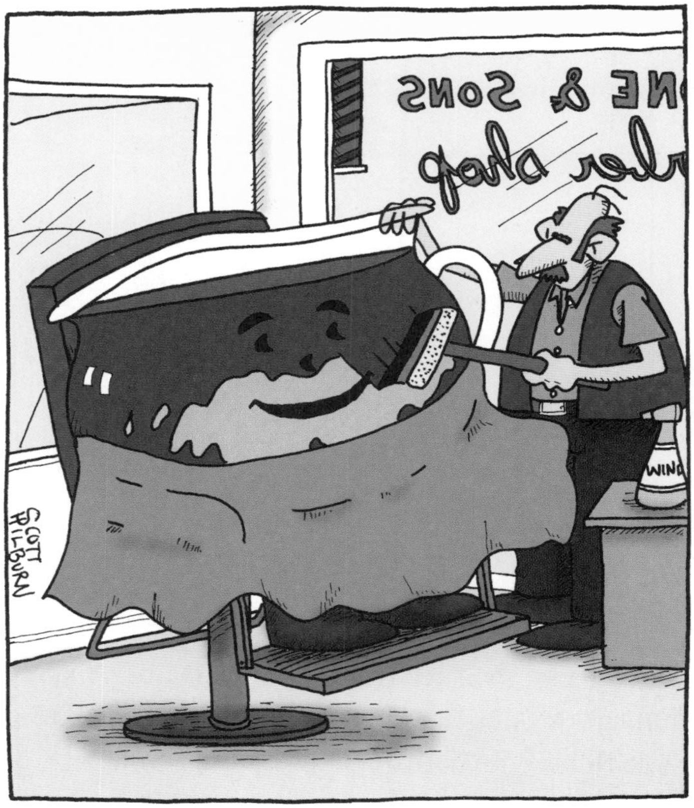
SCOTT HILBURN

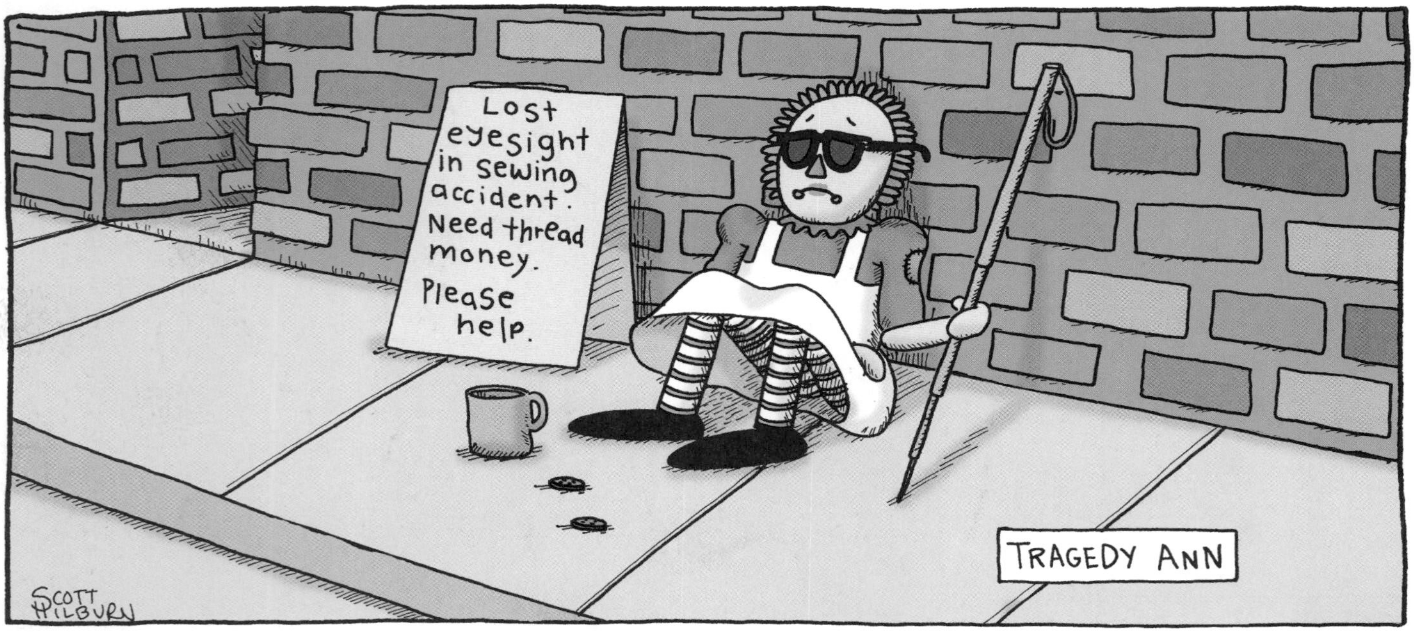
Lost eyesight in sewing accident. Need thread money. Please help.
SCOTT HILBURN

TRAGEDY ANN

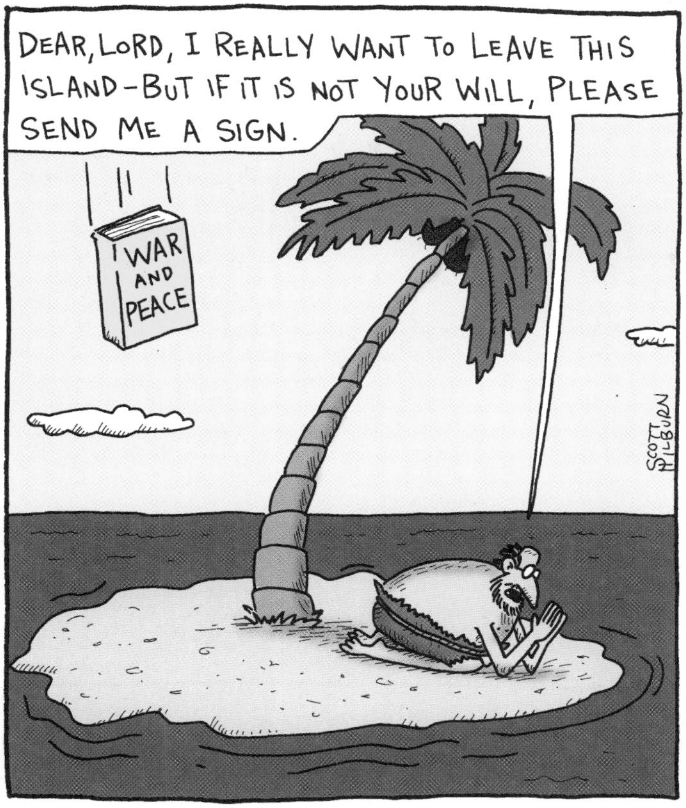
DEAR, LORD, I REALLY WANT TO LEAVE THIS ISLAND - BUT IF IT IS NOT YOUR WILL, PLEASE SEND ME A SIGN.
WAR AND PEACE
SCOTT HILBURN

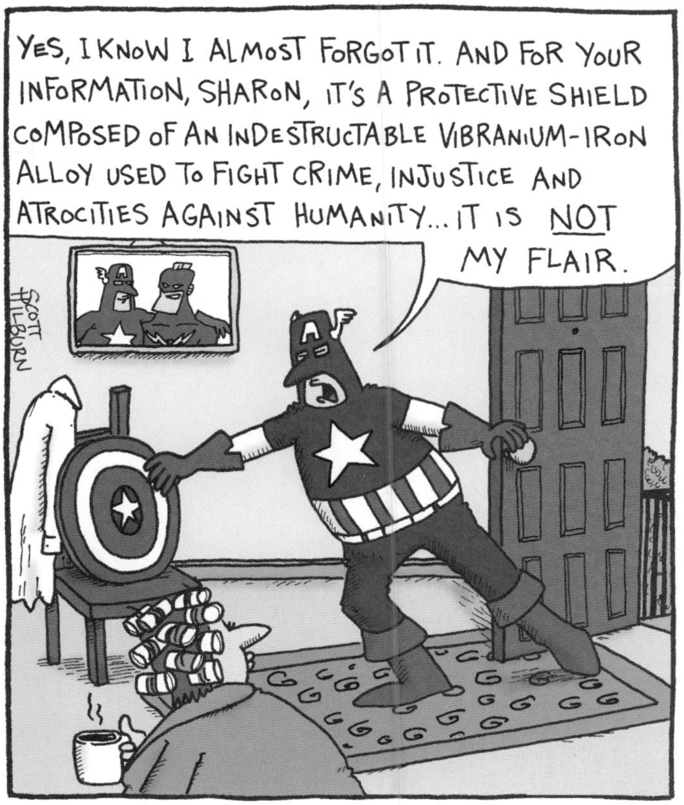
YES, I KNOW I ALMOST FORGOT IT. AND FOR YOUR INFORMATION, SHARON, IT'S A PROTECTIVE SHIELD COMPOSED OF AN INDESTRUCTABLE VIBRANIUM-IRON ALLOY USED TO FIGHT CRIME, INJUSTICE AND ATROCITIES AGAINST HUMANITY... IT IS NOT MY FLAIR.
SCOTT HILBURN

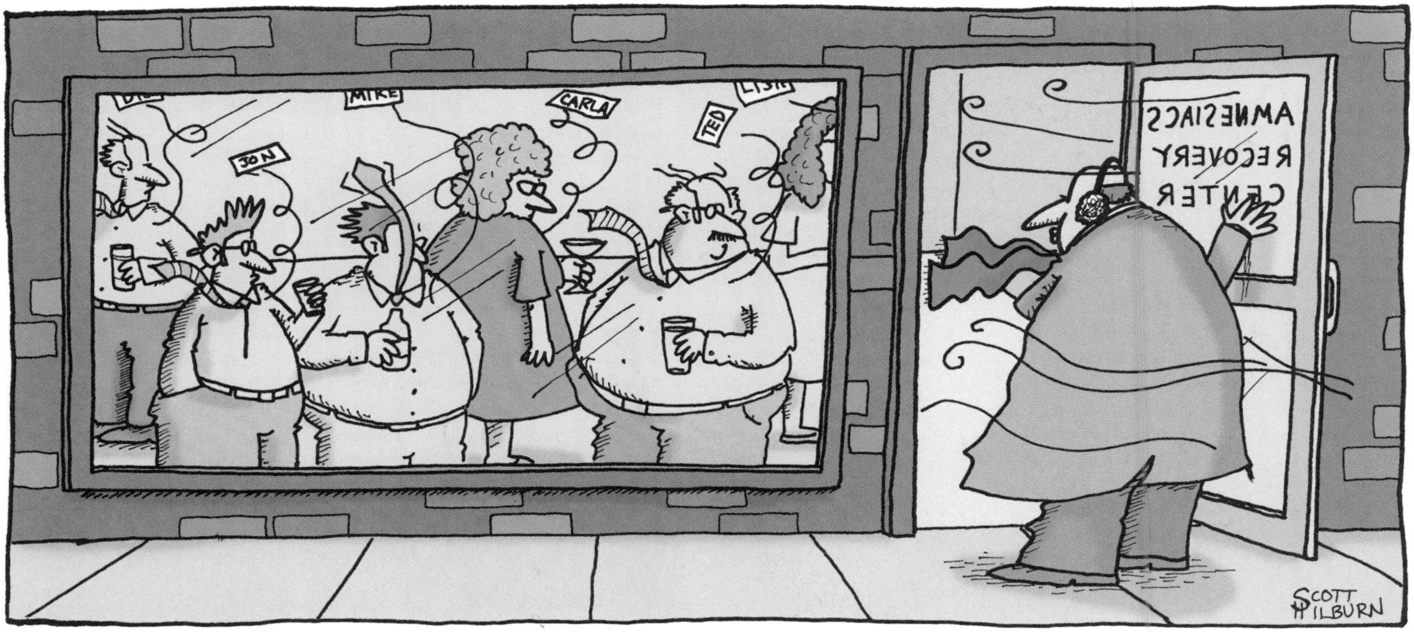
MIKE
CARLA
JON
TED
AMNESIACS RECOVERY CENTER
SCOTT HILBURN

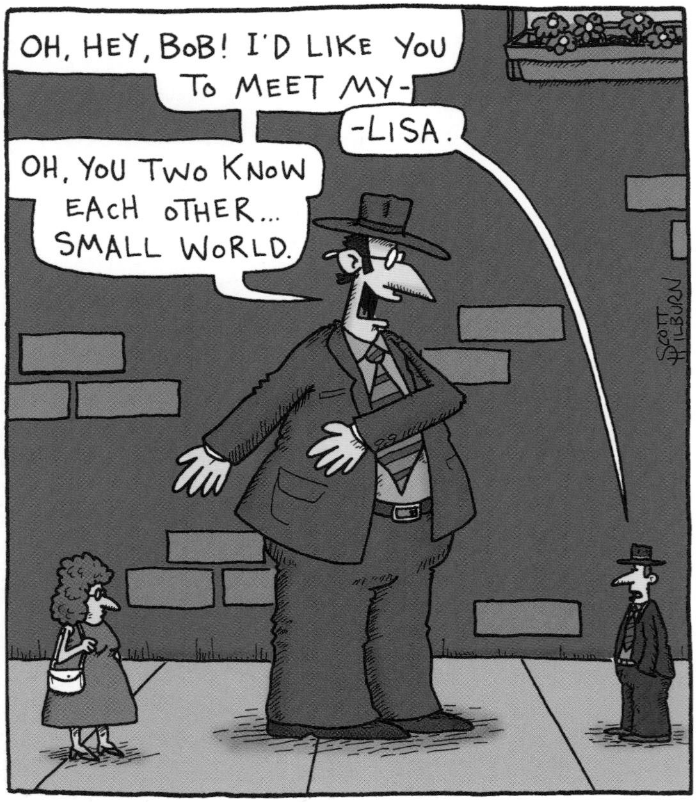
OH, HEY, BOB! I'D LIKE YOU TO MEET MY-
-LISA.
OH, YOU TWO KNOW EACH OTHER... SMALL WORLD.
SCOTT HILBURN

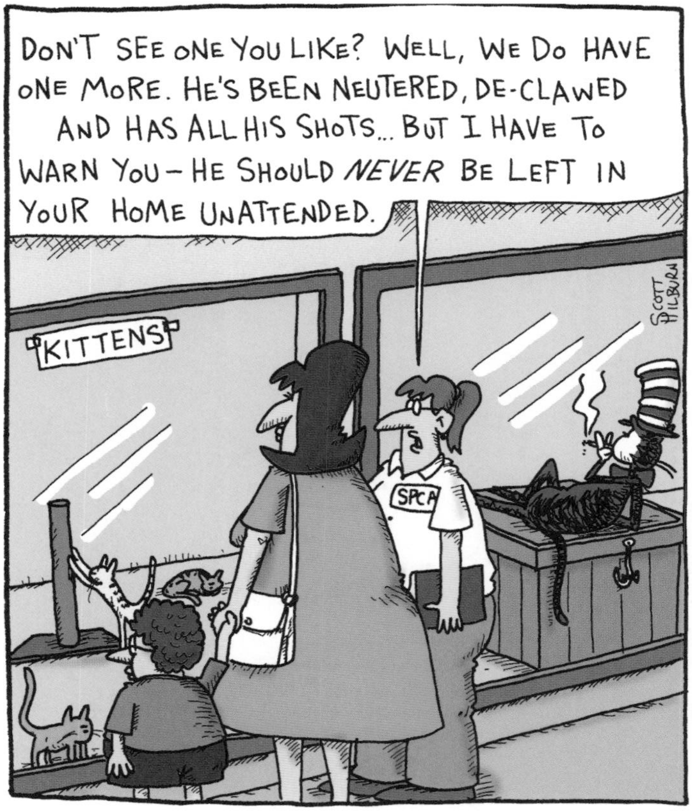
DON'T SEE ONE YOU LIKE? WELL, WE DO HAVE ONE MORE. HE'S BEEN NEUTERED, DE-CLAWED AND HAS ALL HIS SHOTS... BUT I HAVE TO WARN YOU – HE SHOULD *NEVER* BE LEFT IN YOUR HOME UNATTENDED.
KITTENS
SPCA
SCOTT HILBURN

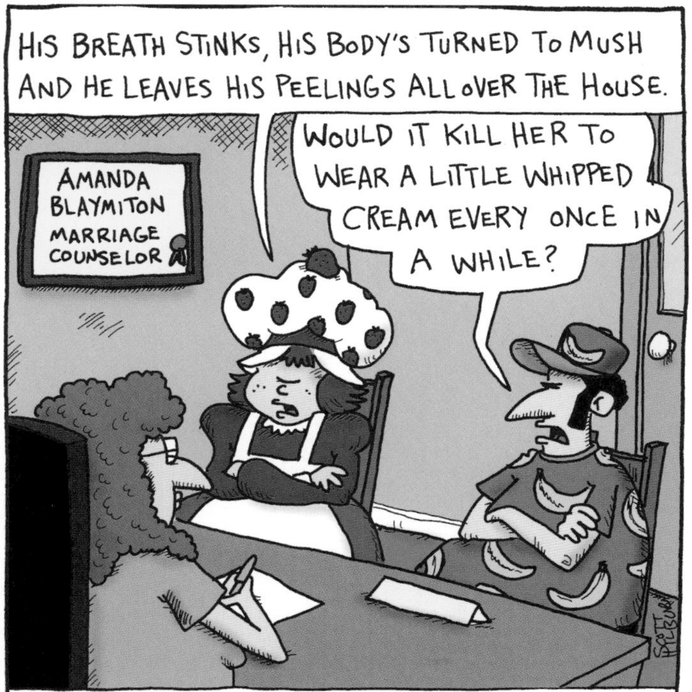
HIS BREATH STINKS, HIS BODY'S TURNED TO MUSH AND HE LEAVES HIS PEELINGS ALL OVER THE HOUSE.
WOULD IT KILL HER TO WEAR A LITTLE WHIPPED CREAM EVERY ONCE IN A WHILE?
AMANDA BLAYMITON MARRIAGE COUNSELOR

THEIR MARRIAGE IN JEOPARDY, STRAWBERRY SHORTCAKE AND BILLY BOB BANANA BREAD SEEK THERAPY.

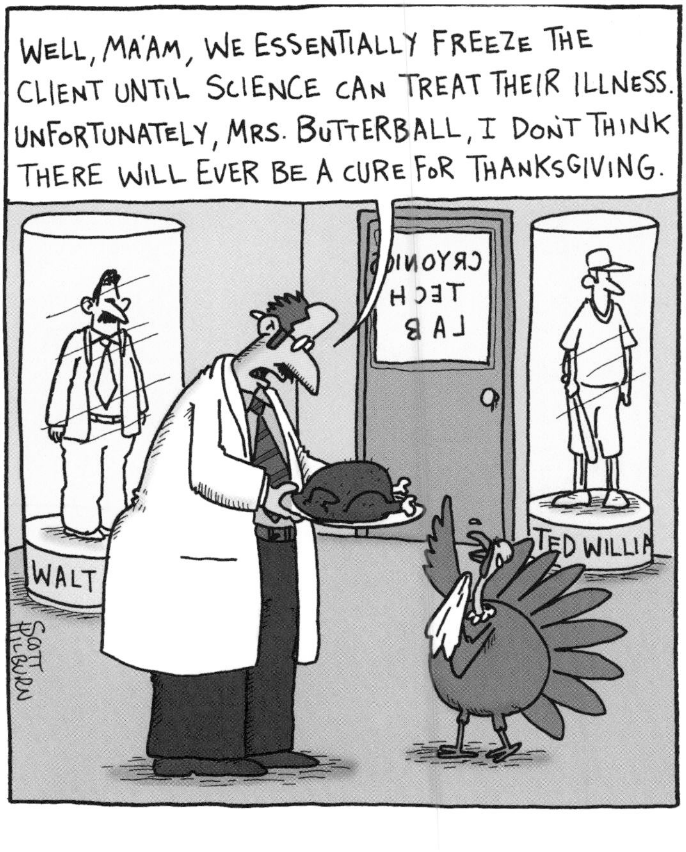
WELL, MA'AM, WE ESSENTIALLY FREEZE THE CLIENT UNTIL SCIENCE CAN TREAT THEIR ILLNESS. UNFORTUNATELY, MRS. BUTTERBALL, I DON'T THINK THERE WILL EVER BE A CURE FOR THANKSGIVING.
WALT
TED WILLIA

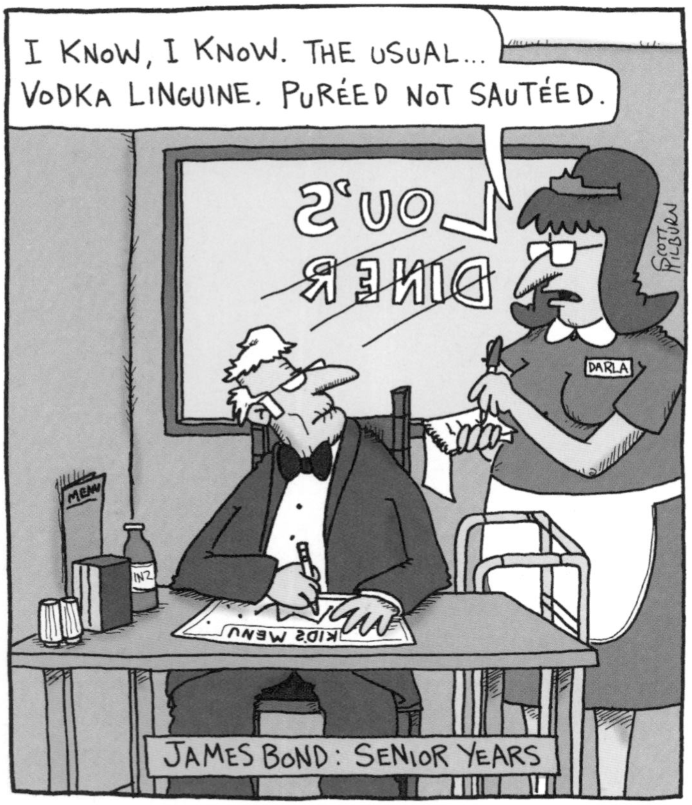
I KNOW, I KNOW. THE USUAL...
VODKA LINGUINE. PURÉED NOT SAUTÉED.
LOU'S DINER
DARLA
MENU
KID'S MENU
SCOTT HILBURN
JAMES BOND: SENIOR YEARS

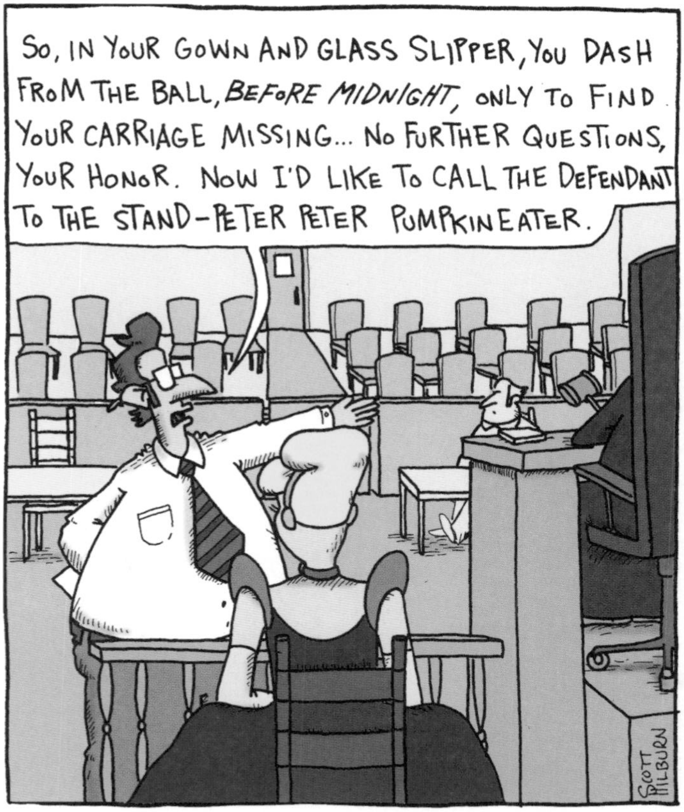
SO, IN YOUR GOWN AND GLASS SLIPPER, YOU DASH FROM THE BALL, *BEFORE MIDNIGHT*, ONLY TO FIND YOUR CARRIAGE MISSING... NO FURTHER QUESTIONS, YOUR HONOR. NOW I'D LIKE TO CALL THE DEFENDANT TO THE STAND—PETER PETER PUMPKIN EATER.
SCOTT HILBURN

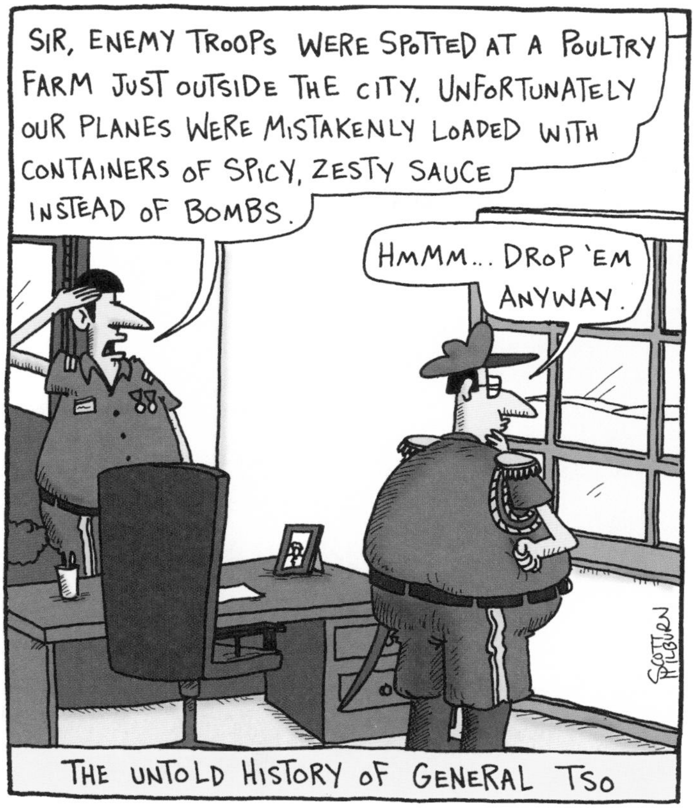
SIR, ENEMY TROOPS WERE SPOTTED AT A POULTRY FARM JUST OUTSIDE THE CITY. UNFORTUNATELY OUR PLANES WERE MISTAKENLY LOADED WITH CONTAINERS OF SPICY, ZESTY SAUCE INSTEAD OF BOMBS.
HMMM... DROP 'EM ANYWAY.
SCOTT HILBURN
THE UNTOLD HISTORY OF GENERAL TSO

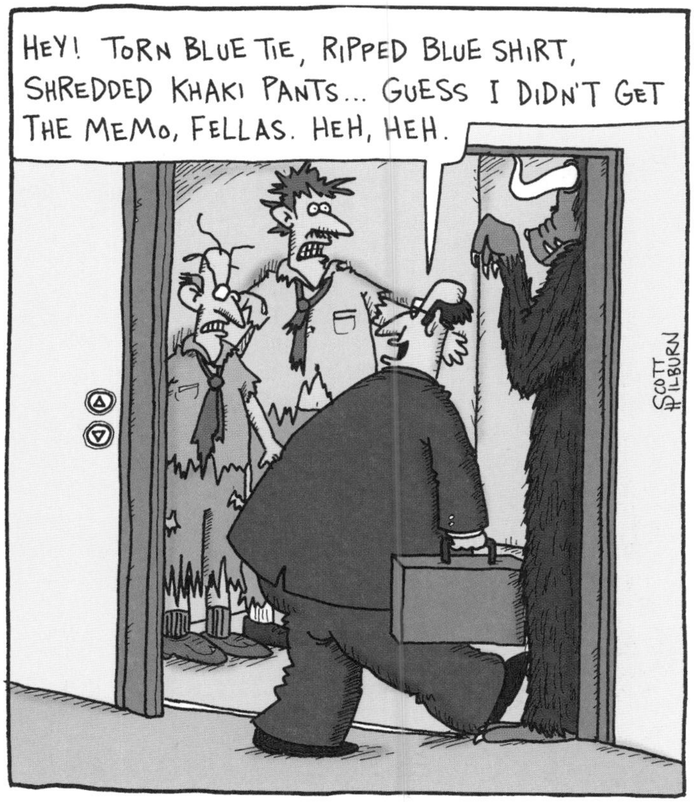
HEY! TORN BLUE TIE, RIPPED BLUE SHIRT, SHREDDED KHAKI PANTS... GUESS I DIDN'T GET THE MEMO, FELLAS. HEH, HEH.
SCOTT HILBURN

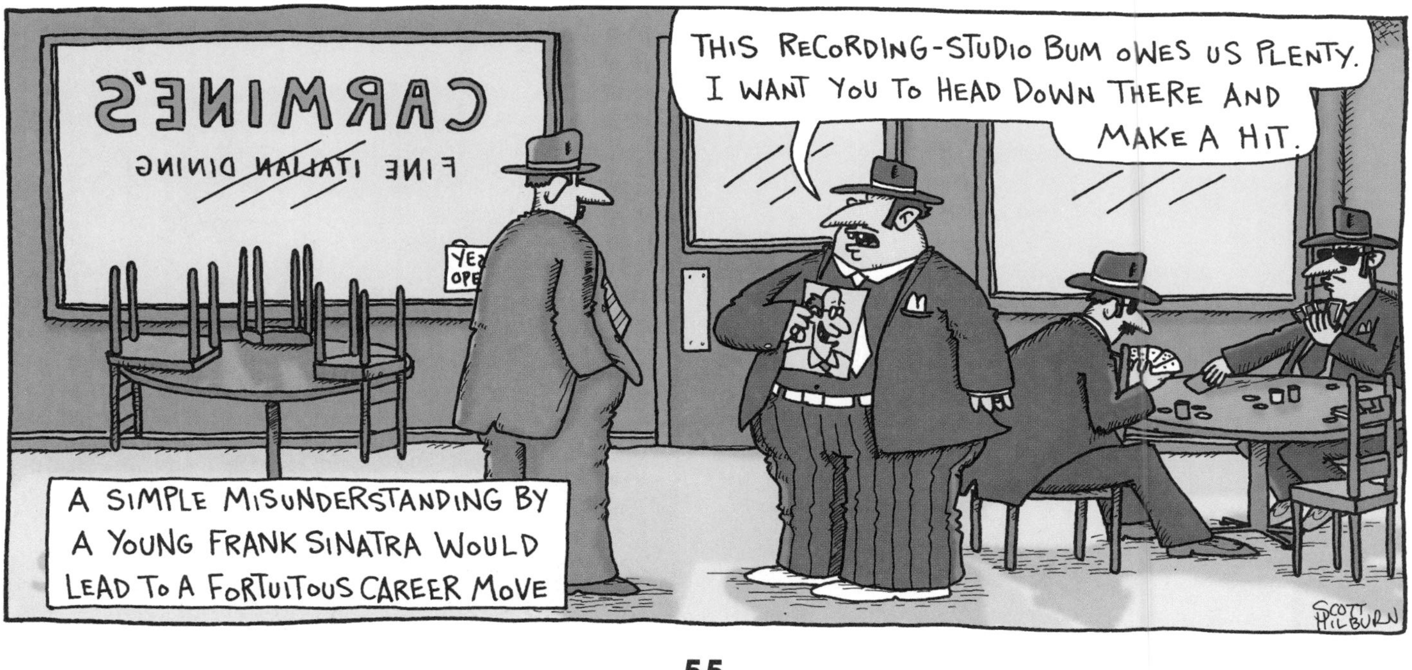
CARMINE'S
FINE ITALIAN DINING
THIS RECORDING-STUDIO BUM OWES US PLENTY. I WANT YOU TO HEAD DOWN THERE AND MAKE A HIT.
SCOTT HILBURN
A SIMPLE MISUNDERSTANDING BY A YOUNG FRANK SINATRA WOULD LEAD TO A FORTUITOUS CAREER MOVE

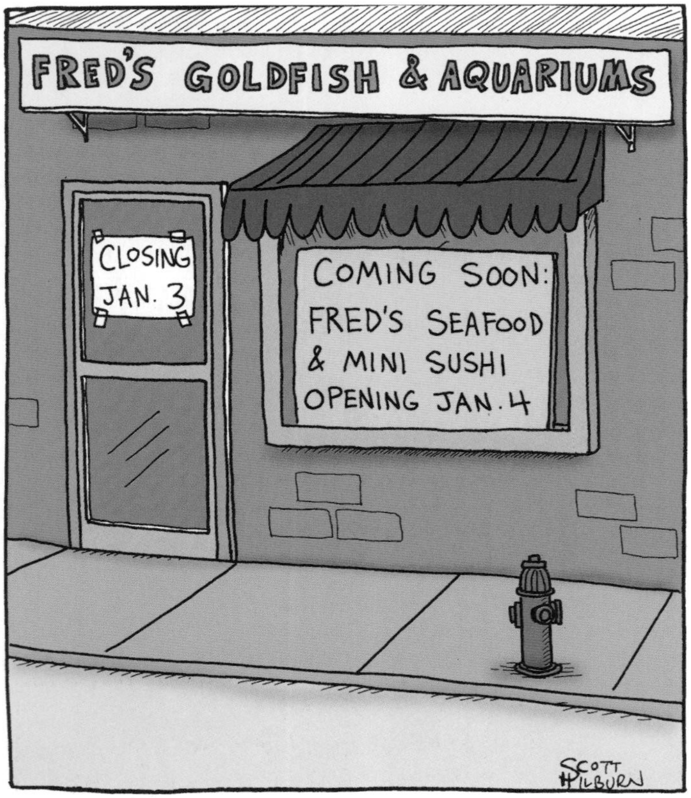
FRED'S GOLDFISH & AQUARIUMS
CLOSING JAN. 3
COMING SOON: FRED'S SEAFOOD & MINI SUSHI OPENING JAN. 4
SCOTT HILBURN

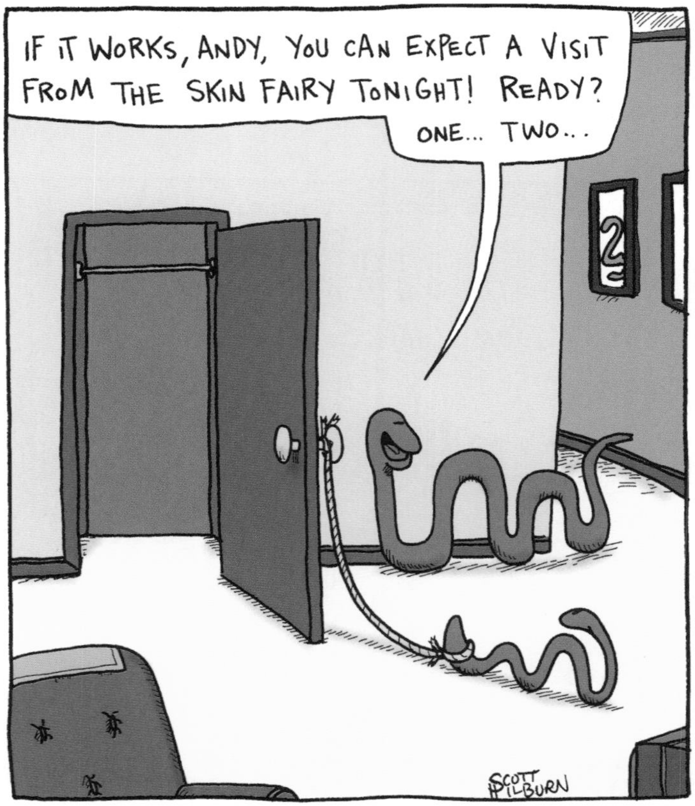
IF IT WORKS, ANDY, YOU CAN EXPECT A VISIT FROM THE SKIN FAIRY TONIGHT! READY? ONE... TWO...
SCOTT HILBURN

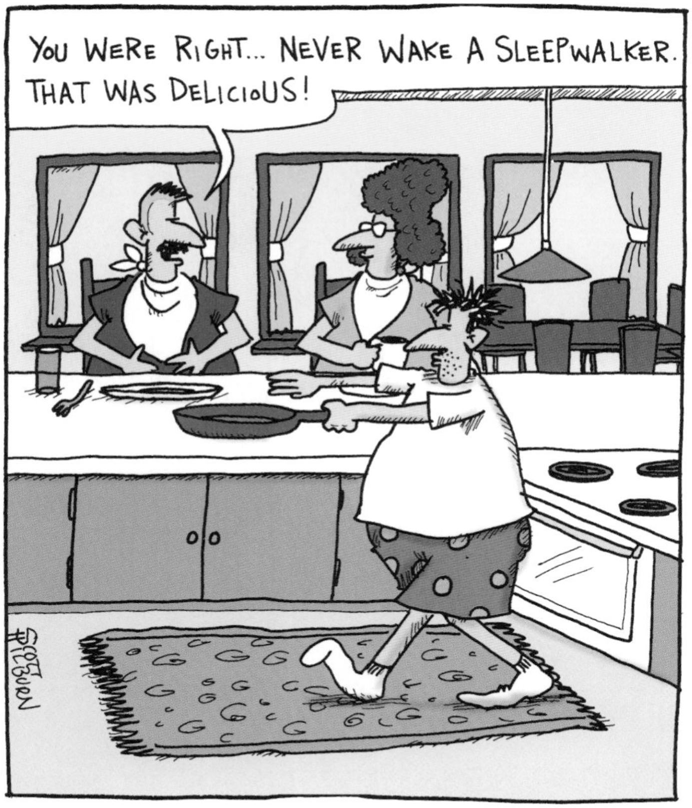
YOU WERE RIGHT... NEVER WAKE A SLEEPWALKER. THAT WAS DELICIOUS!
SCOTT HILBURN

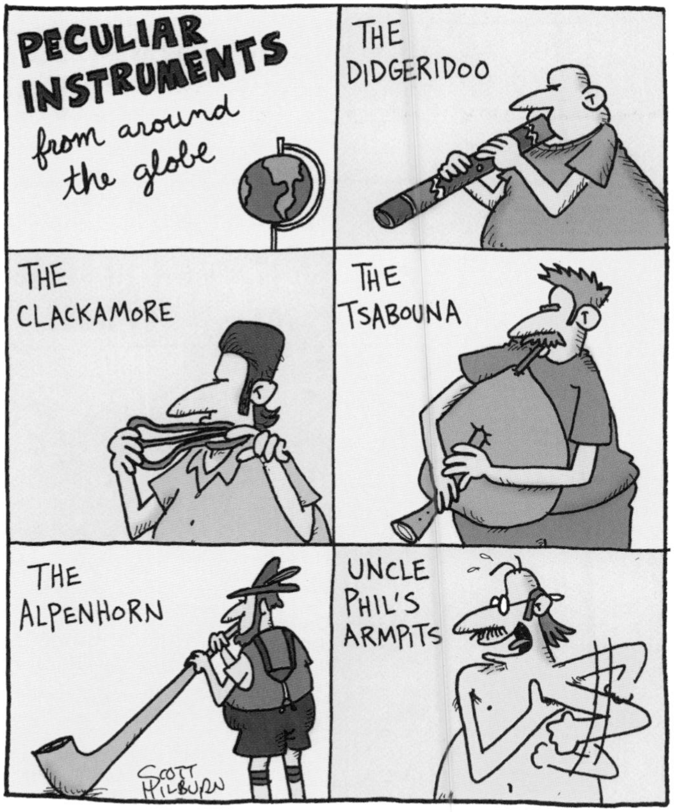
PECULIAR INSTRUMENTS from around the globe
THE DIDGERIDOO
THE CLACKAMORE
THE TSABOUNA
THE ALPENHORN
UNCLE PHIL'S ARMPITS
SCOTT HILBURN

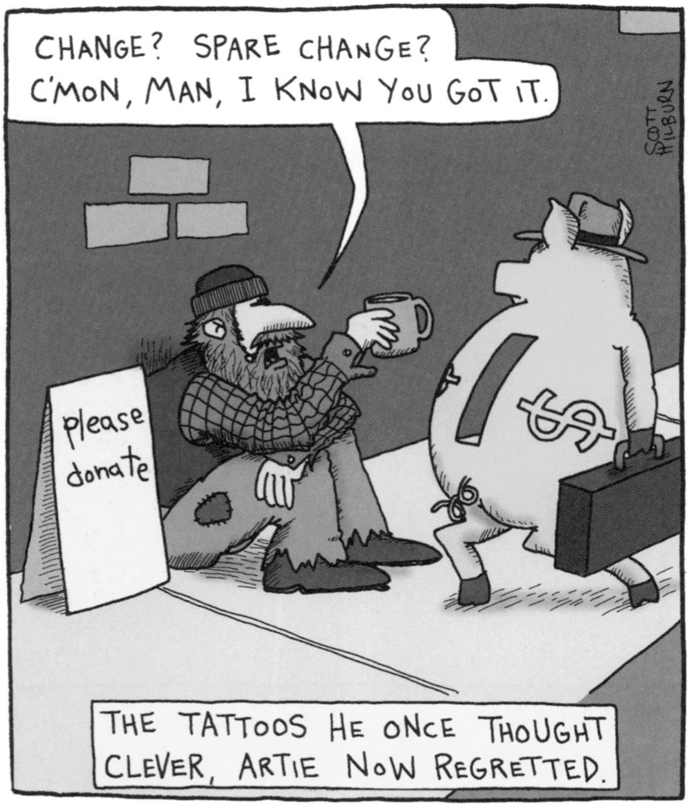
CHANGE? SPARE CHANGE? C'MON, MAN, I KNOW YOU GOT IT.
SCOTT HILBURN
please donate
THE TATTOOS HE ONCE THOUGHT CLEVER, ARTIE NOW REGRETTED.

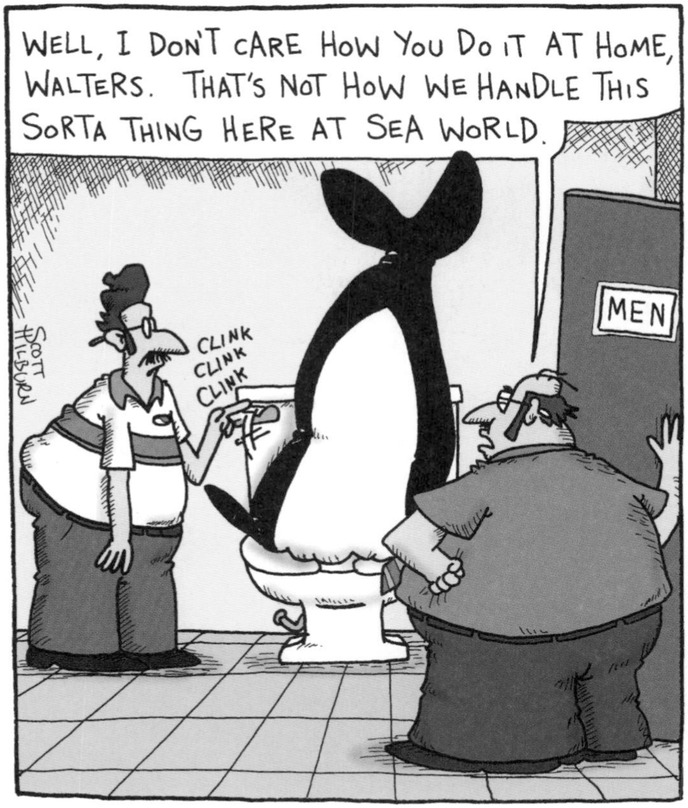
WELL, I DON'T CARE HOW YOU DO IT AT HOME, WALTERS. THAT'S NOT HOW WE HANDLE THIS SORTA THING HERE AT SEA WORLD.
SCOTT HILBURN
CLINK CLINK CLINK
MEN

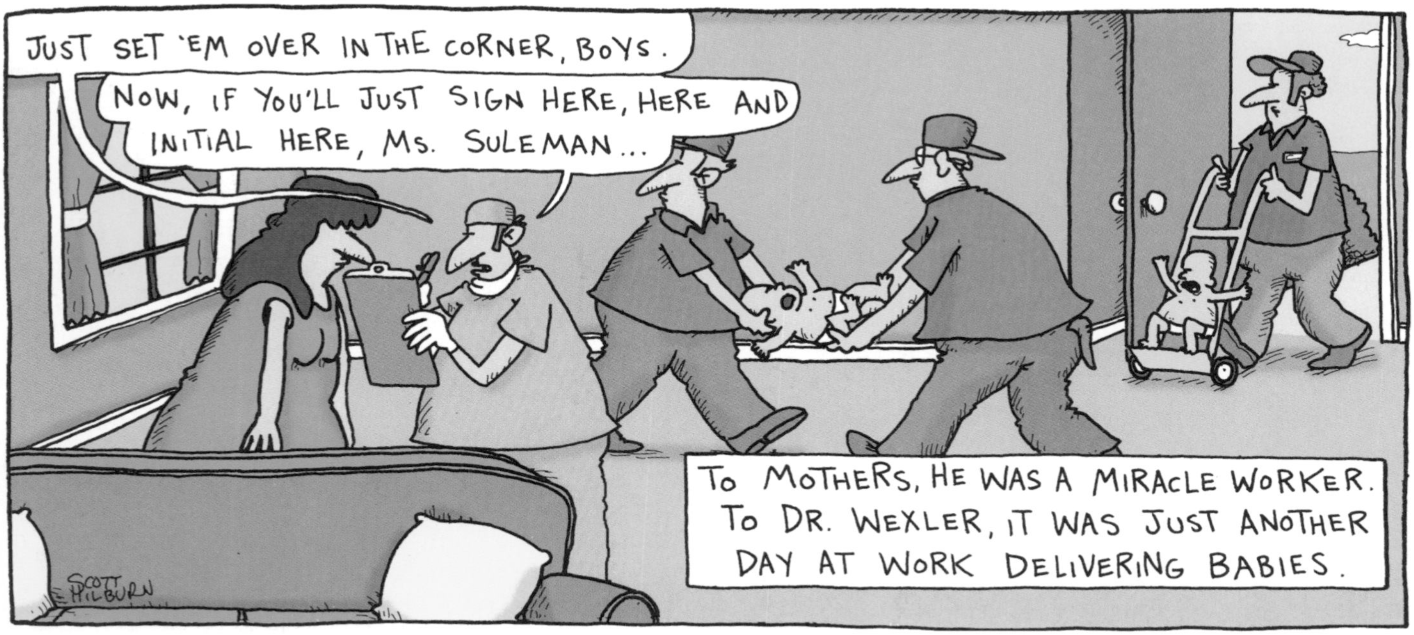
JUST SET 'EM OVER IN THE CORNER, BOYS.
NOW, IF YOU'LL JUST SIGN HERE, HERE AND INITIAL HERE, MS. SULEMAN...
SCOTT HILBURN
TO MOTHERS, HE WAS A MIRACLE WORKER. TO DR. WEXLER, IT WAS JUST ANOTHER DAY AT WORK DELIVERING BABIES.

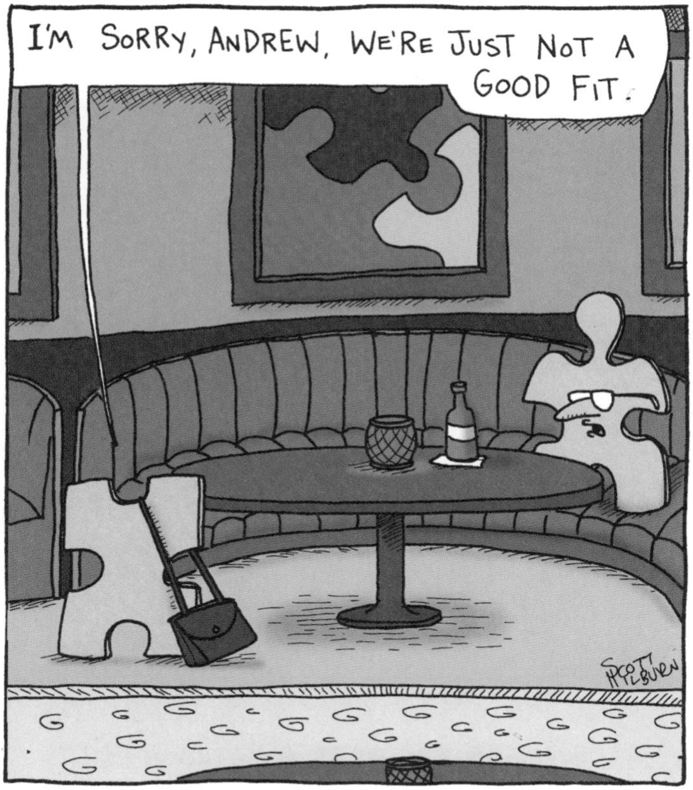
I'M SORRY, ANDREW, WE'RE JUST NOT A GOOD FIT.
SCOTT HILBURN

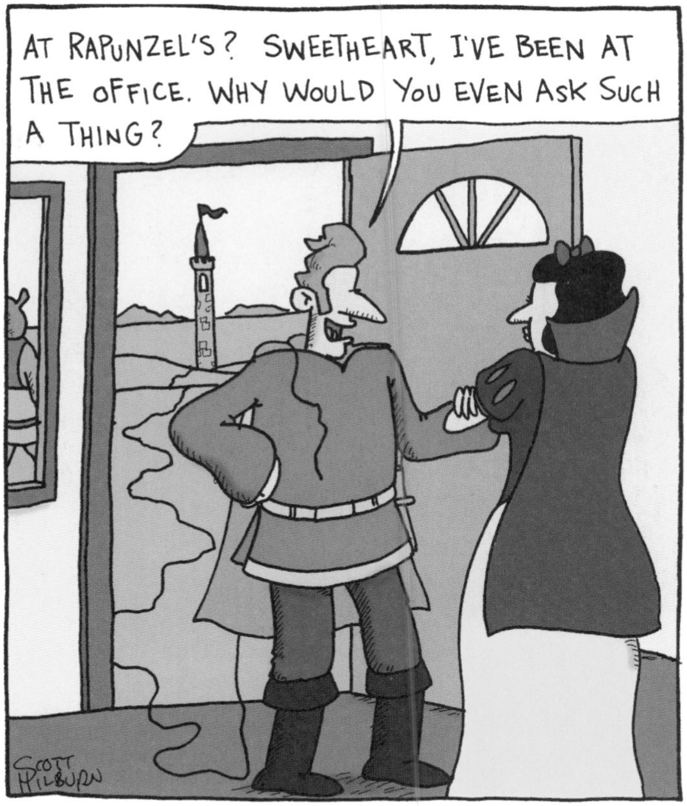
AT RAPUNZEL'S? SWEETHEART, I'VE BEEN AT THE OFFICE. WHY WOULD YOU EVEN ASK SUCH A THING?
SCOTT HILBURN

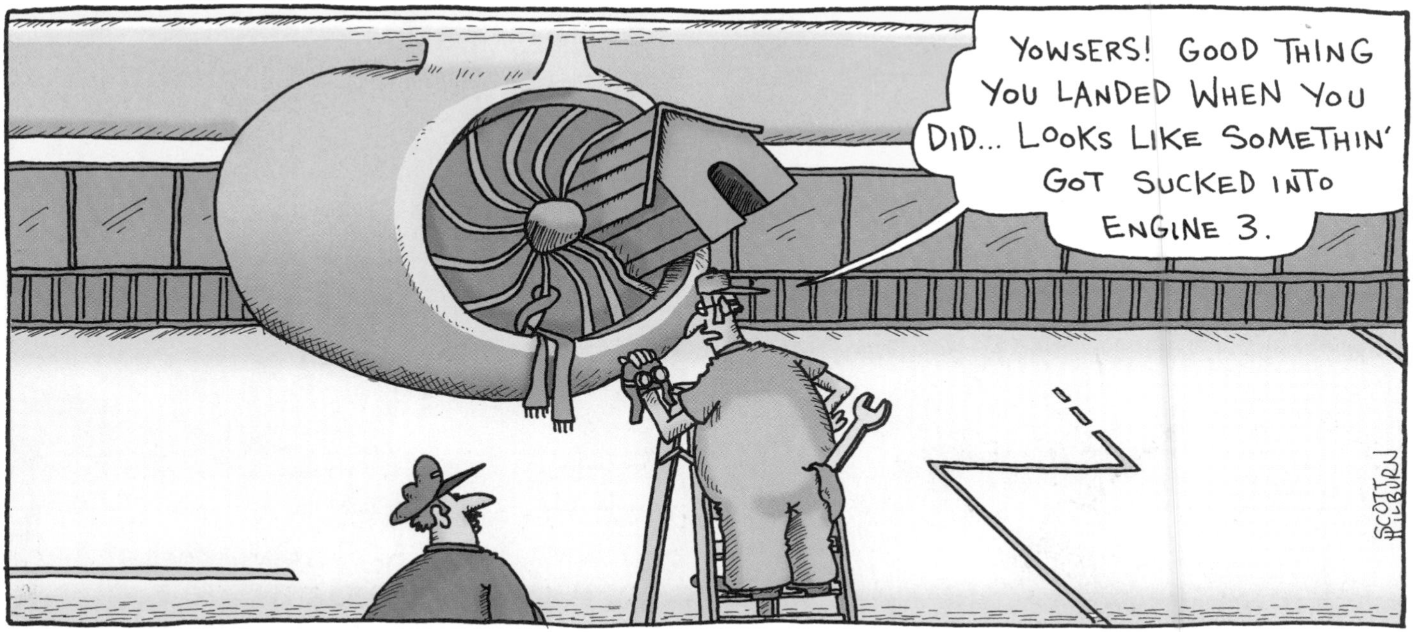
YOWSERS! GOOD THING YOU LANDED WHEN YOU DID... LOOKS LIKE SOMETHIN' GOT SUCKED INTO ENGINE 3.
SCOTT HILBURN

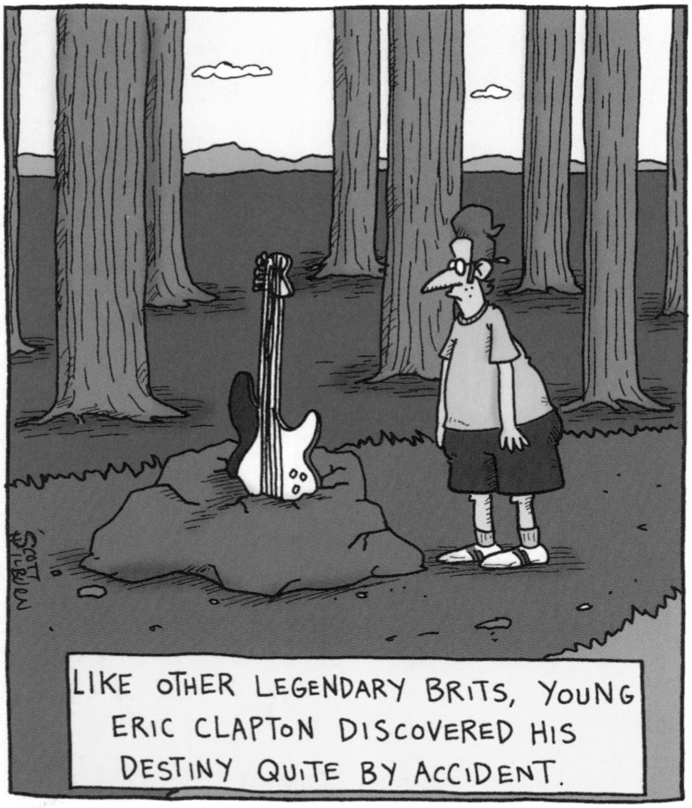
SCOTT HILBURN
LIKE OTHER LEGENDARY BRITS, YOUNG ERIC CLAPTON DISCOVERED HIS DESTINY QUITE BY ACCIDENT.

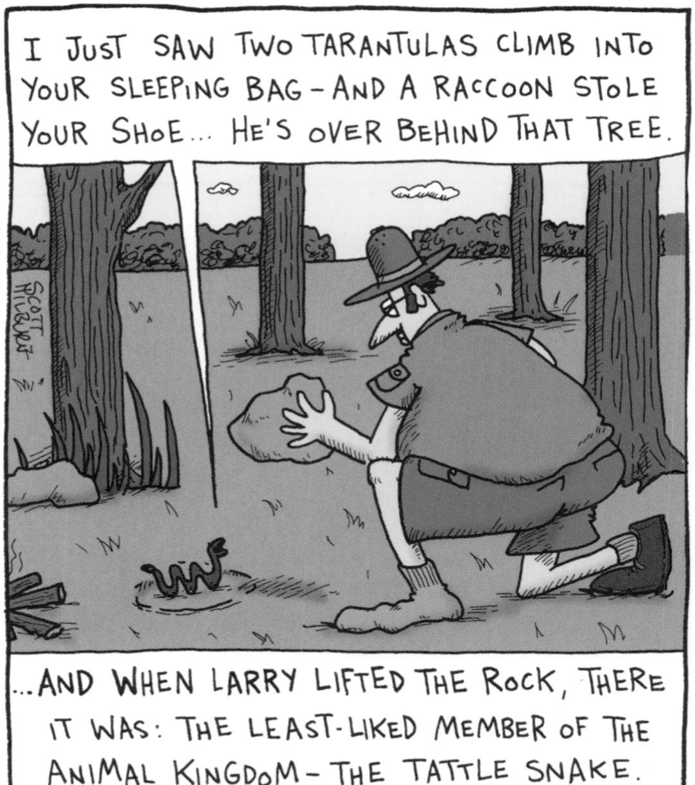
I JUST SAW TWO TARANTULAS CLIMB INTO YOUR SLEEPING BAG - AND A RACCOON STOLE YOUR SHOE... HE'S OVER BEHIND THAT TREE.
SCOTT HILBURN
...AND WHEN LARRY LIFTED THE ROCK, THERE IT WAS: THE LEAST-LIKED MEMBER OF THE ANIMAL KINGDOM - THE TATTLE SNAKE.

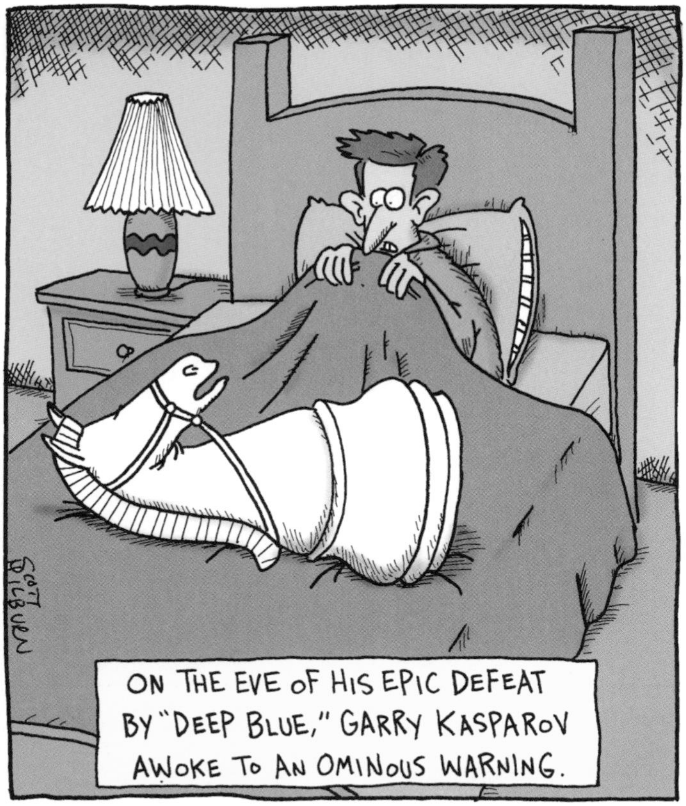
SCOTT HILBURN
ON THE EVE OF HIS EPIC DEFEAT BY "DEEP BLUE," GARRY KASPAROV AWOKE TO AN OMINOUS WARNING.

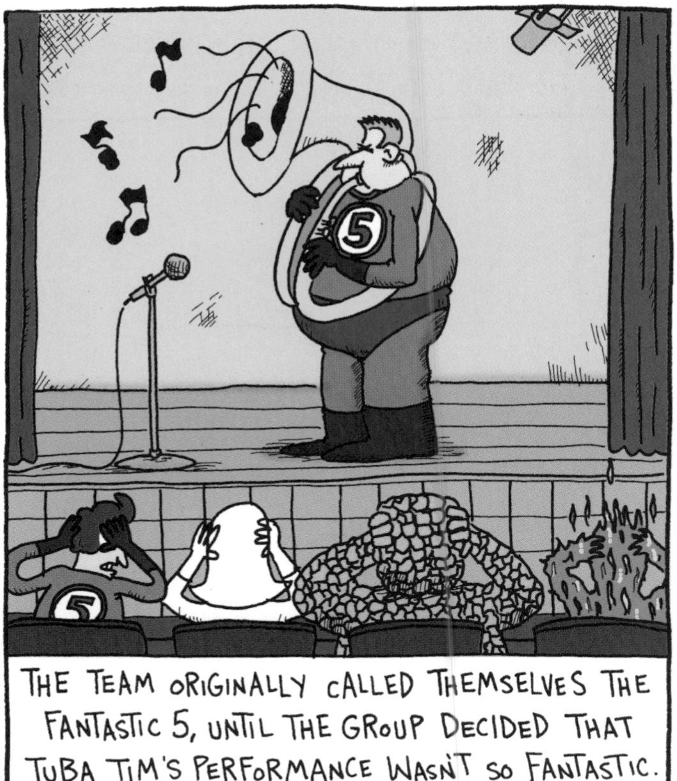
5
THE TEAM ORIGINALLY CALLED THEMSELVES THE FANTASTIC 5, UNTIL THE GROUP DECIDED THAT TUBA TIM'S PERFORMANCE WASN'T SO FANTASTIC.

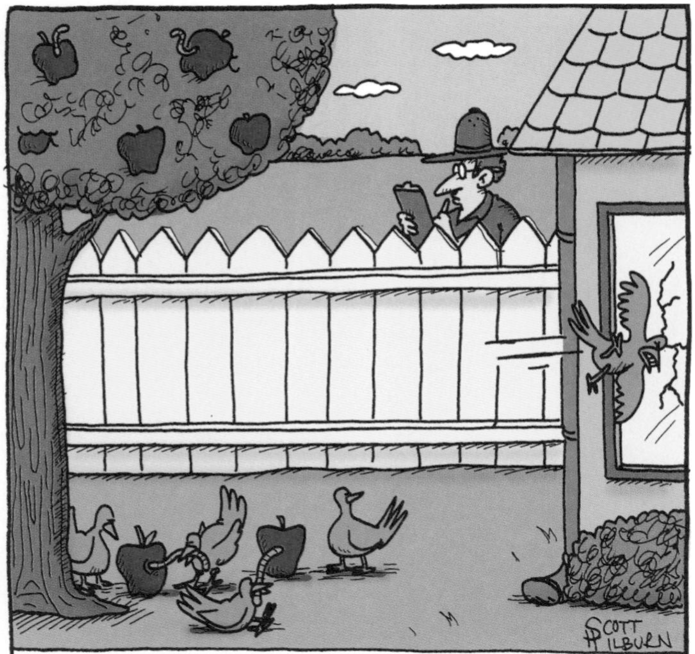
SCOTT HILBURN

ORNITHOLOGICAL STUDIES PERFORMED BY DR. WORTHINGTON PROVED DEFINITIVELY THAT 4 OUT OF 5 BIRDS PREFER APPLES TO WINDOWS.

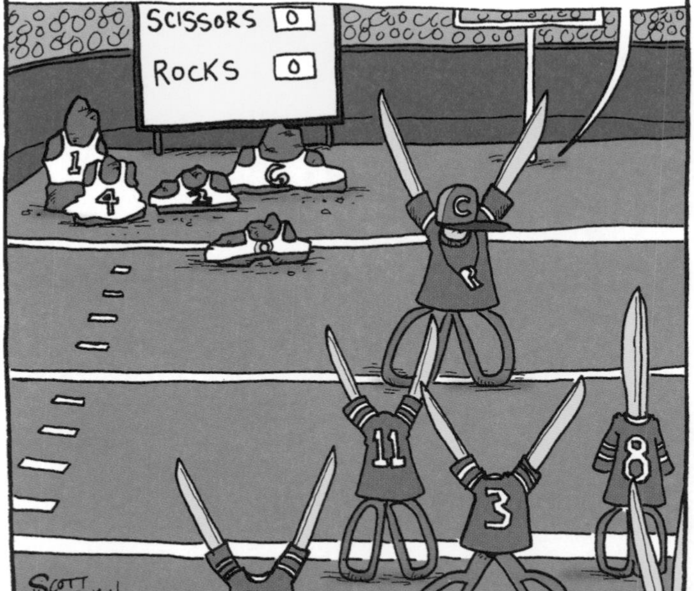
SCISSORS 0
ROCKS 0
SCOTT HILBURN

OKAY, BOYS... PAPER ALREADY BEAT THESE GUYS ONCE – AND WE BEAT PAPER LAST WEEK. WITHOUT GETTING OVERCONFIDENT, IF WE STICK TO OUR GAME, WE SHOULD HAVE NO PROBLEMS.

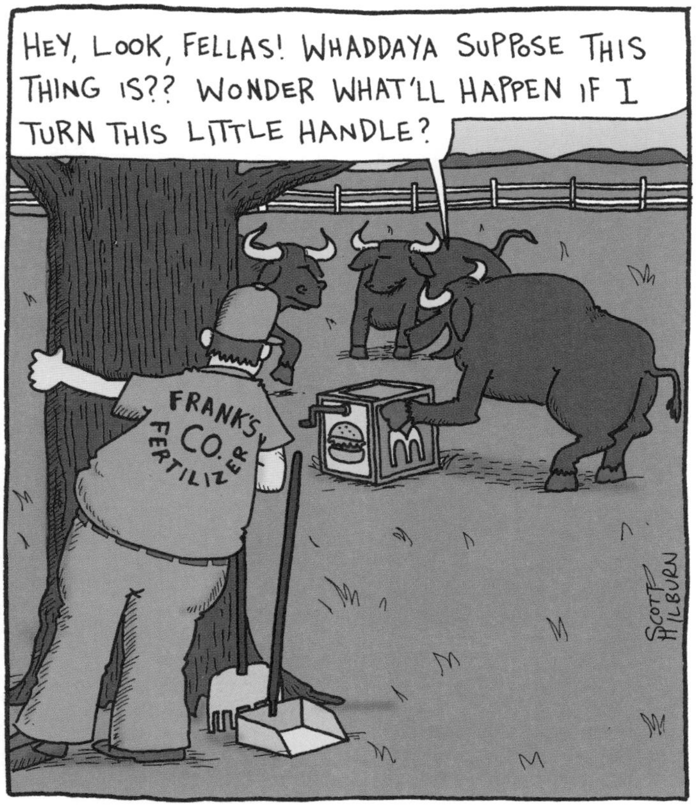
HEY, LOOK, FELLAS! WHADDAYA SUPPOSE THIS THING IS?? WONDER WHAT'LL HAPPEN IF I TURN THIS LITTLE HANDLE?
FRANK'S CO. FERTILIZER
SCOTT HILBURN

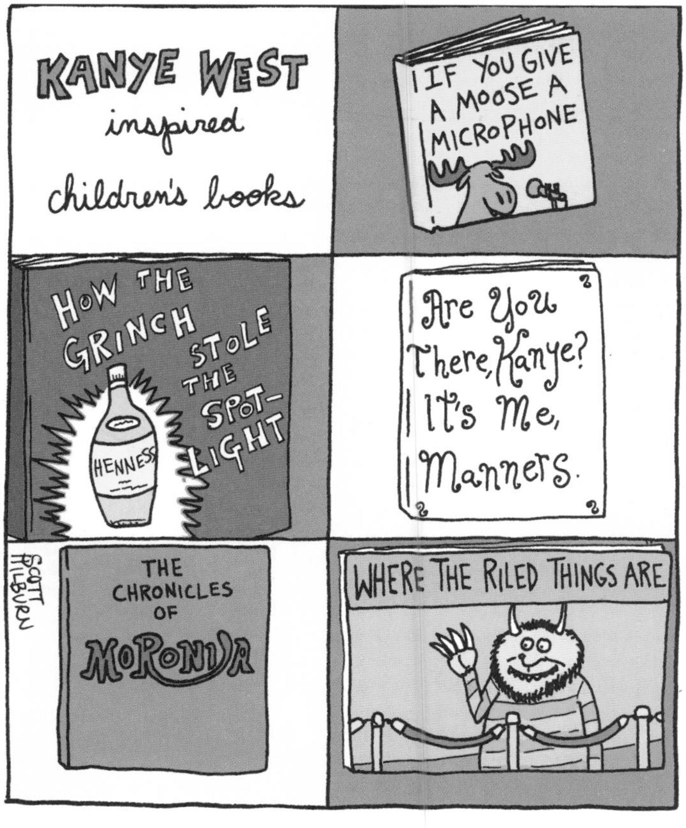
KANYE WEST
inspired
children's books
IF YOU GIVE A MOOSE A MICROPHONE
HOW THE GRINCH STOLE THE SPOT-LIGHT
HENNESS
Are You There, Kanye? It's Me, Manners.
SCOTT HILBURN
THE CHRONICLES OF MORONIA
WHERE THE RILED THINGS ARE

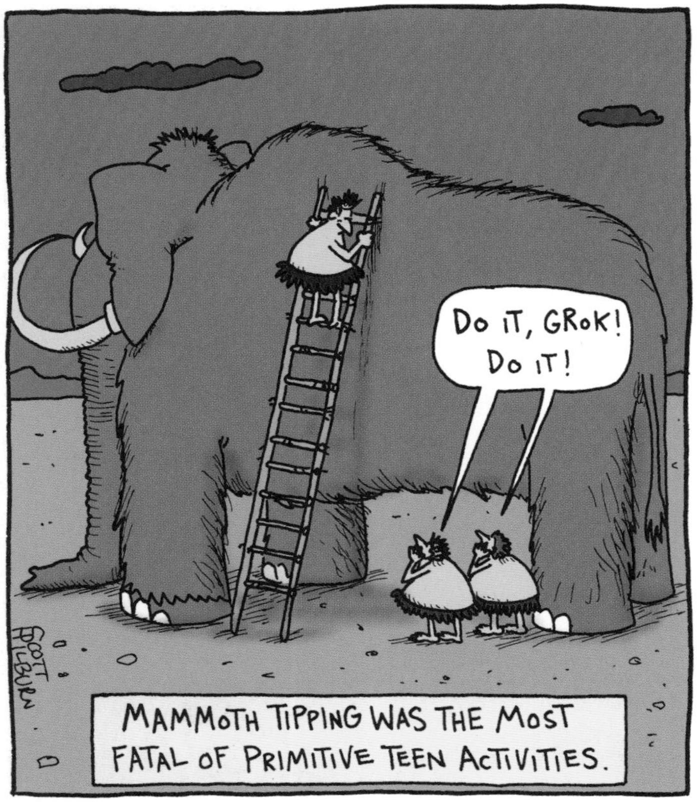
Do iT, GRoK! Do iT!
MAMMOTH TIPPING WAS THE MOST FATAL OF PRIMITIVE TEEN ACTIVITIES.
SCOTT HILBURN

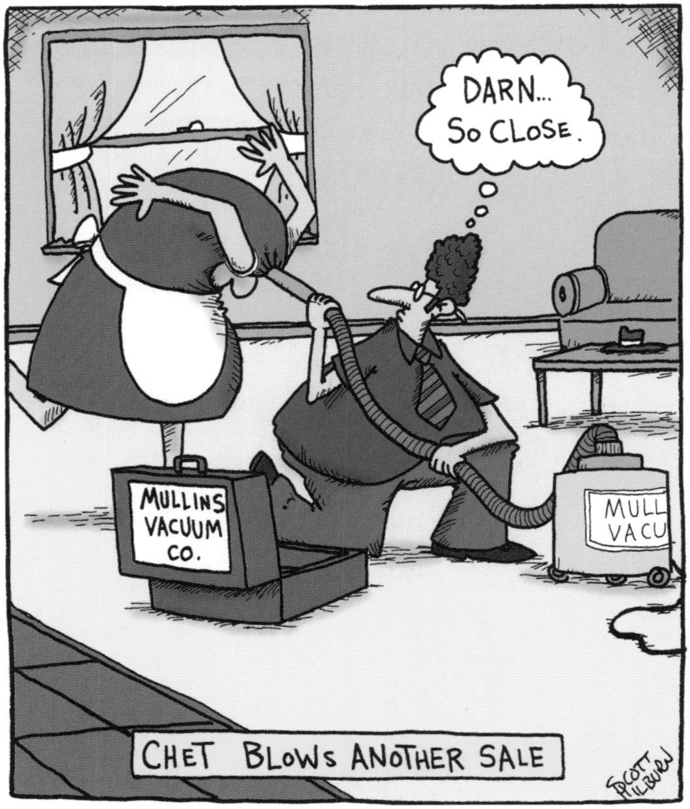
DARN... So CLOSE.
MULLINS VACUUM CO.
MULL VACU
CHET BLOWS ANOTHER SALE
SCOTT HILBURN

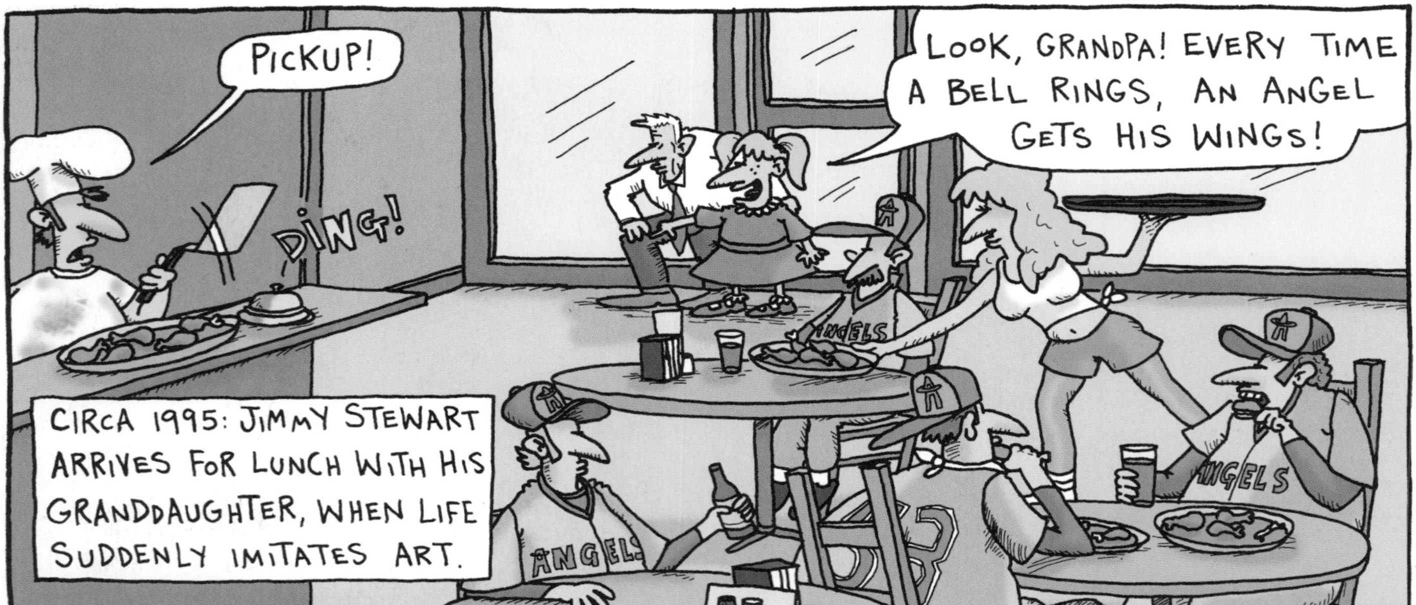
PICKUP!
DiNG!
LOOK, GRANDPA! EVERY TIME A BELL RINGS, AN ANGEL GETS HIS WINGS!
ANGELS
CIRCA 1995: JIMMY STEWART ARRIVES FOR LUNCH WITH HIS GRANDDAUGHTER, WHEN LIFE SUDDENLY IMITATES ART.

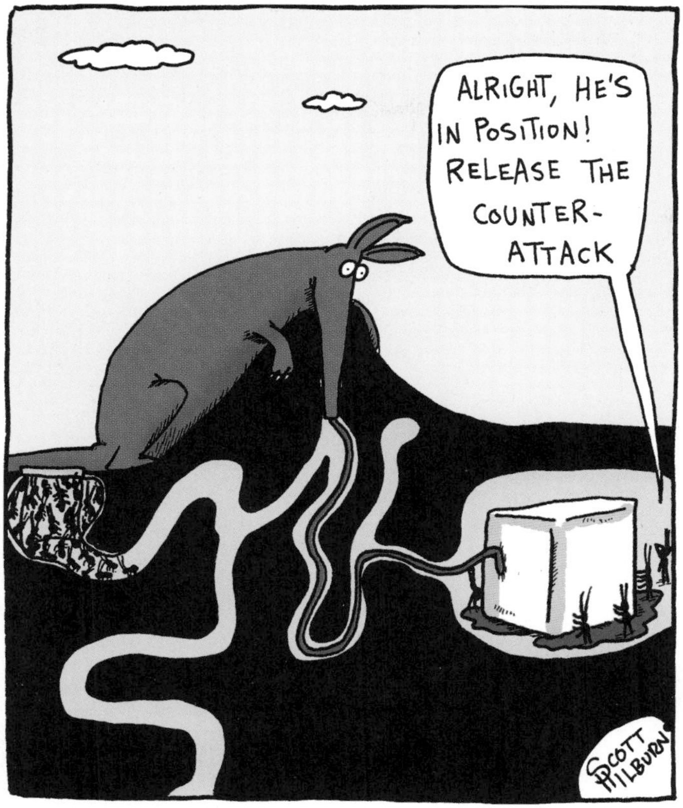
ALRIGHT, HE'S IN POSITION! RELEASE THE COUNTER-ATTACK
SCOTT HILBURN

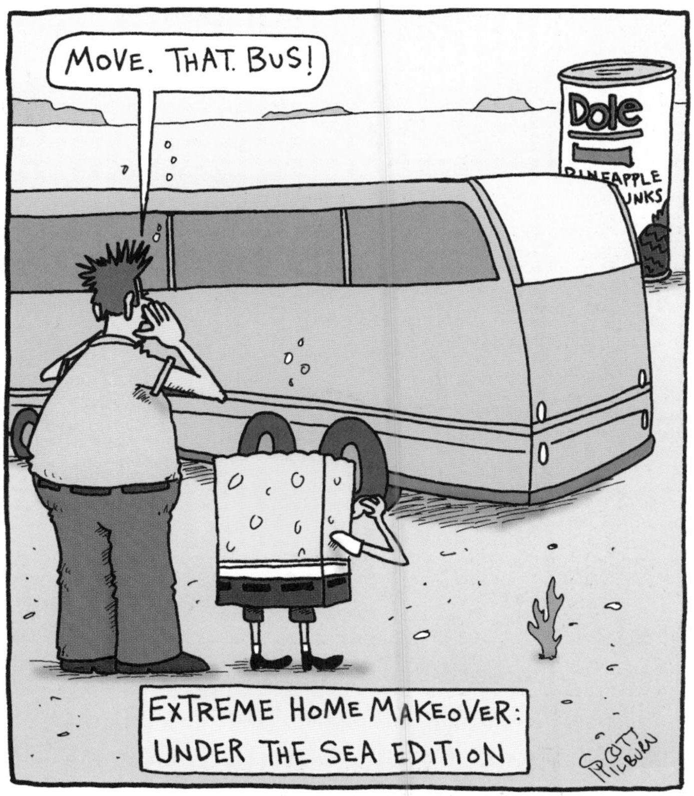
MOVE. THAT. BUS!
Dole
PINEAPPLE CHUNKS
EXTREME HOME MAKEOVER: UNDER THE SEA EDITION
SCOTT HILBURN

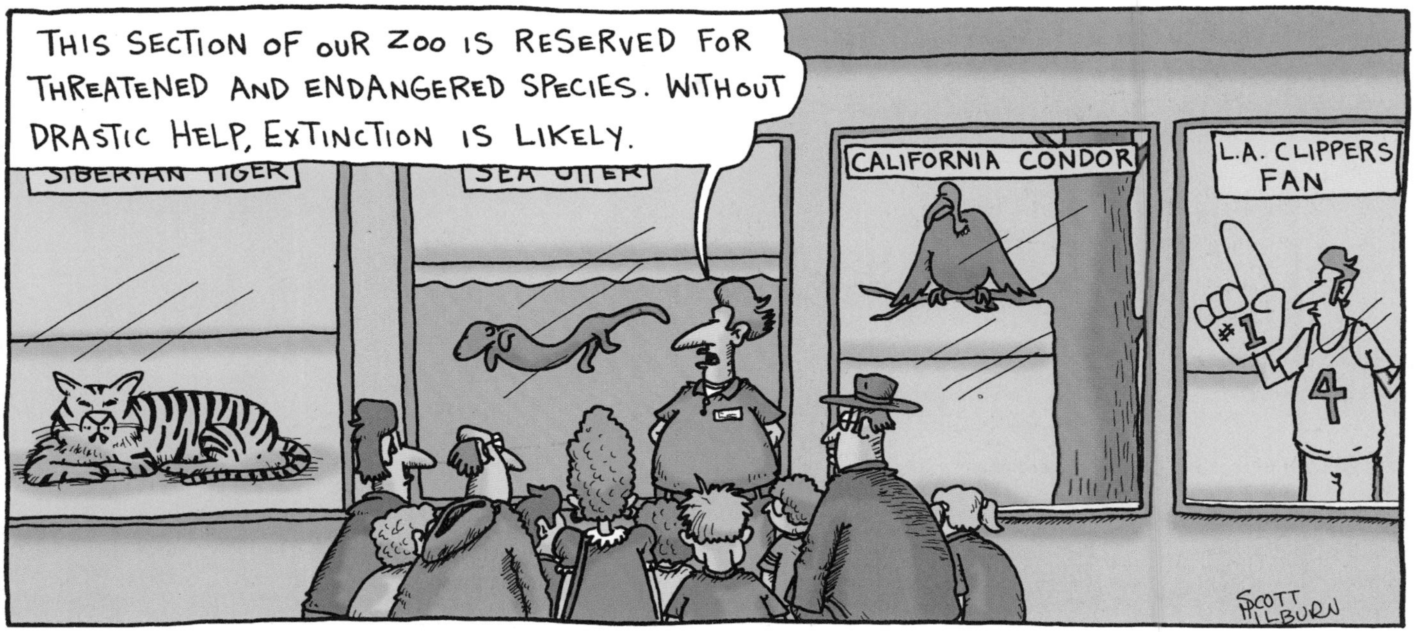
THIS SECTION OF OUR ZOO IS RESERVED FOR THREATENED AND ENDANGERED SPECIES. WITHOUT DRASTIC HELP, EXTINCTION IS LIKELY.
SIBERIAN TIGER
SEA OTTER
CALIFORNIA CONDOR
L.A. CLIPPERS FAN
#1
4
SCOTT HILBURN

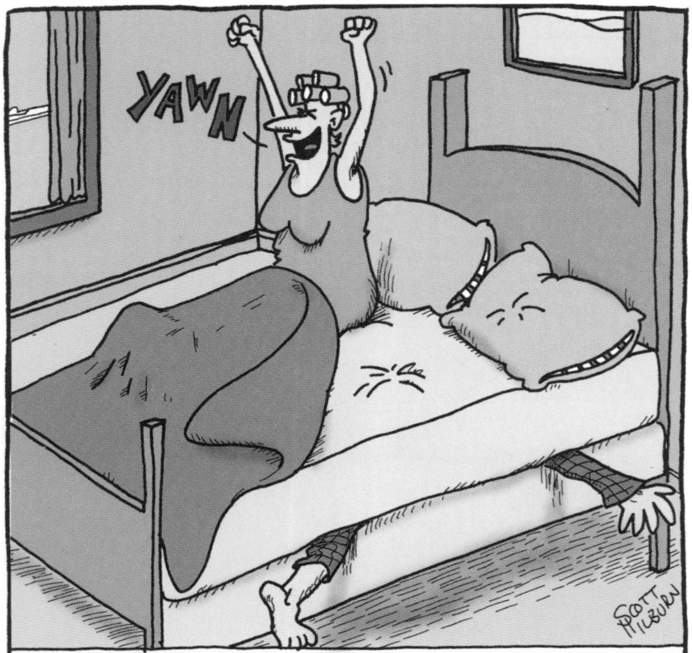
YAWN
SCOTT HILBURN

FOR THE THIRD TIME IN AS MANY MORNINGS, AMY STARTS HER DAY IN A GOOD MOOD, WHILE TED AGAIN WAKES UP ON THE WRONG SIDE OF THE BED.

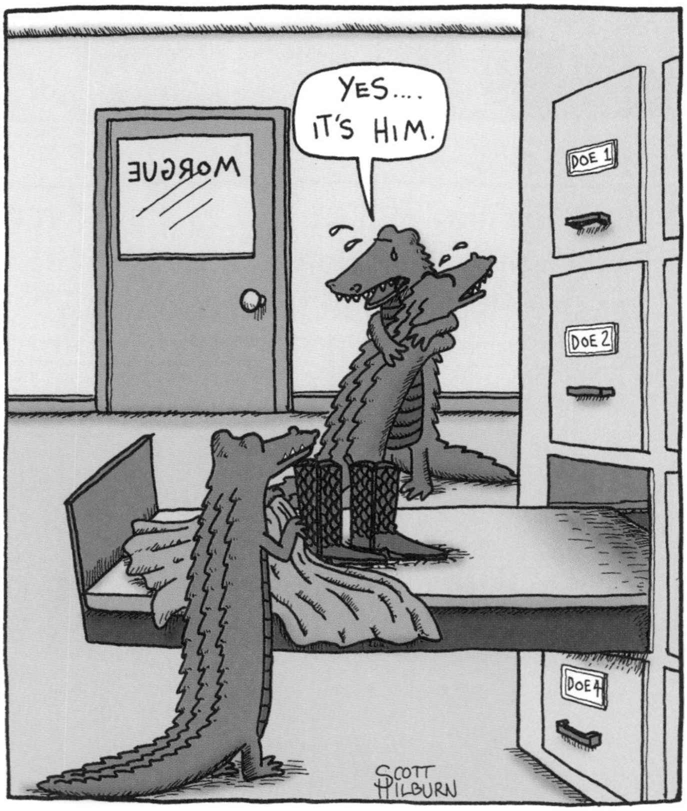
YES....
IT'S HIM.
MORGUE
DOE 1
DOE 2
DOE 4
SCOTT HILBURN

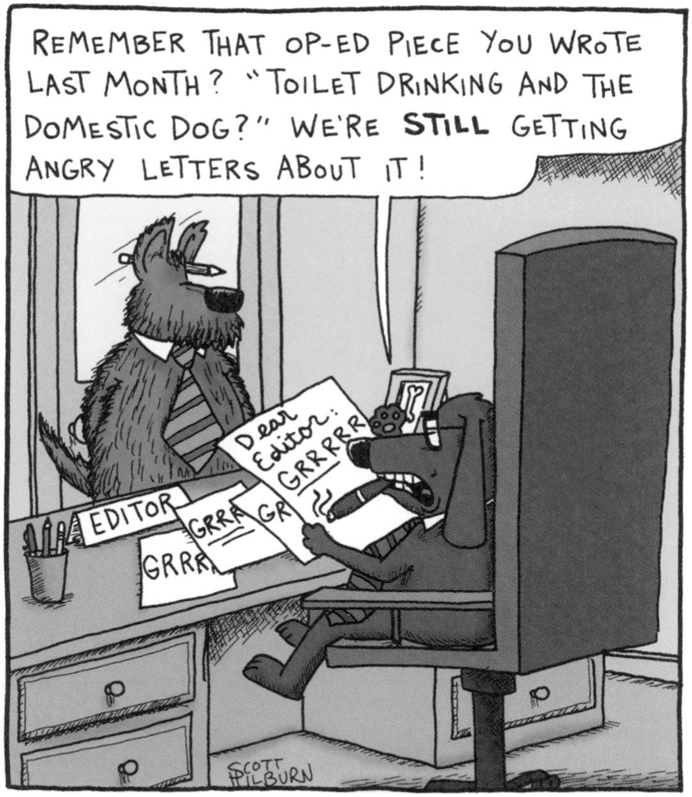
REMEMBER THAT OP-ED PIECE YOU WROTE LAST MONTH? "TOILET DRINKING AND THE DOMESTIC DOG?" WE'RE **STILL** GETTING ANGRY LETTERS ABOUT IT!
EDITOR
Dear Editor: GRRRRR
GRRR
GRR
GRRR
SCOTT HILBURN

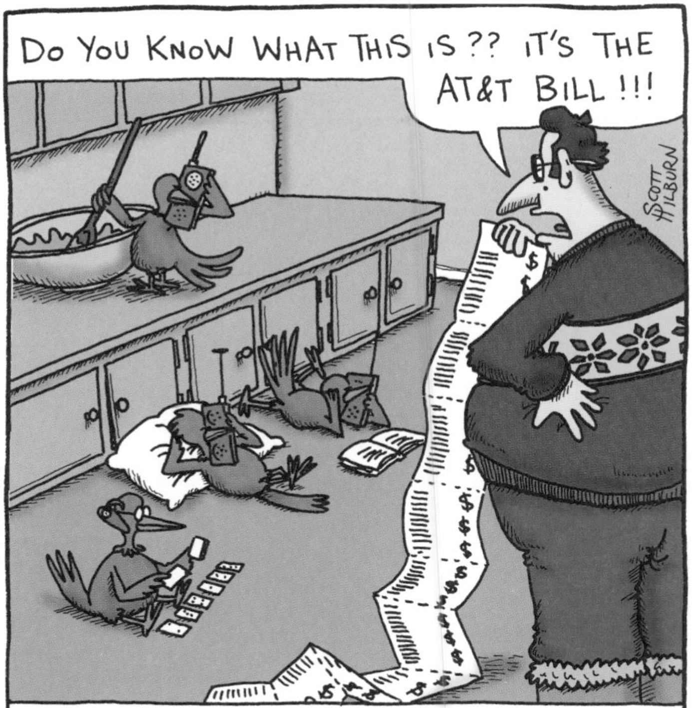
DO YOU KNOW WHAT THIS IS?? IT'S THE AT&T BILL!!!
SCOTT HILBURN

CONRAD GREW TO RESENT THE FOUR CALLING BIRDS HIS TRUE LOVE GAVE TO HIM.

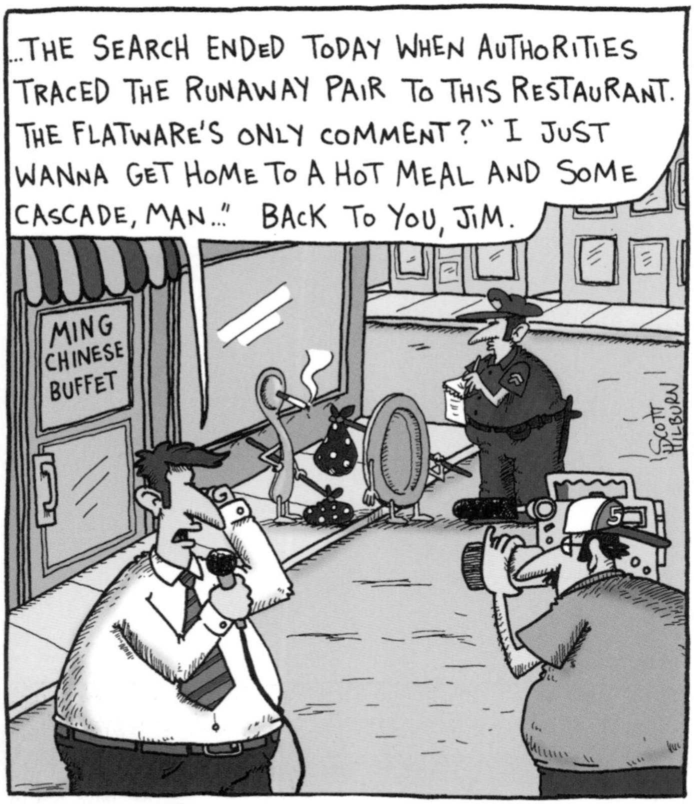
...THE SEARCH ENDED TODAY WHEN AUTHORITIES TRACED THE RUNAWAY PAIR TO THIS RESTAURANT. THE FLATWARE'S ONLY COMMENT? "I JUST WANNA GET HOME TO A HOT MEAL AND SOME CASCADE, MAN..." BACK TO YOU, JIM.
MING CHINESE BUFFET
SCOTT HILBURN

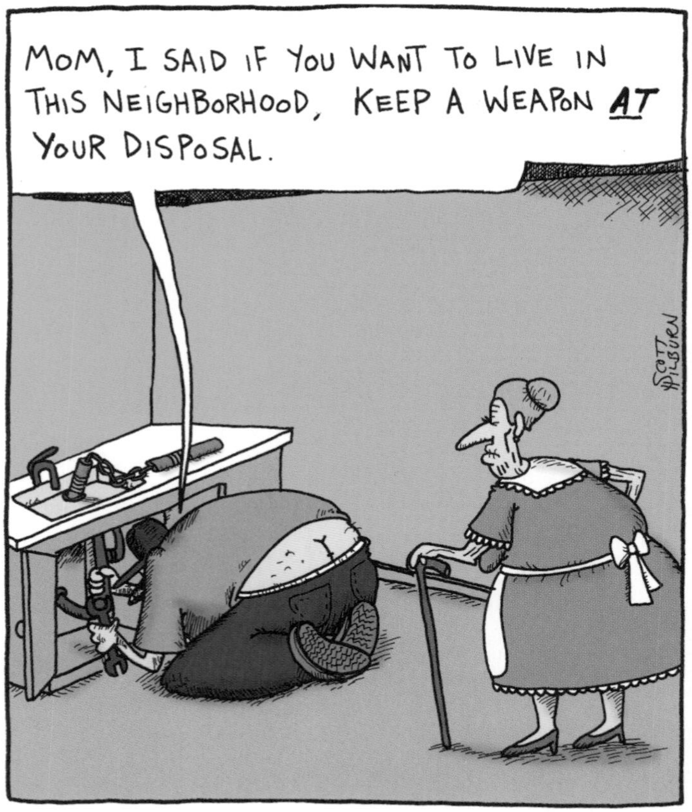
MOM, I SAID IF YOU WANT TO LIVE IN THIS NEIGHBORHOOD, KEEP A WEAPON AT YOUR DISPOSAL.
SCOTT HILBURN

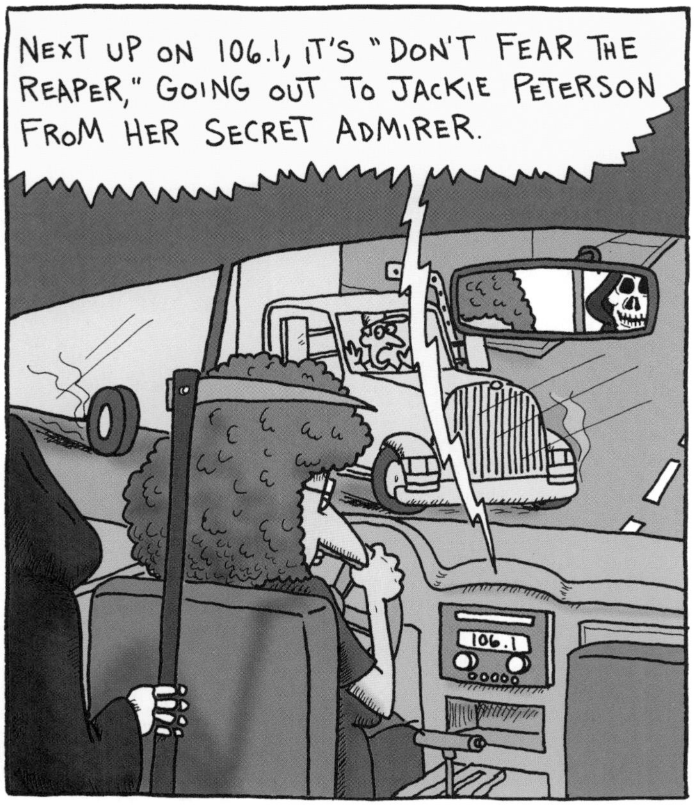
NEXT UP ON 106.1, IT'S "DON'T FEAR THE REAPER," GOING OUT TO JACKIE PETERSON FROM HER SECRET ADMIRER.
106.1

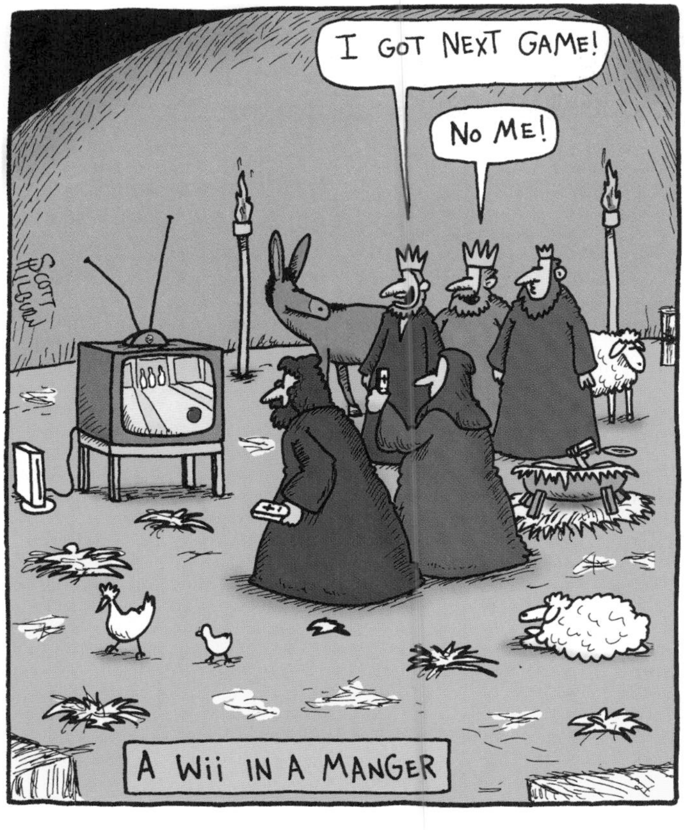
I GOT NEXT GAME!
NO ME!
SCOTT HILBURN

A Wii IN A MANGER

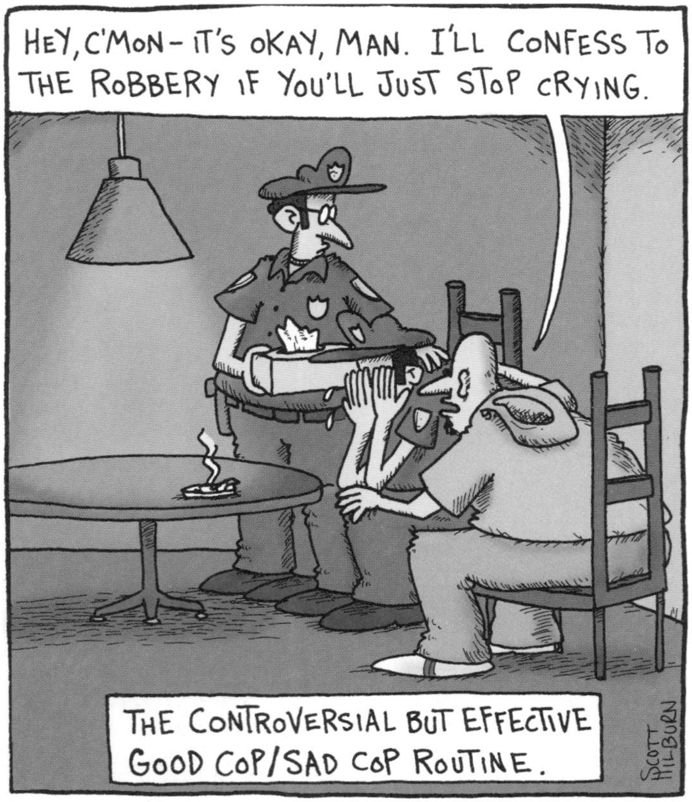
HEY, C'MON– IT'S OKAY, MAN. I'LL CONFESS TO THE ROBBERY IF YOU'LL JUST STOP CRYING.
THE CONTROVERSIAL BUT EFFECTIVE GOOD COP/SAD COP ROUTINE.
SCOTT HILBURN

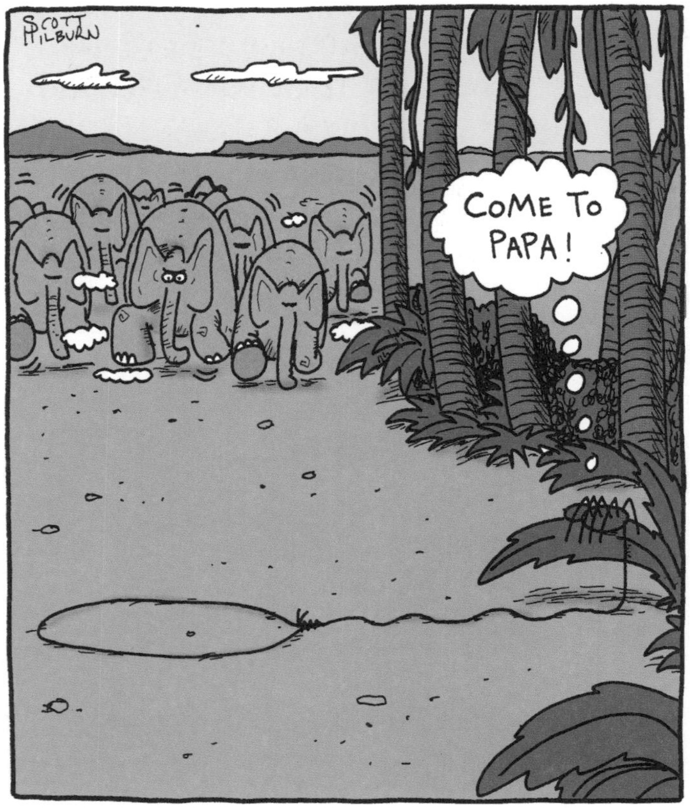
SCOTT HILBURN
COME TO PAPA!

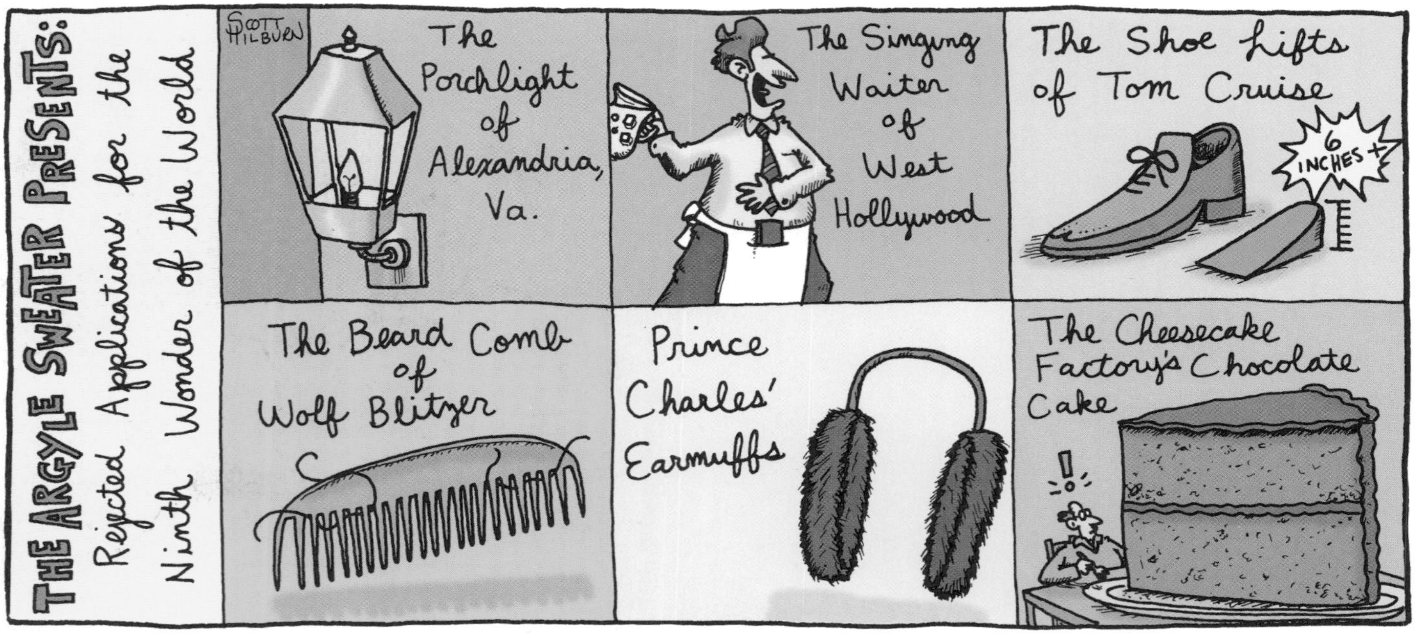
THE ARGYLE SWEATER PRESENTS:
Rejected Applications for the Ninth Wonder of the World
SCOTT HILBURN
The Porchlight of Alexandria, Va.
The Singing Waiter of West Hollywood
The Shoe Lifts of Tom Cruise
6 INCHES +
The Beard Comb of Wolf Blitzer
Prince Charles' Earmuffs
The Cheesecake Factory's Chocolate Cake
!

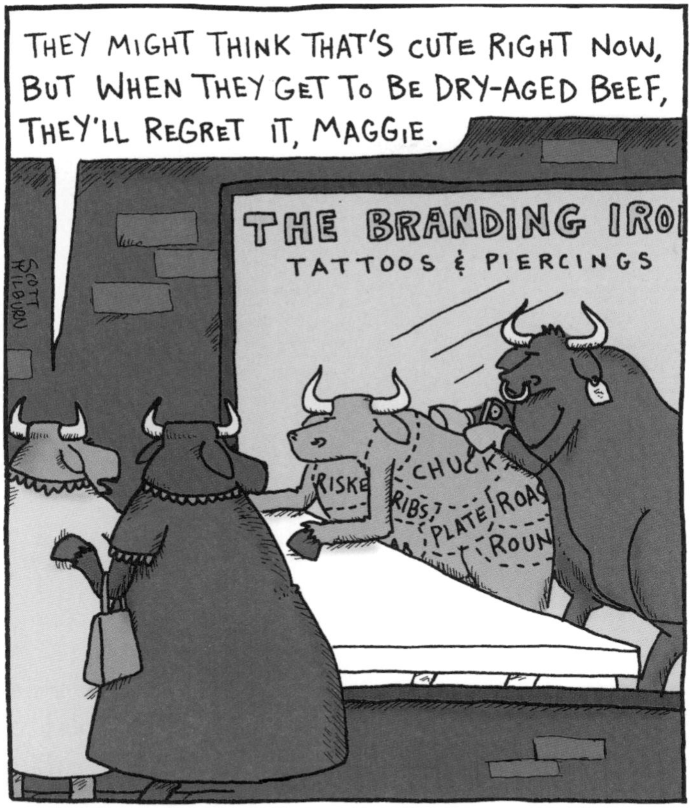
THEY MIGHT THINK THAT'S CUTE RIGHT NOW, BUT WHEN THEY GET TO BE DRY-AGED BEEF, THEY'LL REGRET IT, MAGGIE.
THE BRANDING IRO
TATTOOS & PIERCINGS

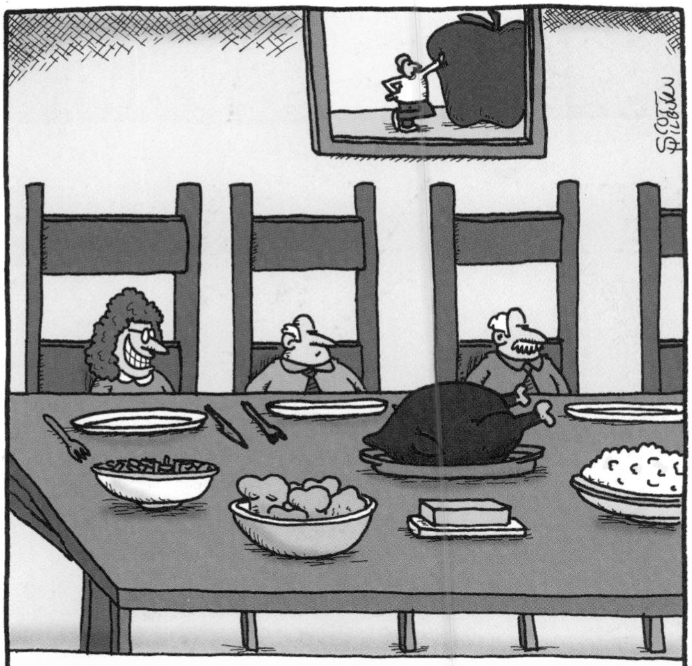

NO LONGER A CHILD, MAUREEN IS EXCITED TO EXPERIENCE HER FIRST HOLIDAY DINNER AT THE BIG TABLE.

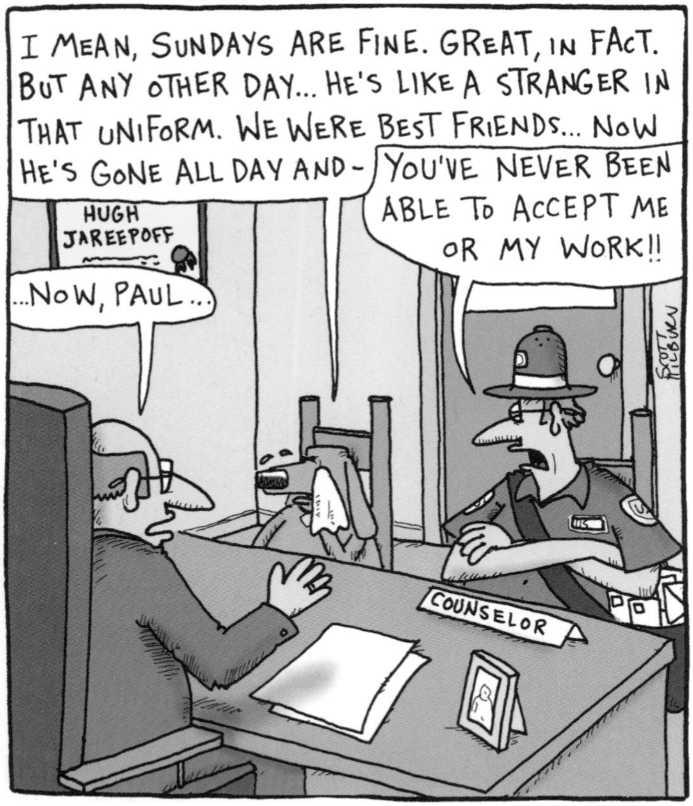
I MEAN, SUNDAYS ARE FINE. GREAT, IN FACT. BUT ANY OTHER DAY... HE'S LIKE A STRANGER IN THAT UNIFORM. WE WERE BEST FRIENDS... NOW HE'S GONE ALL DAY AND-
YOU'VE NEVER BEEN ABLE TO ACCEPT ME OR MY WORK!!
HUGH JAREEPOFF
...NOW, PAUL...
COUNSELOR
SCOTT HILBURN

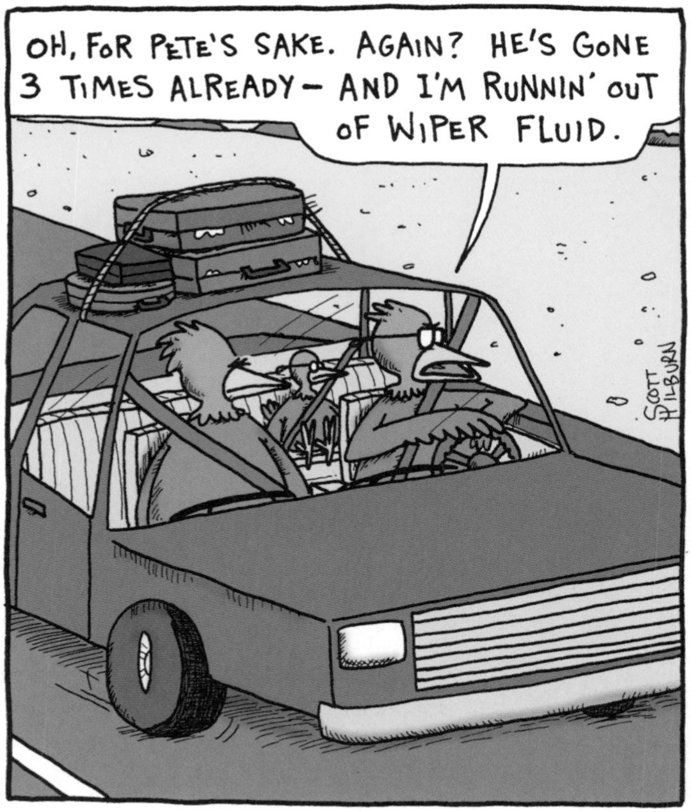
OH, FOR PETE'S SAKE. AGAIN? HE'S GONE 3 TIMES ALREADY- AND I'M RUNNIN' OUT OF WIPER FLUID.
SCOTT HILBURN

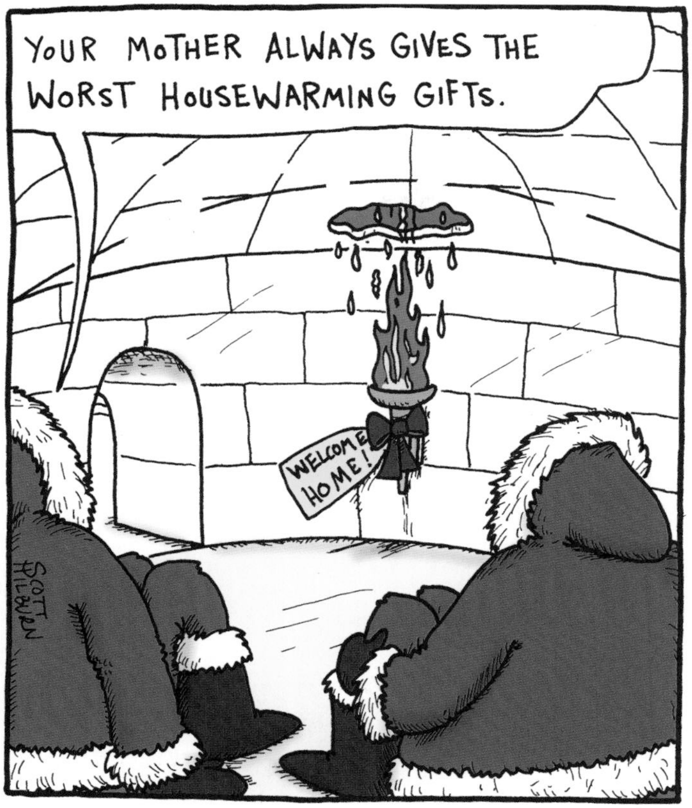
YOUR MOTHER ALWAYS GIVES THE WORST HOUSEWARMING GIFTS.
WELCOME HOME!
SCOTT HILBURN

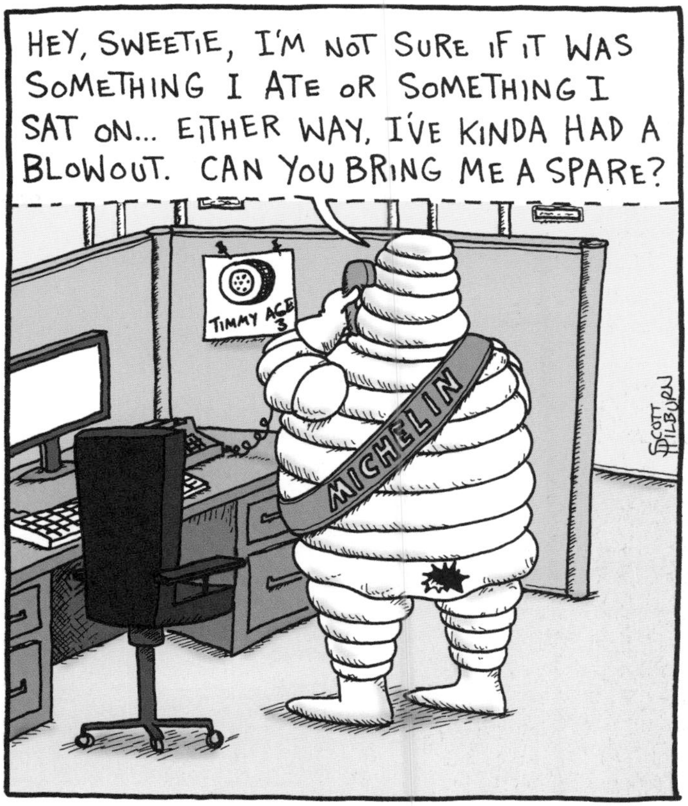
HEY, SWEETIE, I'M NOT SURE IF IT WAS SOMETHING I ATE OR SOMETHING I SAT ON... EITHER WAY, I'VE KINDA HAD A BLOWOUT. CAN YOU BRING ME A SPARE?
TIMMY AGE 3
MICHELIN
SCOTT HILBURN

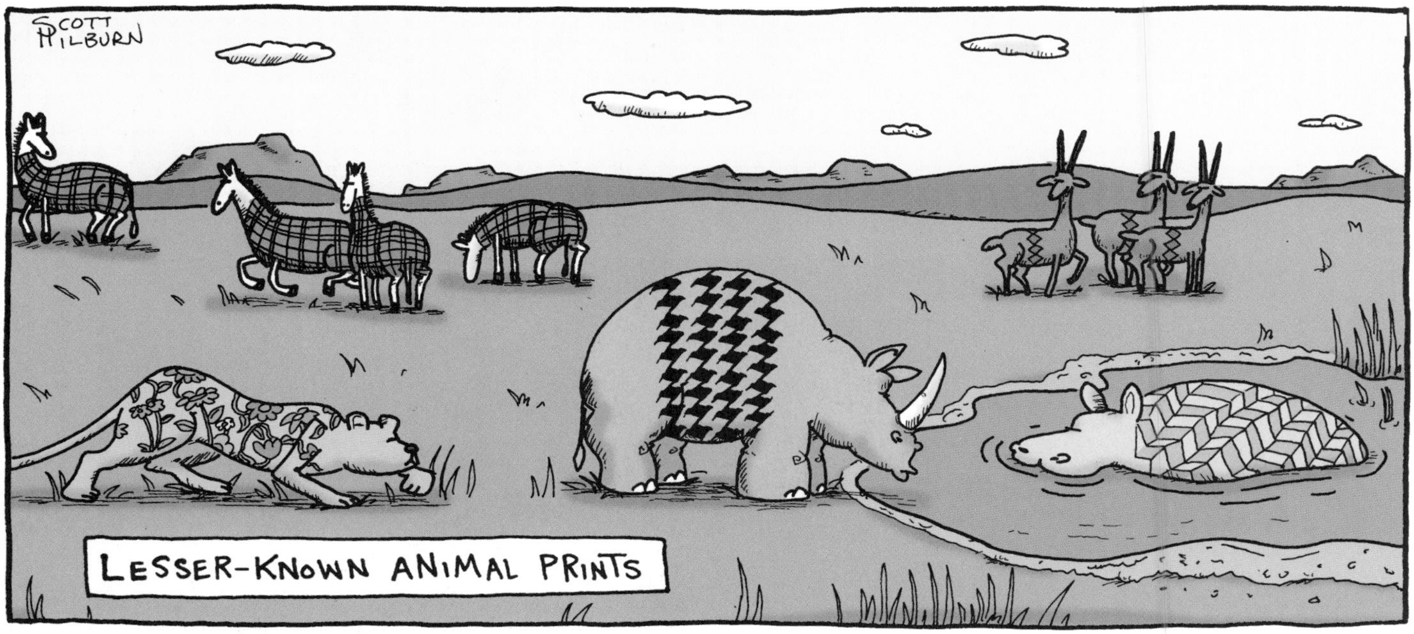
SCOTT HILBURN

LESSER-KNOWN ANIMAL PRINTS

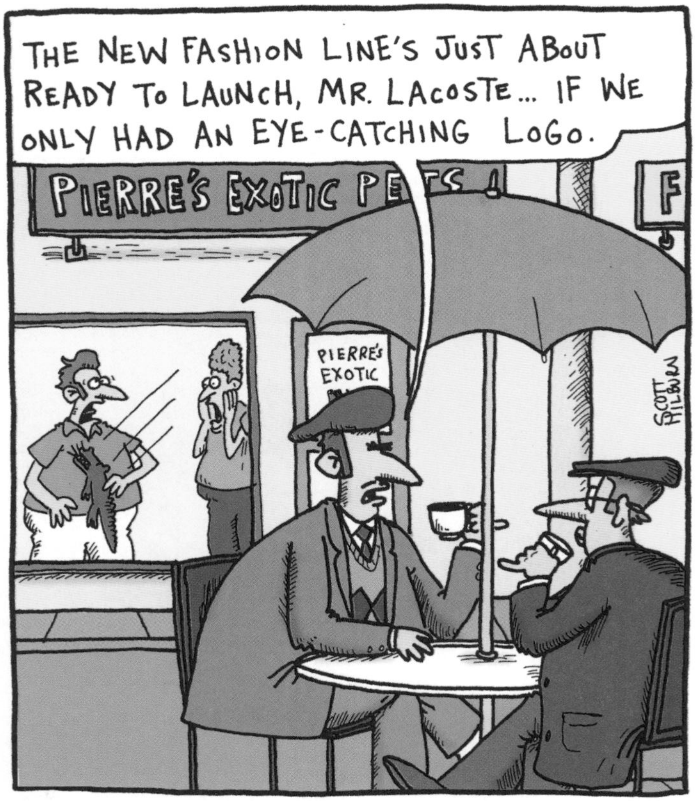
THE NEW FASHION LINE'S JUST ABOUT READY TO LAUNCH, MR. LACOSTE... IF WE ONLY HAD AN EYE-CATCHING LOGO.
PIERRE'S EXOTIC PE
F
PIERRE'S EXOTIC
SCOTT HILBURN

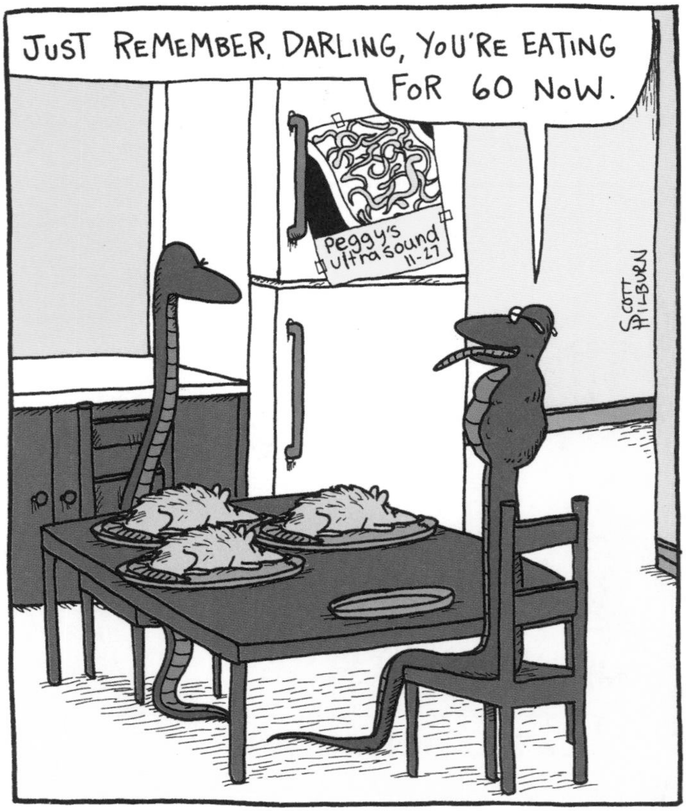
JUST REMEMBER, DARLING, YOU'RE EATING FOR 60 NOW.
Peggy's ultrasound 11-27
SCOTT HILBURN

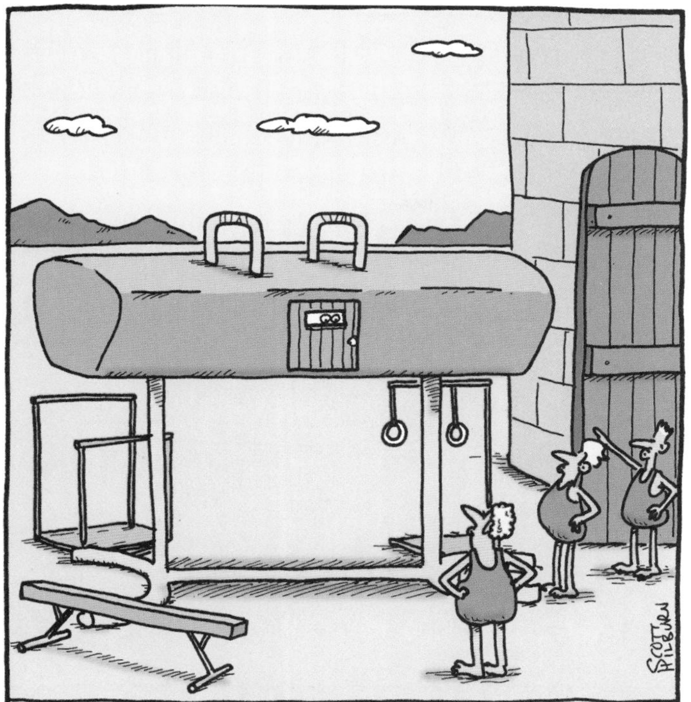
SCOTT HILBURN

TROY'S RENOWNED GYMNASTICS TEAM HAD NEVER BEFORE RECEIVED A GIFT OF SUCH GENEROSITY.

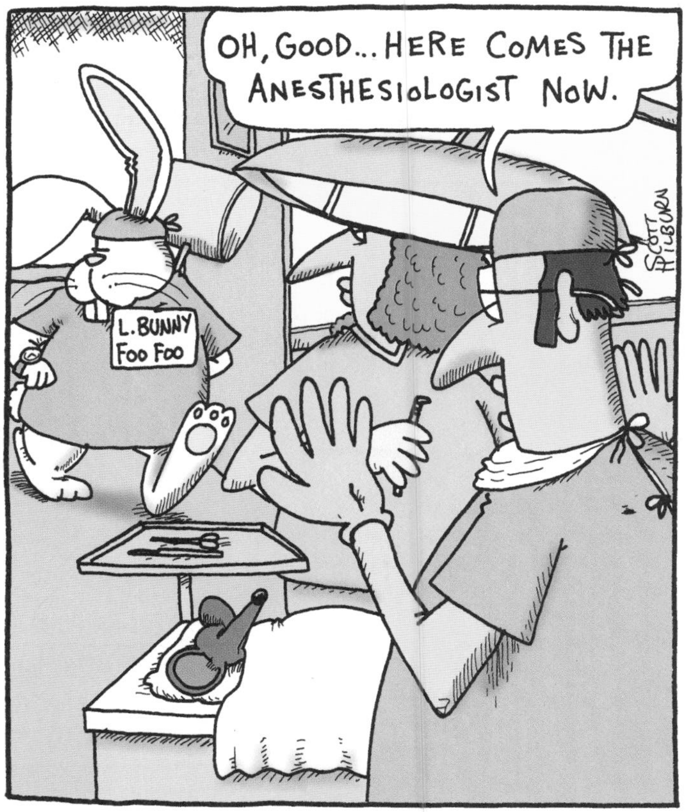
OH, GOOD... HERE COMES THE ANESTHESIOLOGIST NOW.
L. BUNNY Foo Foo
SCOTT HILBURN

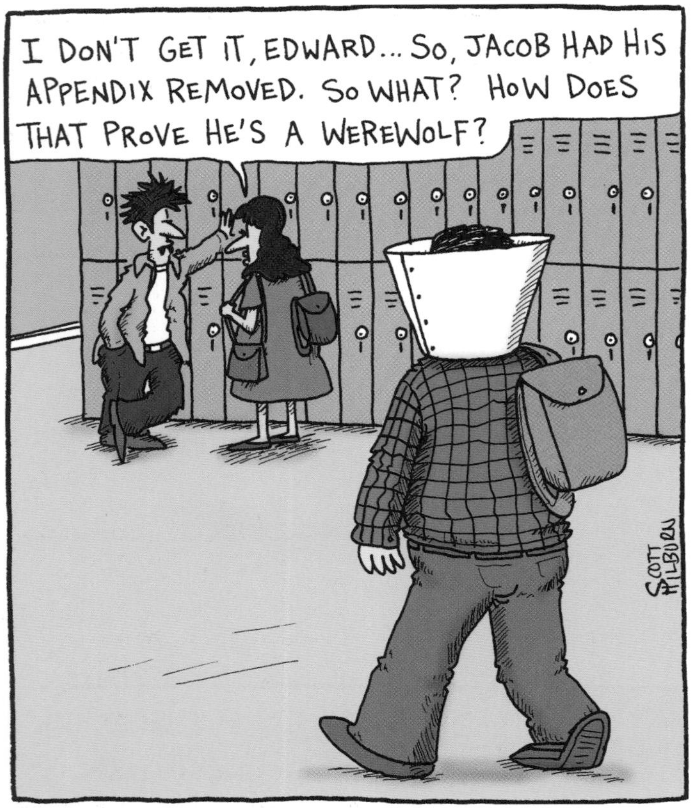
I DON'T GET IT, EDWARD... SO, JACOB HAD HIS APPENDIX REMOVED. SO WHAT? HOW DOES THAT PROVE HE'S A WEREWOLF?
SCOTT HILBURN

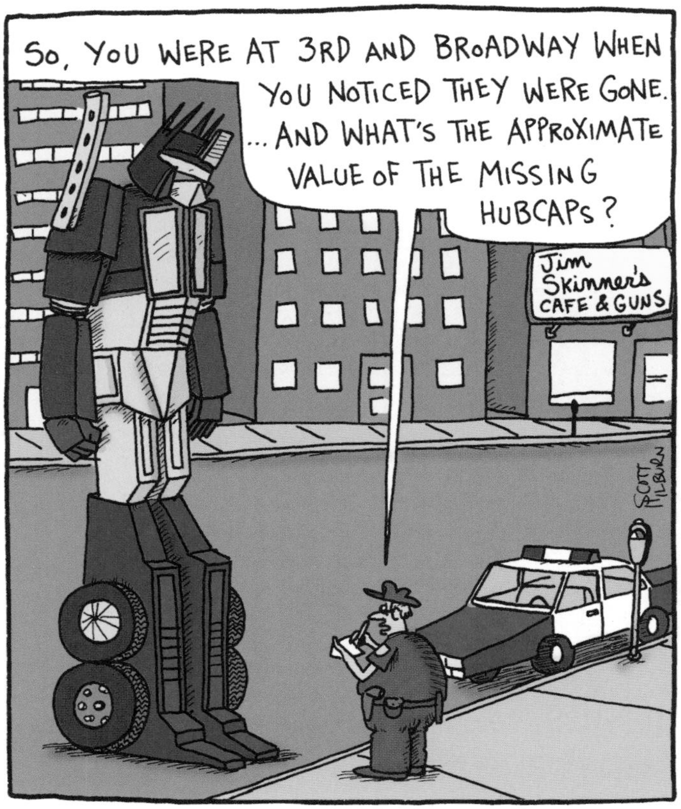
SO, YOU WERE AT 3RD AND BROADWAY WHEN YOU NOTICED THEY WERE GONE. ...AND WHAT'S THE APPROXIMATE VALUE OF THE MISSING HUBCAPS?
Jim Skinner's CAFE & GUNS
SCOTT HILBURN

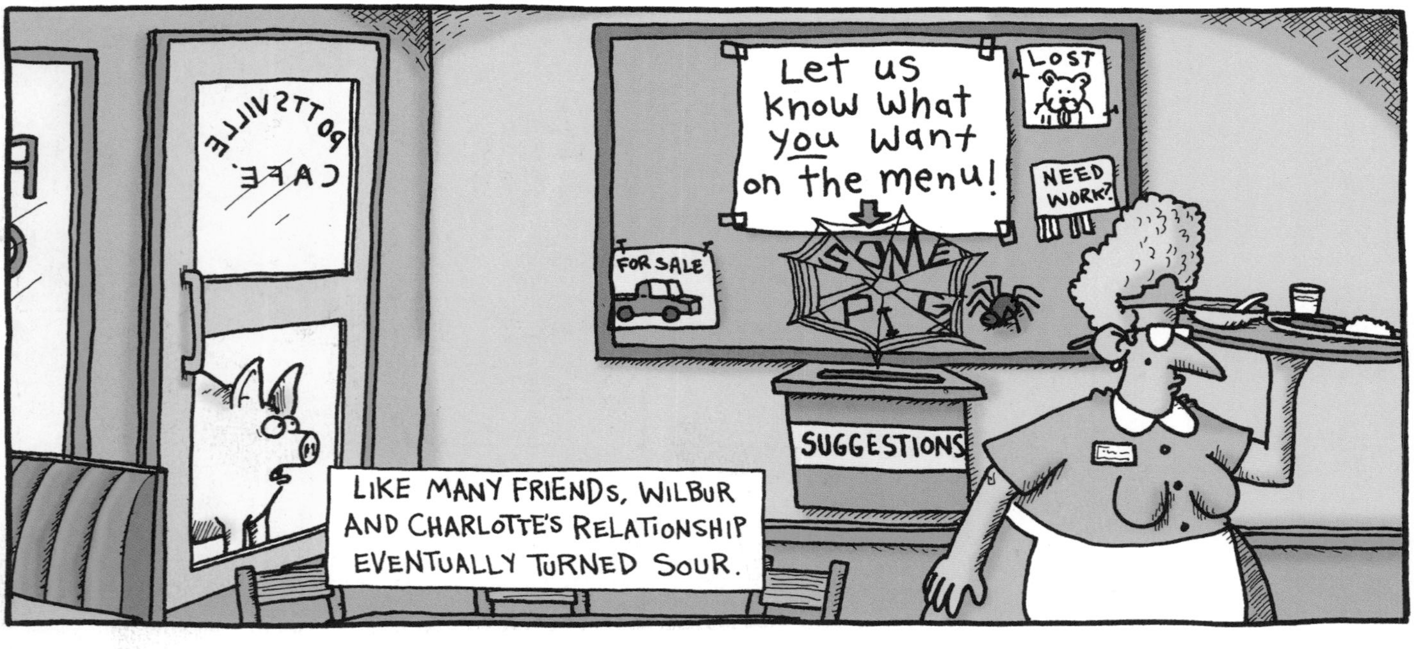
POTTSVILLE CAFE
Let us know what you want on the menu!
LOST
NEED WORK?
FOR SALE
SOME PIG
SUGGESTIONS
LIKE MANY FRIENDS, WILBUR AND CHARLOTTE'S RELATIONSHIP EVENTUALLY TURNED SOUR.

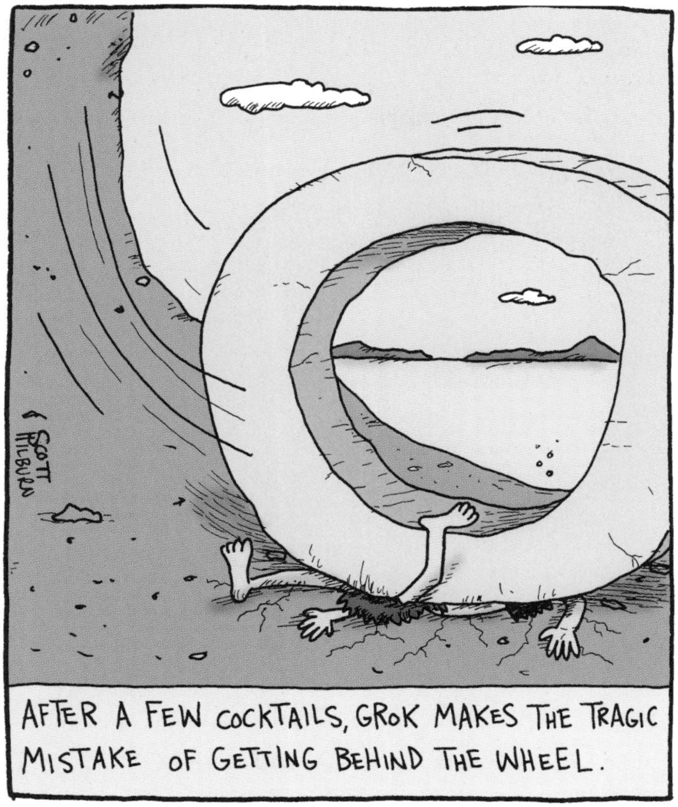
SCOTT HILBURN
AFTER A FEW COCKTAILS, GROK MAKES THE TRAGIC MISTAKE OF GETTING BEHIND THE WHEEL.

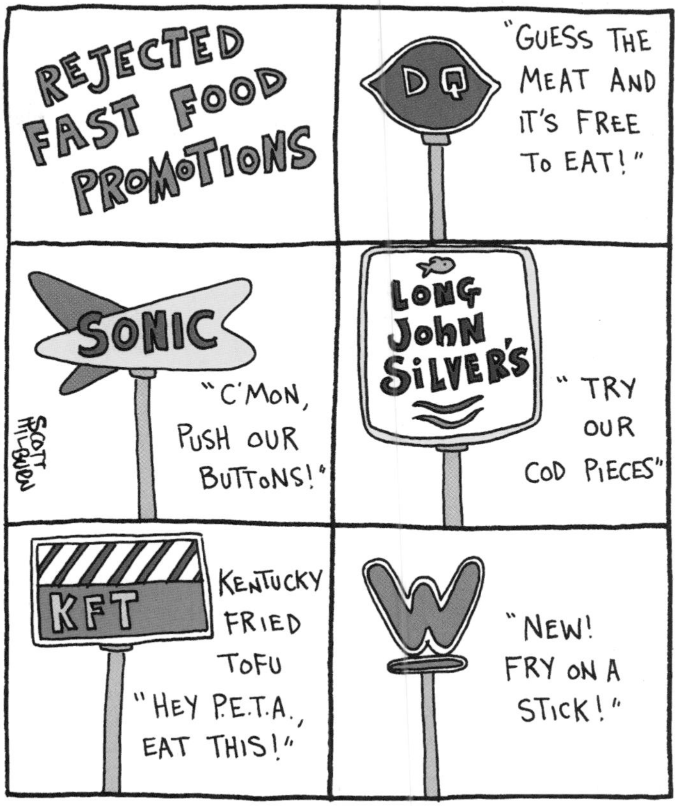
REJECTED FAST FOOD PROMOTIONS
DQ
"GUESS THE MEAT AND IT'S FREE TO EAT!"
SONIC
"C'MON, PUSH OUR BUTTONS!"
SCOTT HILBURN
LONG JOHN SILVER'S
"TRY TRY OUR COD PIECES"
KFT
KENTUCKY FRIED TOFU
"HEY P.E.T.A., EAT THIS!"
W
"NEW! FRY ON A STICK!"

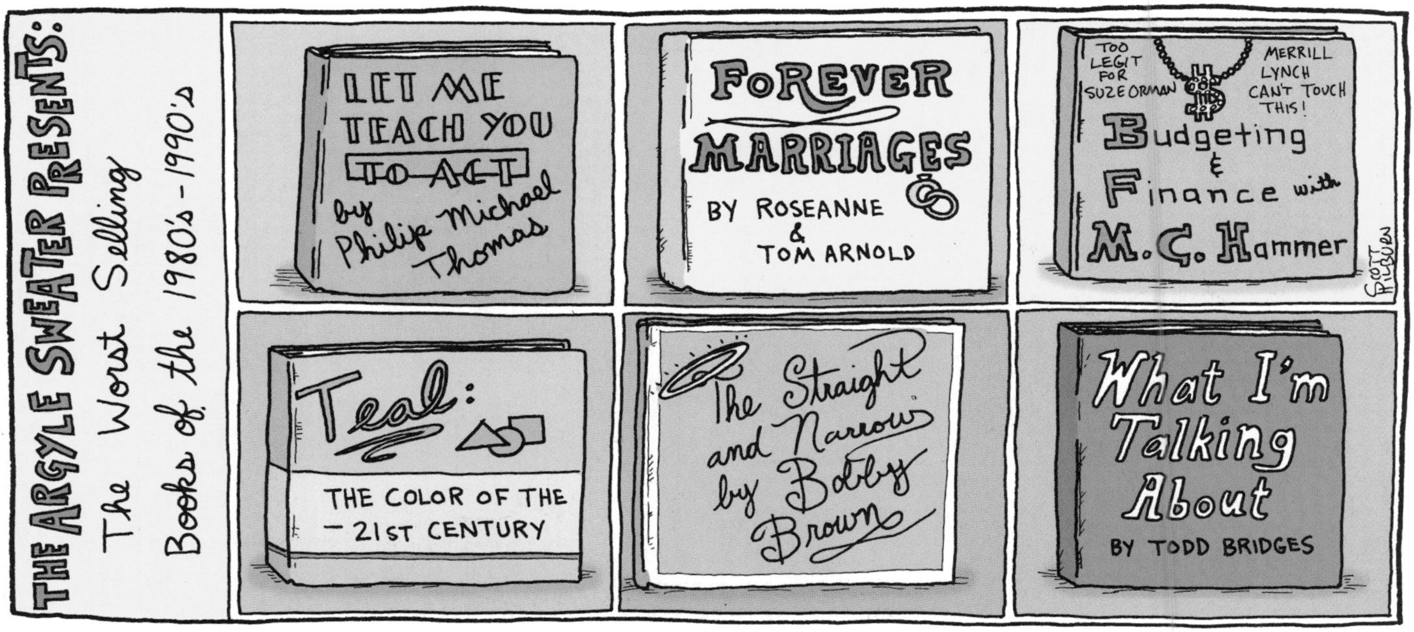
THE ARGYLE SWEATER PRESENTS:
The Worst Selling Books of the 1980's–1990's
LET ME TEACH YOU TO ACT by Philip Michael Thomas
FOREVER MARRIAGES BY ROSEANNE & TOM ARNOLD
TOO LEGIT FOR SUZE ORMAN
MERRILL LYNCH CAN'T TOUCH THIS!
Budgeting & Finance with M.C. Hammer
SCOTT HILBURN
Teal: THE COLOR OF THE 21ST CENTURY
The Straight and Narrow by Bobby Brown
What I'm Talking About BY TODD BRIDGES

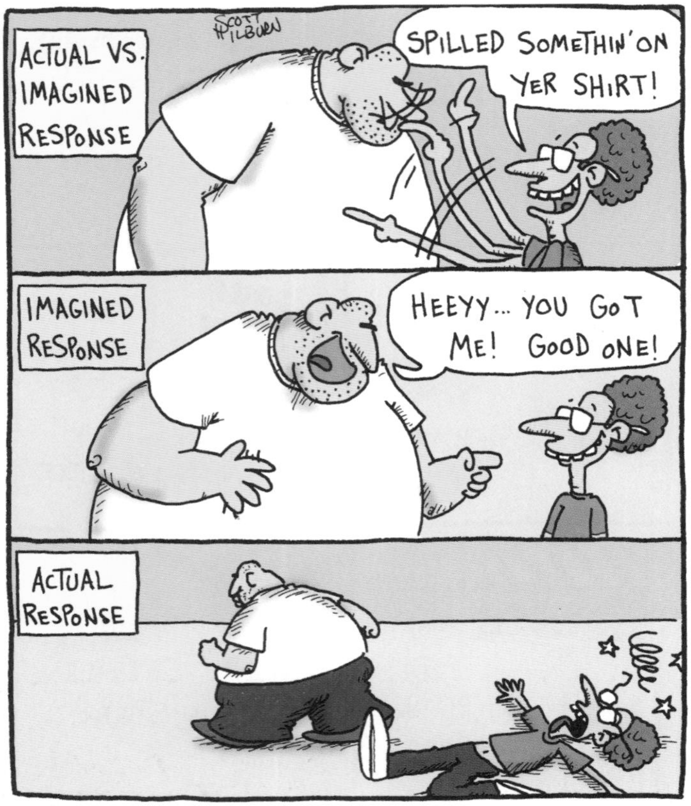
SCOTT HILBURN
ACTUAL VS. IMAGINED RESPONSE
SPILLED SOMETHIN' ON YER SHIRT!
IMAGINED RESPONSE
HEEYY... YOU GOT ME! GOOD ONE!
ACTUAL RESPONSE

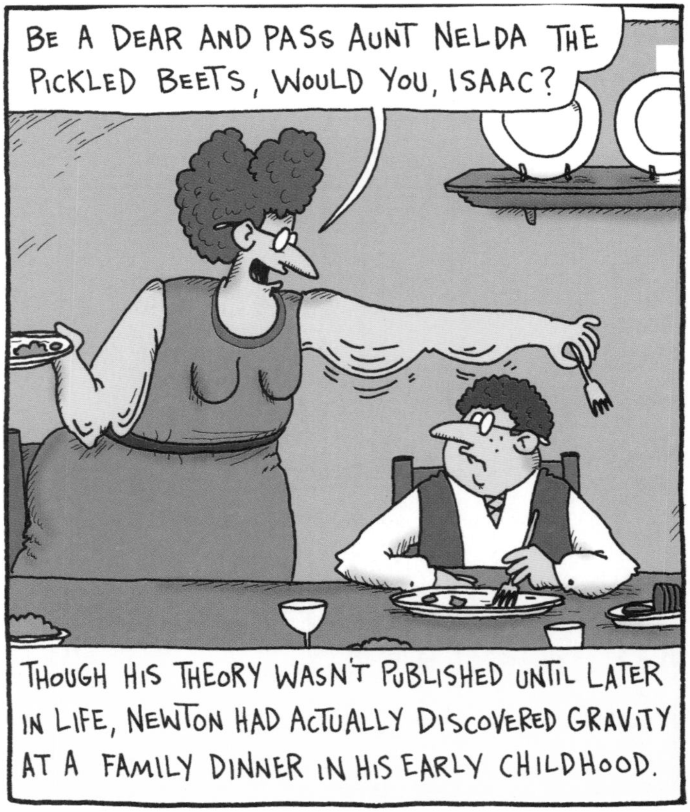
BE A DEAR AND PASS AUNT NELDA THE PICKLED BEETS, WOULD YOU, ISAAC?
THOUGH HIS THEORY WASN'T PUBLISHED UNTIL LATER IN LIFE, NEWTON HAD ACTUALLY DISCOVERED GRAVITY AT A FAMILY DINNER IN HIS EARLY CHILDHOOD.

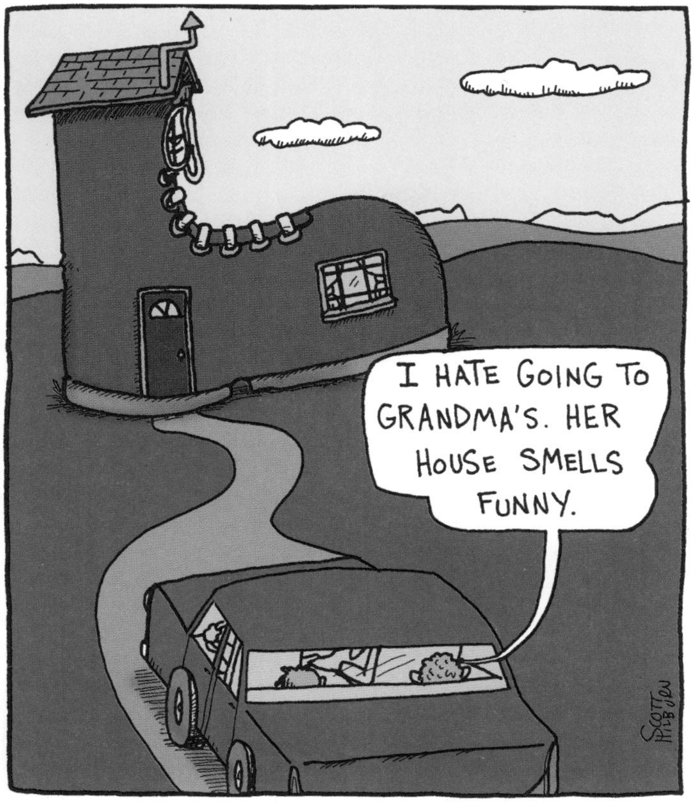
I HATE GOING TO GRANDMA'S. HER HOUSE SMELLS FUNNY.
SCOTT HILBURN

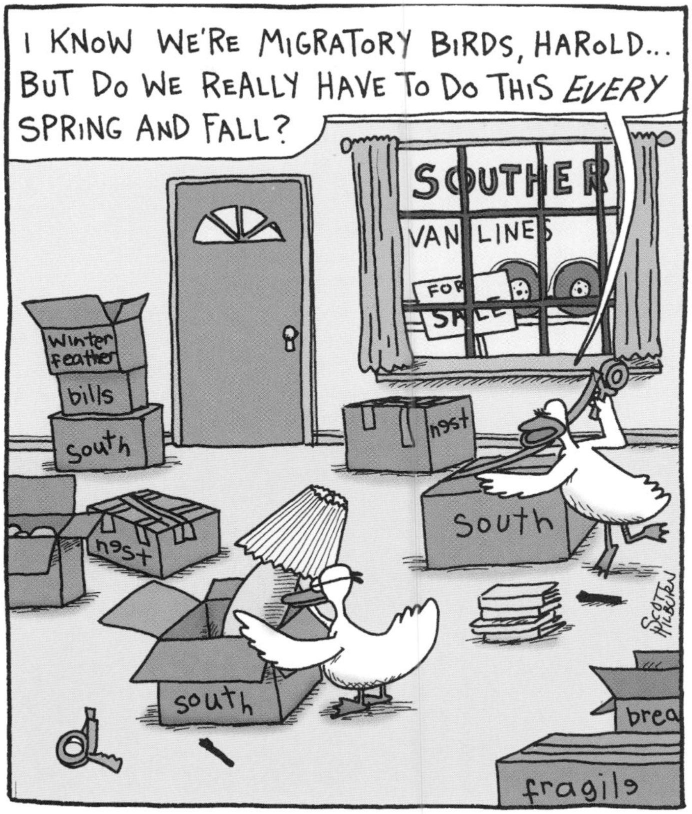
I KNOW WE'RE MIGRATORY BIRDS, HAROLD... BUT DO WE REALLY HAVE TO DO THIS *EVERY* SPRING AND FALL?
SOUTHER
VAN LINES
FOR
winter feather
bills
south
nest
nest
south
south
brea
SCOTT HILBURN

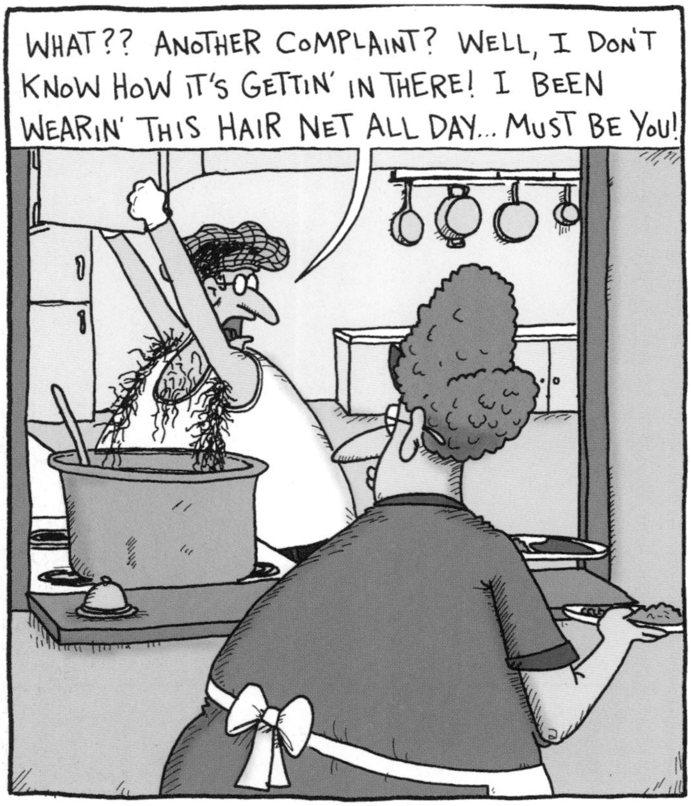
WHAT?? ANOTHER COMPLAINT? WELL, I DON'T KNOW HOW IT'S GETTIN' IN THERE! I BEEN WEARIN' THIS HAIR NET ALL DAY... MUST BE YOU!

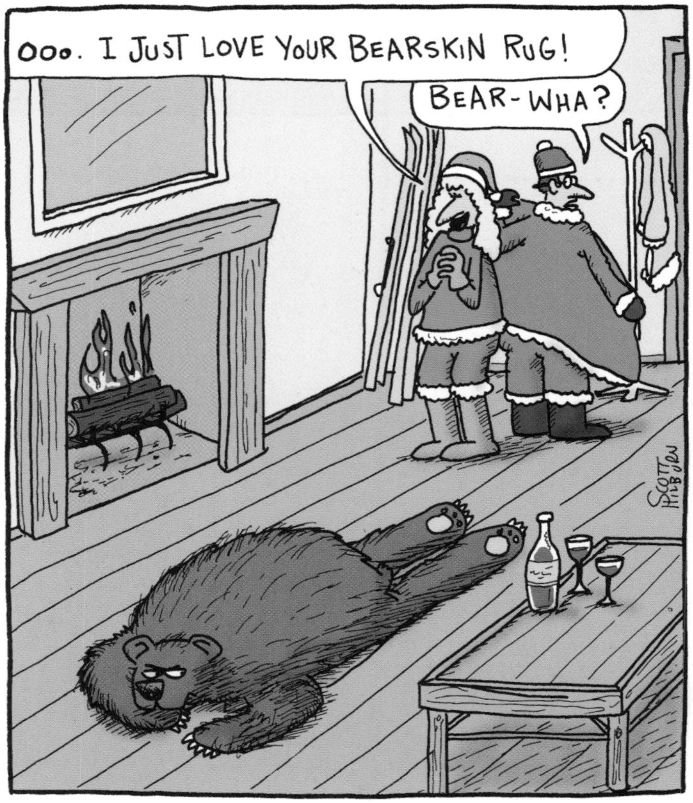
Ooo. I JUST LOVE YOUR BEARSKIN RUG!
BEAR-WHA?
SCOTT HILBURN

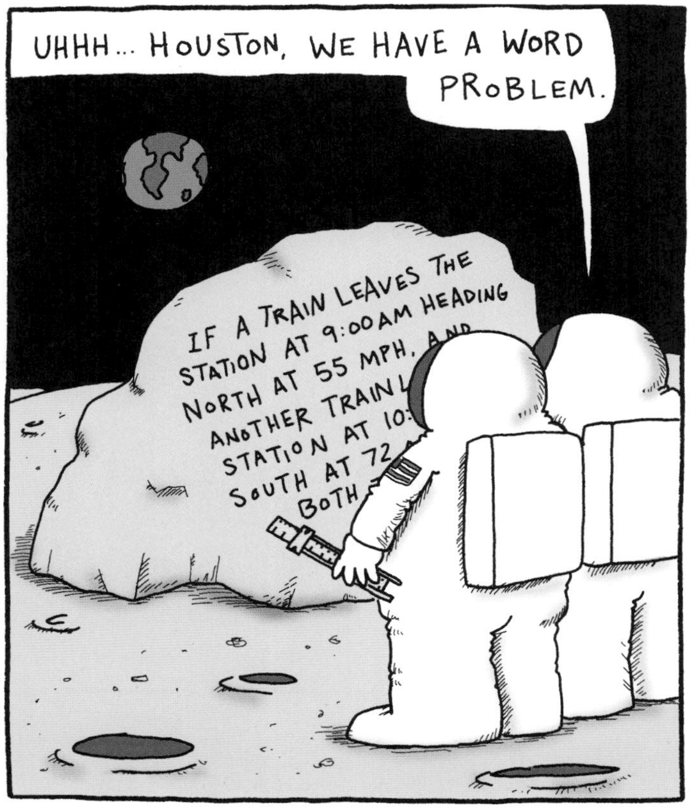
UHHH... HOUSTON, WE HAVE A WORD PROBLEM.
IF A TRAIN LEAVES THE
STATION AT 9:00AM HEADING
NORTH AT 55 MPH,
ANOTHER TRAIN
STATION AT
SOUTH AT 72
BOTH

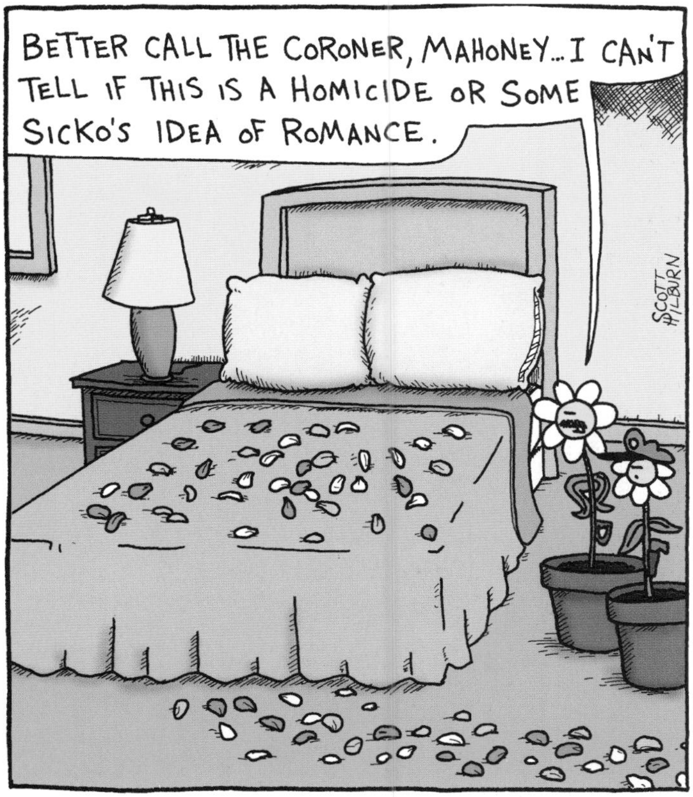
BETTER CALL THE CORONER, MAHONEY... I CAN'T TELL IF THIS IS A HOMICIDE OR SOME SICKO'S IDEA OF ROMANCE.
SCOTT HILBURN

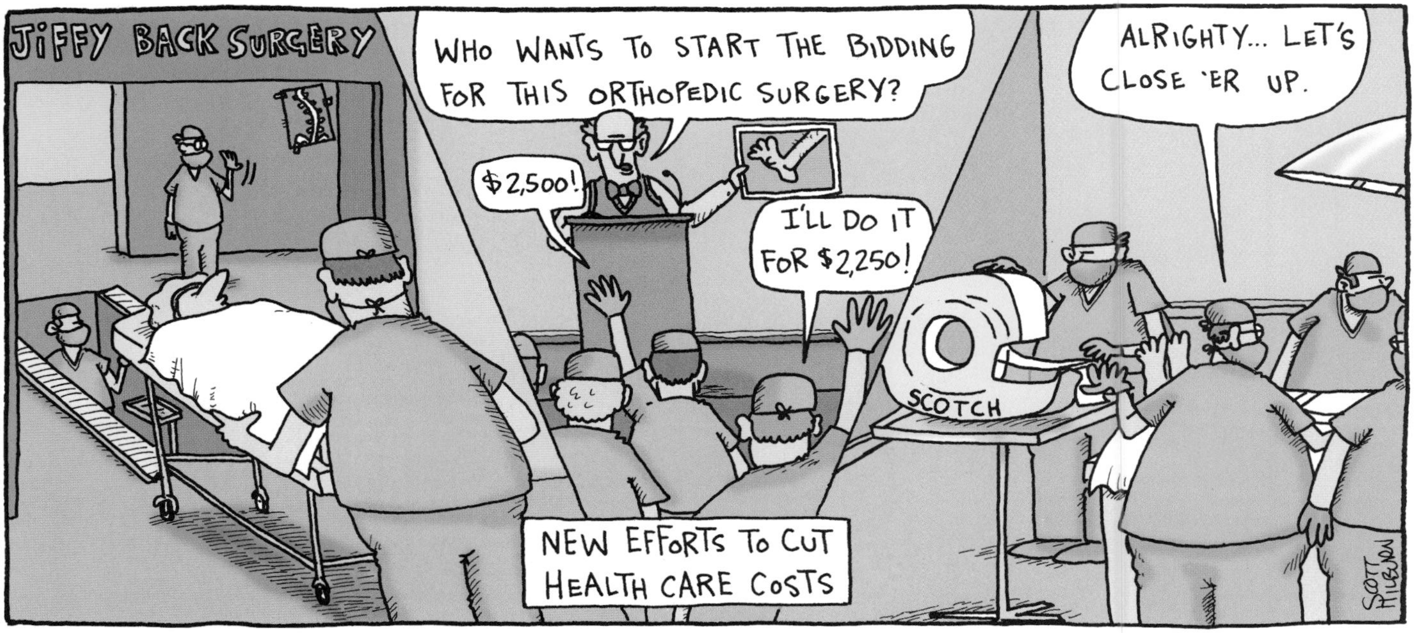
JIFFY BACK SURGERY
WHO WANTS TO START THE BIDDING FOR THIS ORTHOPEDIC SURGERY?
$2,500!
I'LL DO IT FOR $2,250!
ALRIGHTY... LET'S CLOSE 'ER UP.
SCOTCH
NEW EFFORTS TO CUT HEALTH CARE COSTS
SCOTT HILBURN

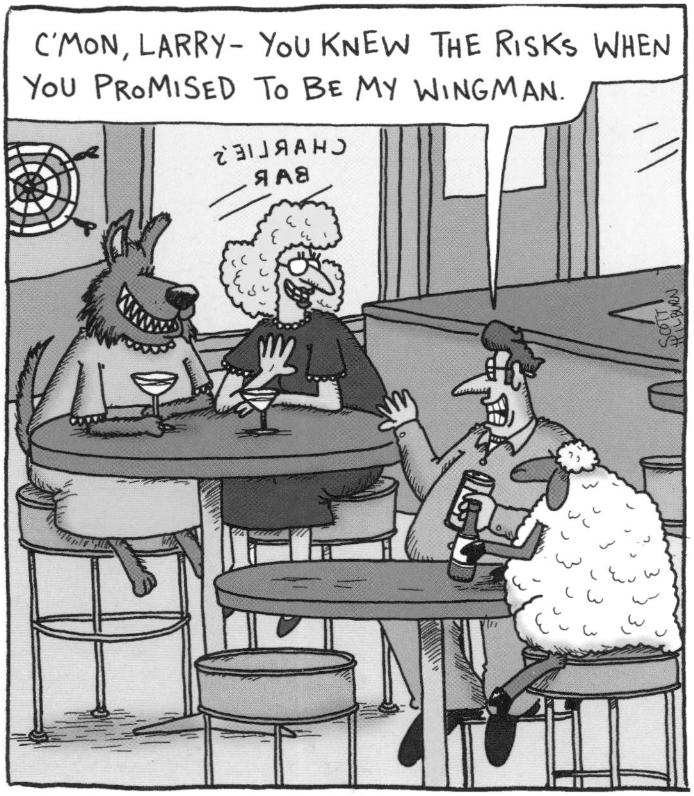
C'MON, LARRY- YOU KNEW THE RISKS WHEN YOU PROMISED TO BE MY WINGMAN.

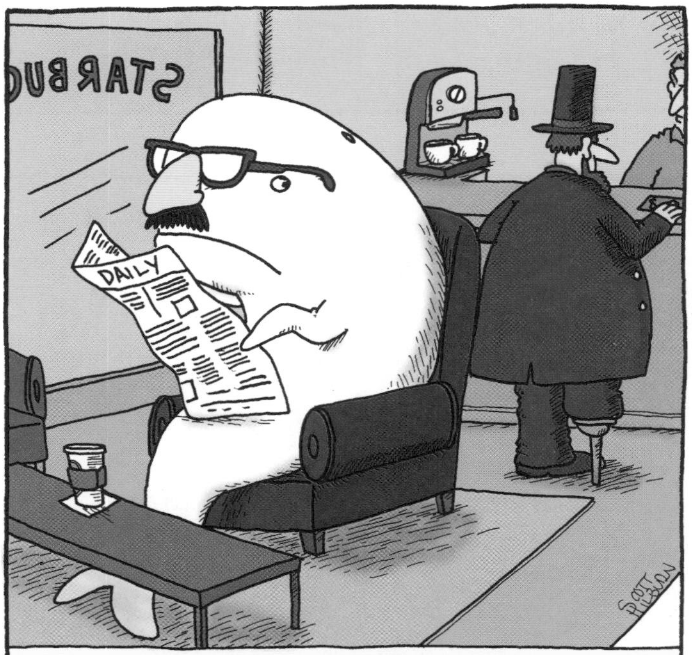
DAILY

WHILE HIS NEMESIS ORDERED A SCONE, LEVI WAS AGAIN SAVED BY THE F.B.I.'S HIGH-BUDGET WITNESS PROTECTION PROGRAM-ISSUED DISGUISES.

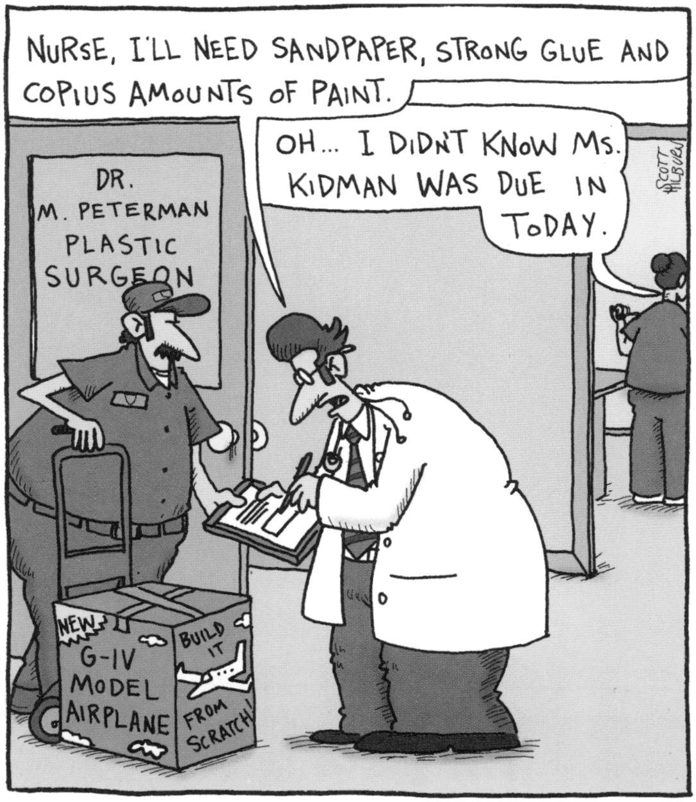
NURSE, I'LL NEED SANDPAPER, STRONG GLUE AND COPIUS AMOUNTS OF PAINT.
OH... I DIDN'T KNOW MS. KIDMAN WAS DUE IN TODAY.
DR. M. PETERMAN PLASTIC SURGEON
NEW G-IV MODEL AIRPLANE
BUILD IT FROM SCRATCH!
SCOTT HILBURN

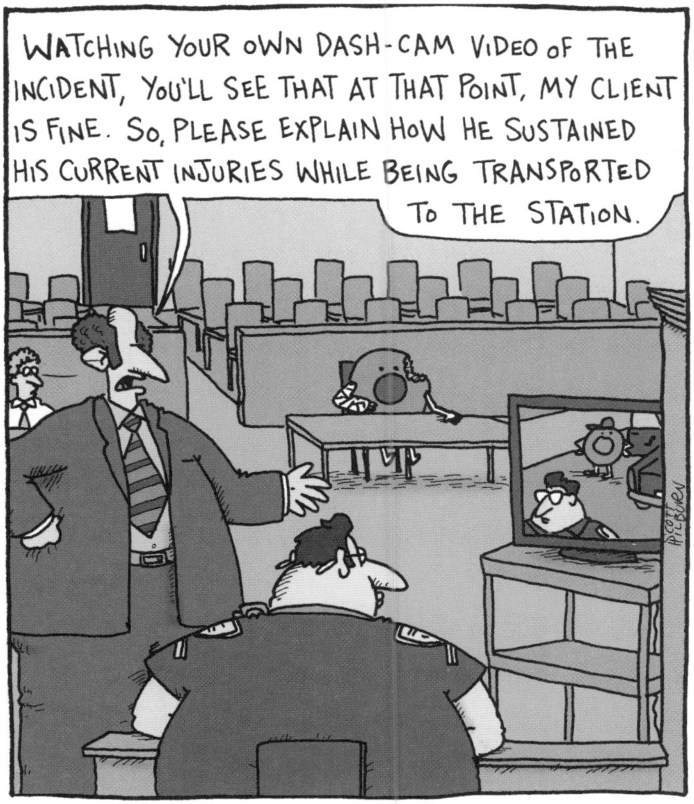
WATCHING YOUR OWN DASH-CAM VIDEO OF THE INCIDENT, YOU'LL SEE THAT AT THAT POINT, MY CLIENT IS FINE. SO, PLEASE EXPLAIN HOW HE SUSTAINED HIS CURRENT INJURIES WHILE BEING TRANSPORTED TO THE STATION.
SCOTT HILBURN

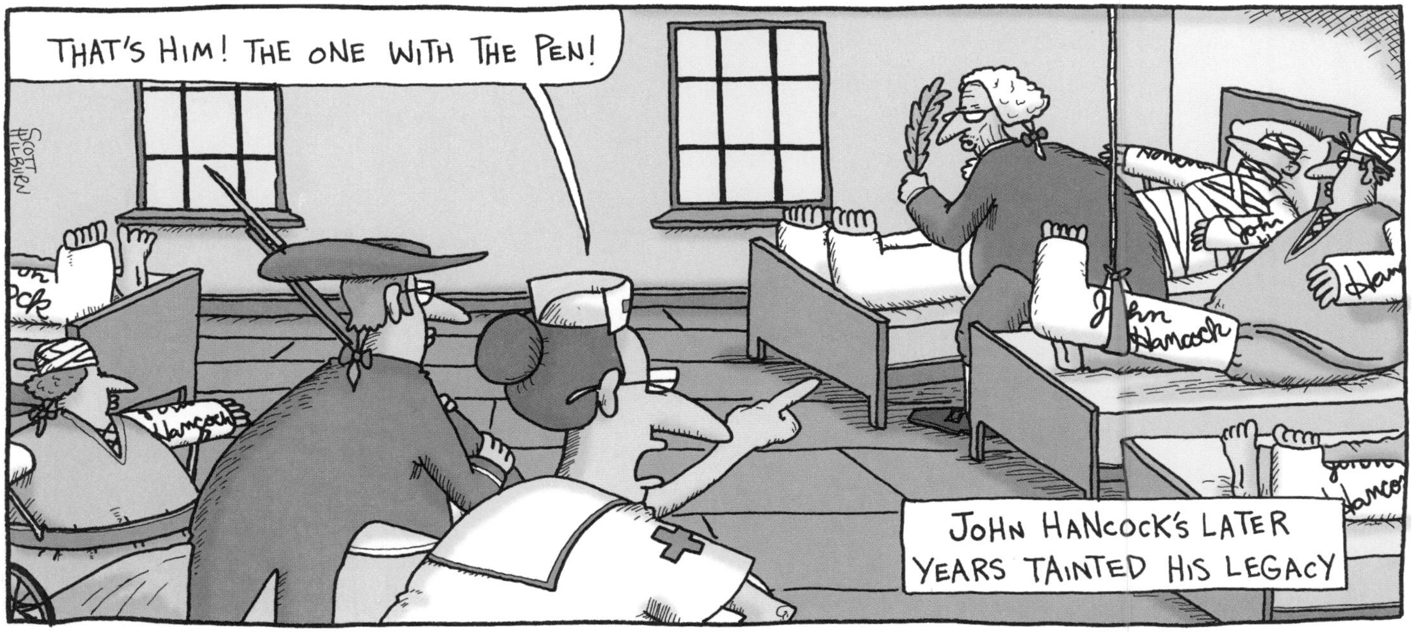
THAT'S HIM! THE ONE WITH THE PEN!
SCOTT HILBURN
John Hancock

JOHN HANCOCK'S LATER YEARS TAINTED HIS LEGACY

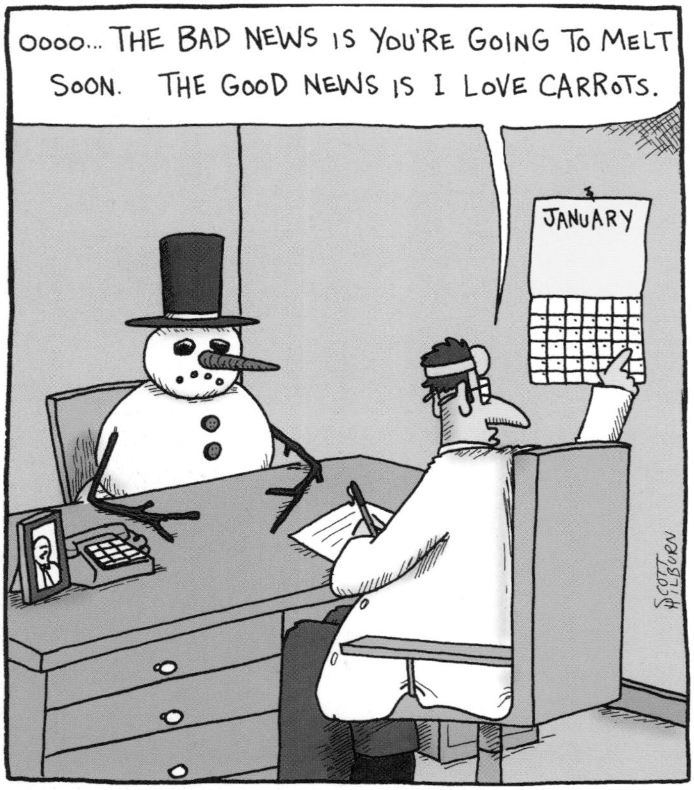
OOOO... THE BAD NEWS IS YOU'RE GOING TO MELT SOON. THE GOOD NEWS IS I LOVE CARROTS.
JANUARY
SCOTT HILBURN

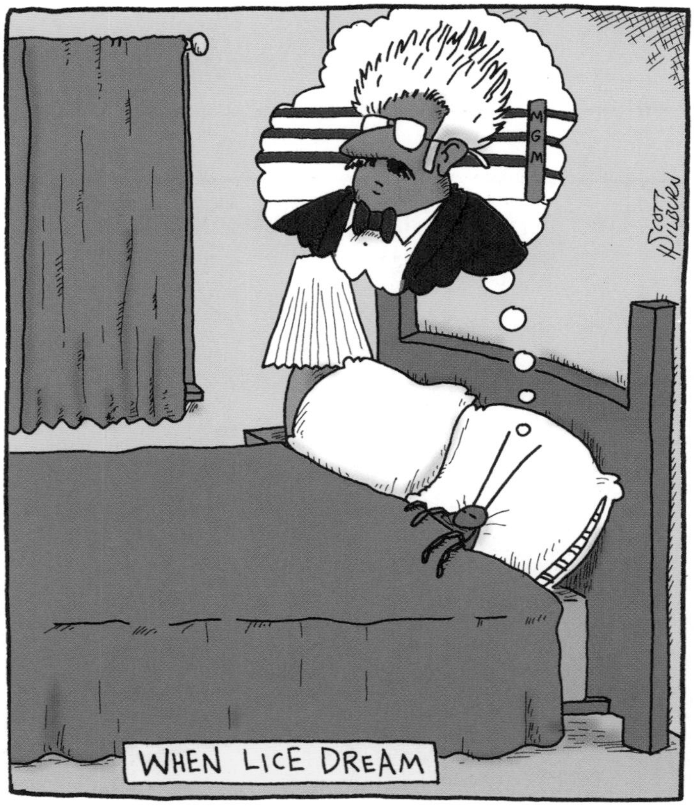
MGM
SCOTT HILBURN
WHEN LICE DREAM

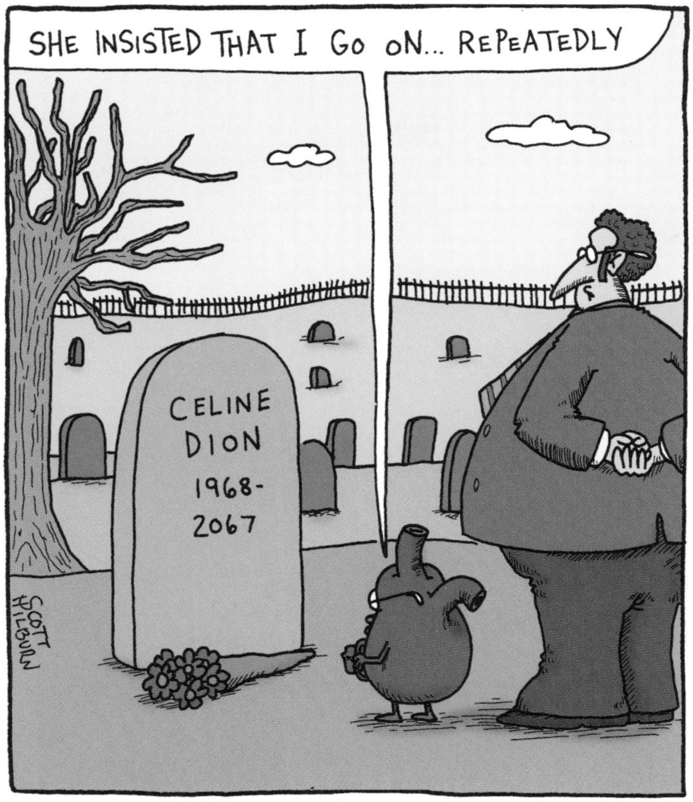
SHE INSISTED THAT I GO ON... REPEATEDLY
CELINE DION 1968-2067
SCOTT HILBURN

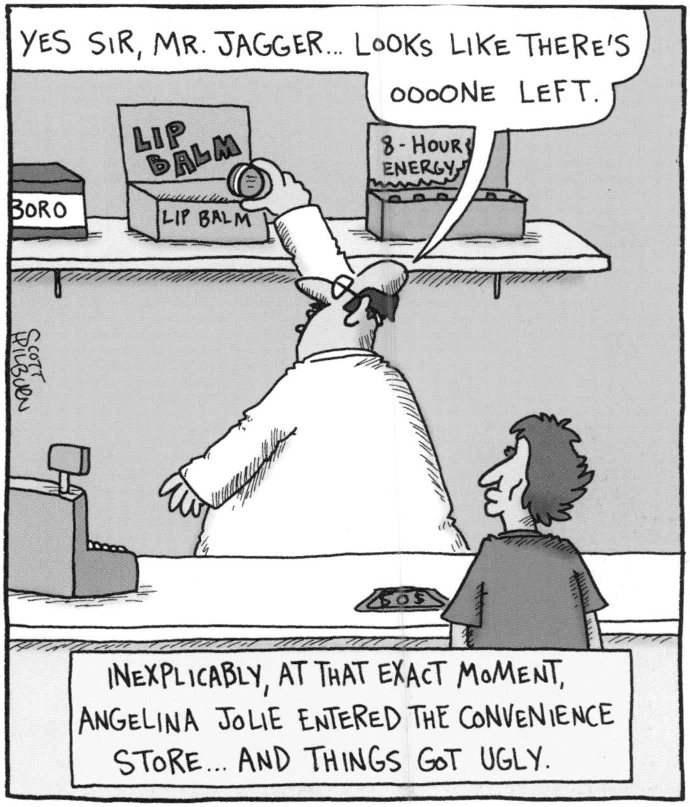
YES SIR, MR. JAGGER... LOOKS LIKE THERE'S OOOONE LEFT.
LIP BALM
LIP BALM
8-HOUR ENERGY
BORO
SCOTT HILBURN
INEXPLICABLY, AT THAT EXACT MOMENT, ANGELINA JOLIE ENTERED THE CONVENIENCE STORE... AND THINGS GOT UGLY.

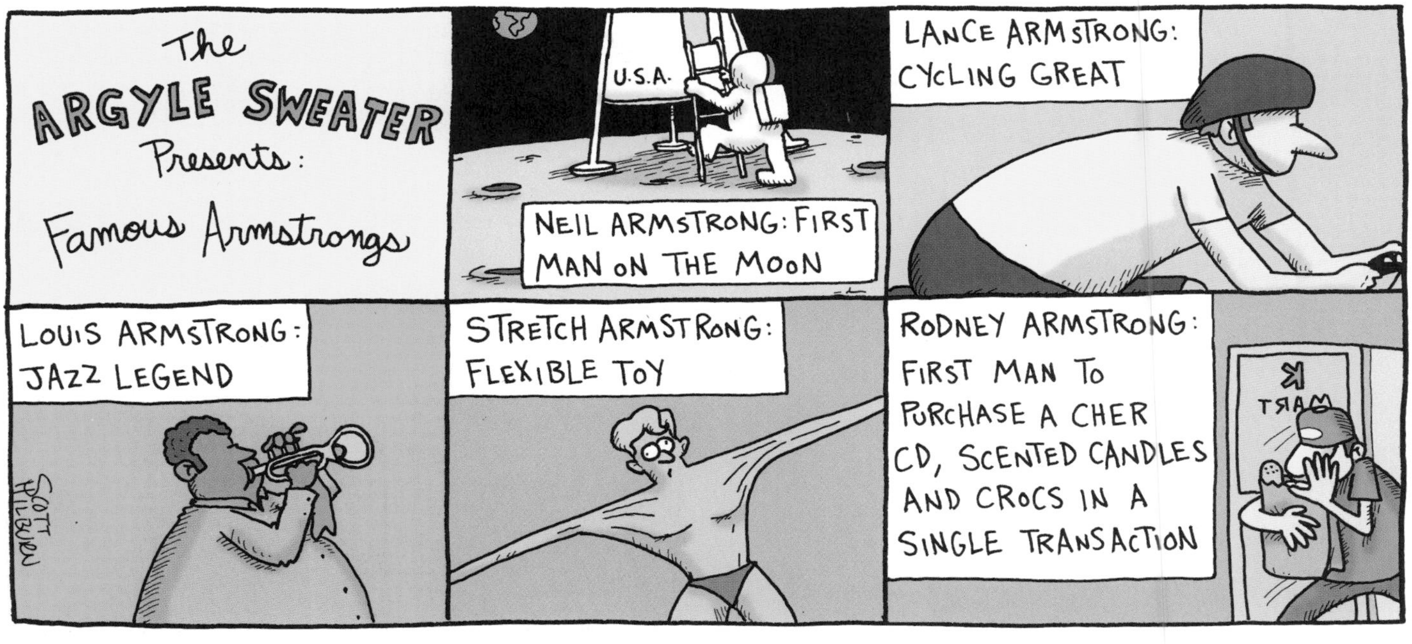
The ARGYLE SWEATER Presents: Famous Armstrongs
U.S.A.
NEIL ARMSTRONG: FIRST MAN ON THE MOON
LANCE ARMSTRONG: CYCLING GREAT
LOUIS ARMSTRONG: JAZZ LEGEND
SCOTT HILBURN
STRETCH ARMSTRONG: FLEXIBLE TOY
RODNEY ARMSTRONG: FIRST MAN TO PURCHASE A CHER CD, SCENTED CANDLES AND CROCS IN A SINGLE TRANSACTION

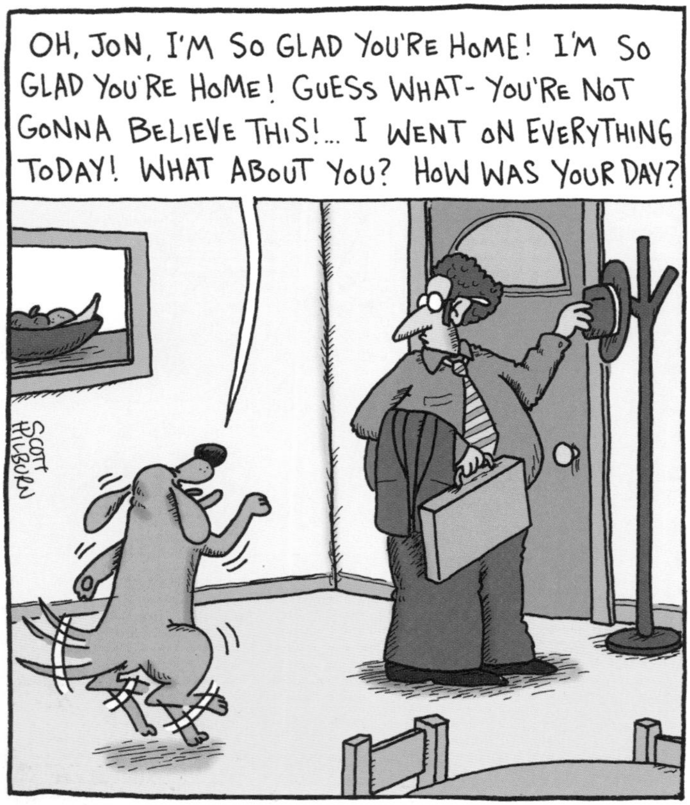
OH, JON, I'M SO GLAD YOU'RE HOME! I'M SO GLAD YOU'RE HOME! GUESS WHAT- YOU'RE NOT GONNA BELIEVE THIS!... I WENT ON EVERYTHING TODAY! WHAT ABOUT YOU? HOW WAS YOUR DAY?
SCOTT HILBURN

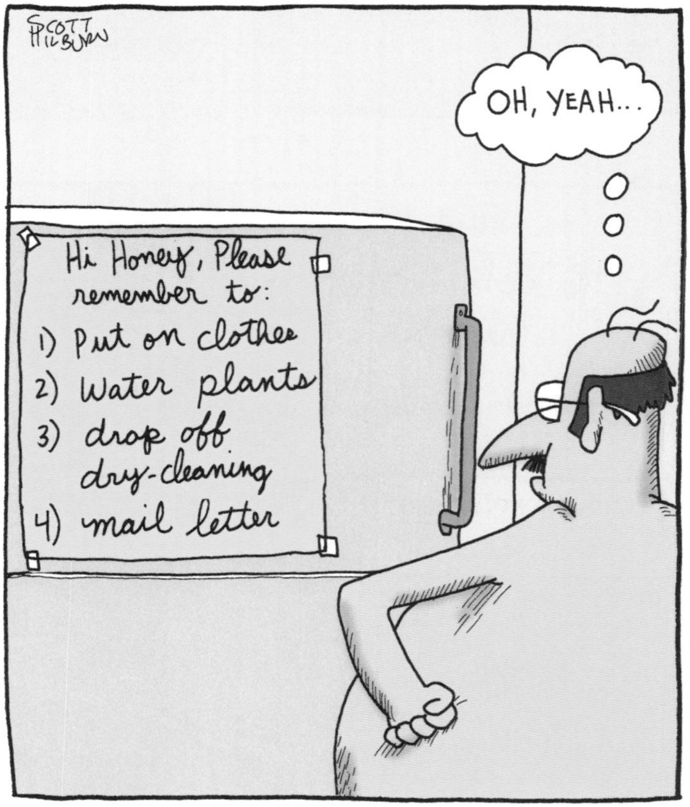
SCOTT HILBURN
OH, YEAH...
Hi Honey, Please remember to:
1) Put on clothes
2) Water plants
3) drop off dry-cleaning
4) mail letter

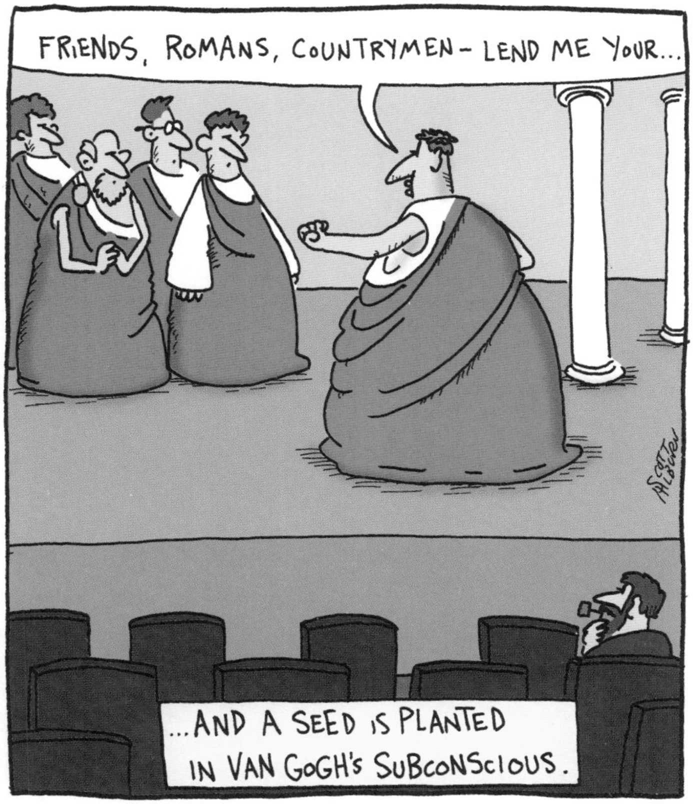
FRIENDS, ROMANS, COUNTRYMEN - LEND ME YOUR...
...AND A SEED IS PLANTED IN VAN GOGH'S SUBCONSCIOUS.
SCOTT HILBURN

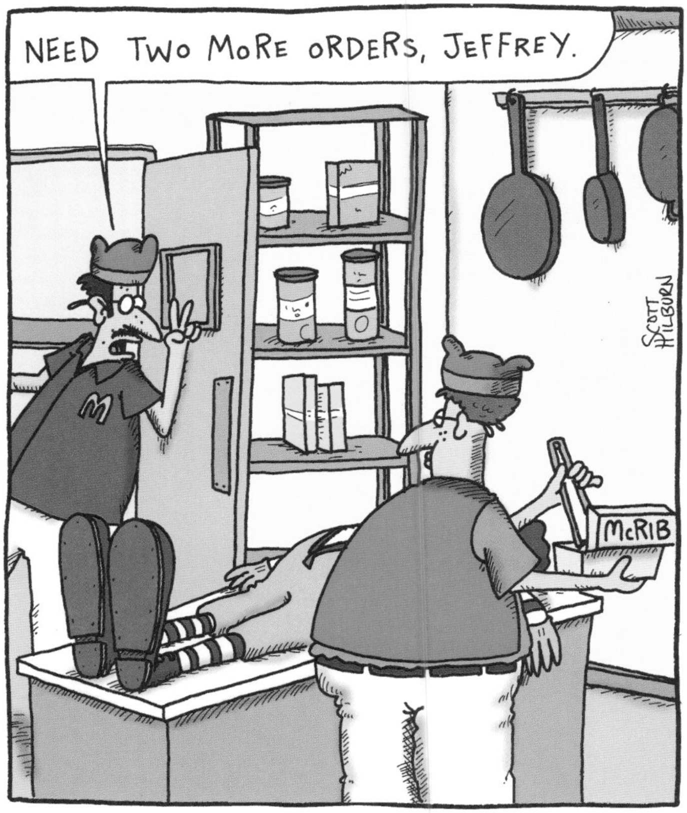
NEED TWO MORE ORDERS, JEFFREY.
McRIB
SCOTT HILBURN

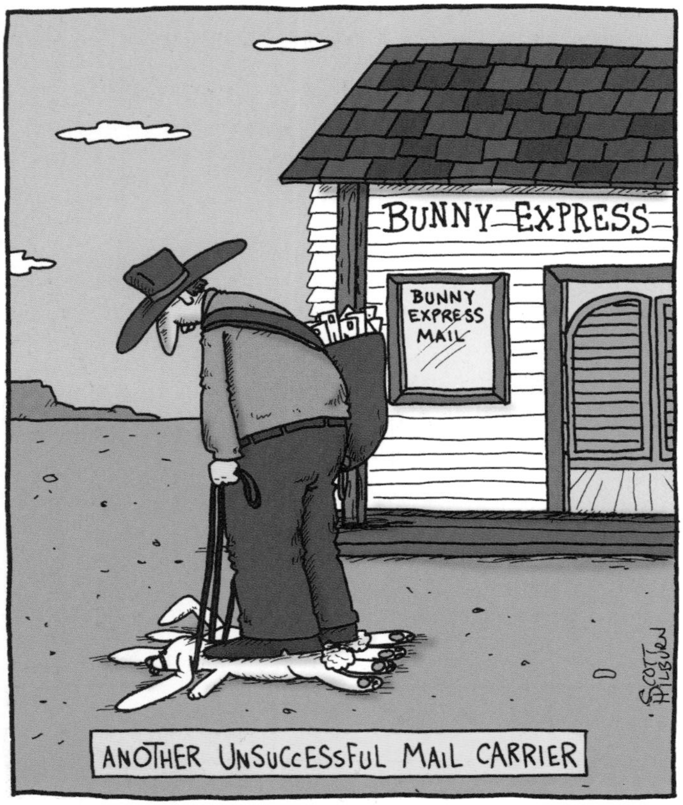
BUNNY EXPRESS
BUNNY EXPRESS MAIL
SCOTT HILBURN
ANOTHER UNSUCCESSFUL MAIL CARRIER

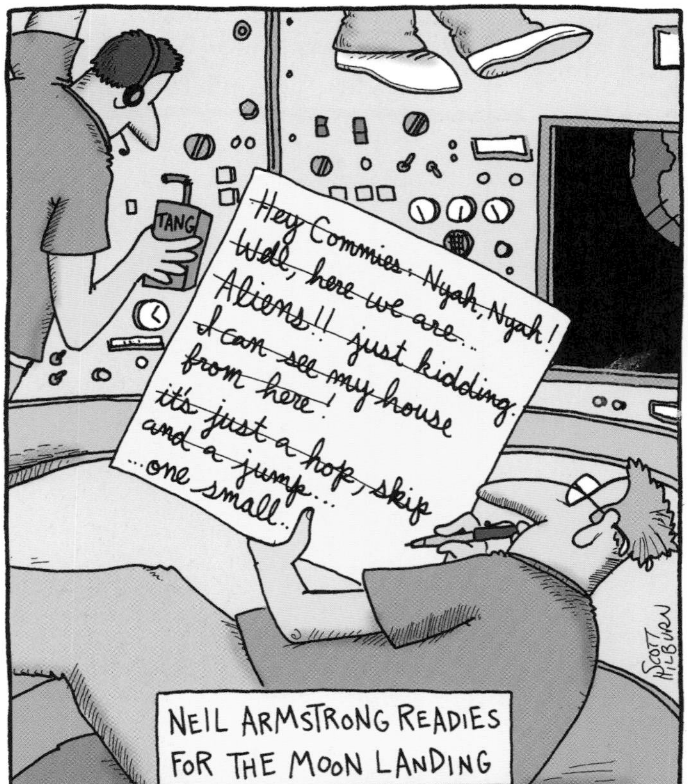
TANG
Hey Commies, Nyah, Nyah!
Well, here we are...
Aliens!! just kidding.
I can see my house
from here!
it's just a hop, skip
and a jump...
...one small...
SCOTT HILBURN
NEIL ARMSTRONG READIES FOR THE MOON LANDING

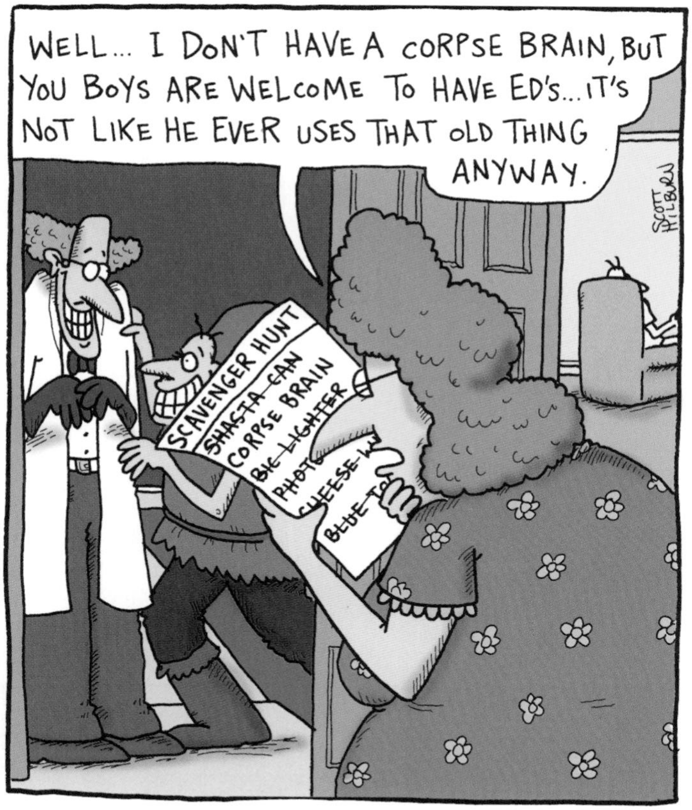
WELL... I DON'T HAVE A CORPSE BRAIN, BUT YOU BOYS ARE WELCOME TO HAVE ED'S... IT'S NOT LIKE HE EVER USES THAT OLD THING ANYWAY.
SCAVENGER HUNT
SHASTA CAN
CORPSE BRAIN
BIG LIGHTER
SCOTT HILBURN

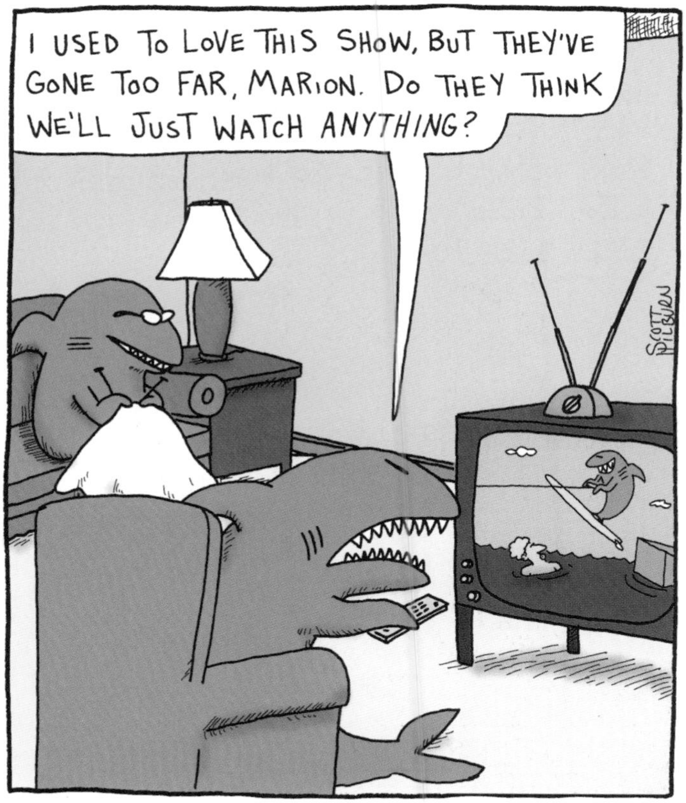
I USED TO LOVE THIS SHOW, BUT THEY'VE GONE TOO FAR, MARION. DO THEY THINK WE'LL JUST WATCH *ANYTHING*?
SCOTT HILBURN

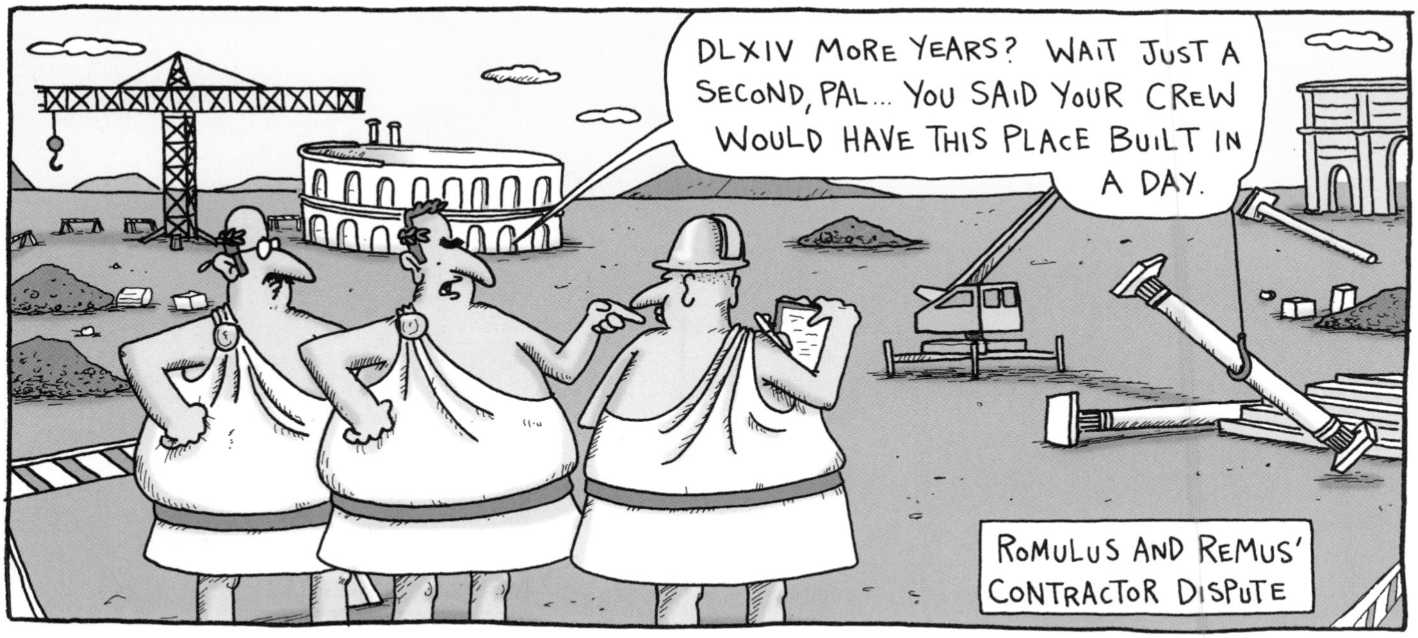
DLXIV MORE YEARS? WAIT JUST A SECOND, PAL... YOU SAID YOUR CREW WOULD HAVE THIS PLACE BUILT IN A DAY.
ROMULUS AND REMUS' CONTRACTOR DISPUTE

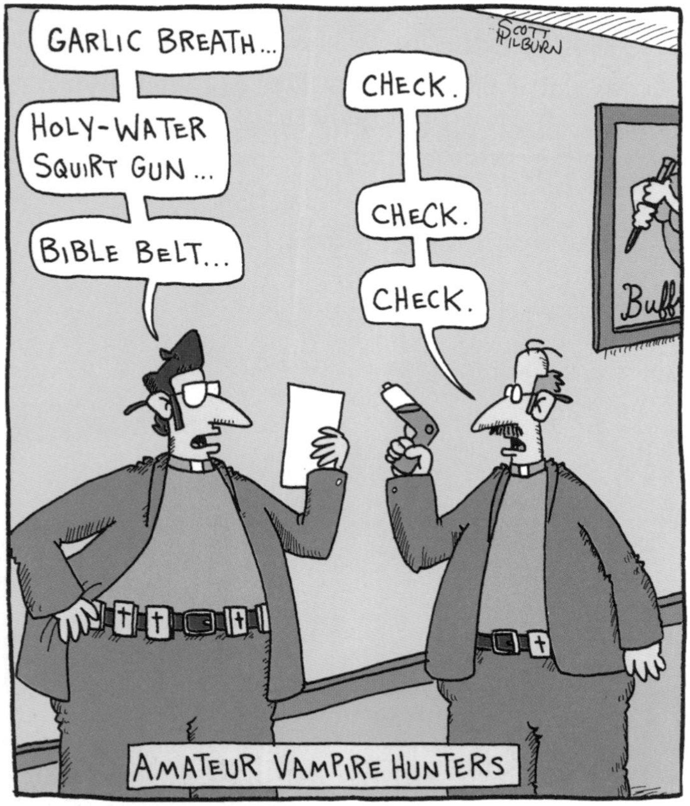
SCOTT HILBURN
GARLIC BREATH...
CHECK.
HOLY-WATER SQUIRT GUN...
CHECK.
BIBLE BELT...
CHECK.
AMATEUR VAMPIRE HUNTERS

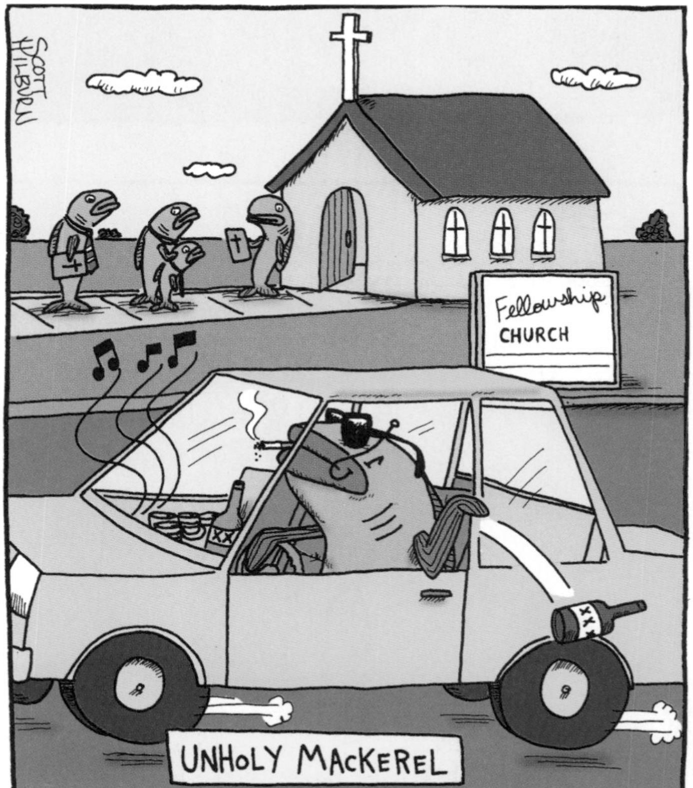
SCOTT HILBURN
Fellowship CHURCH
UNHOLY MACKEREL

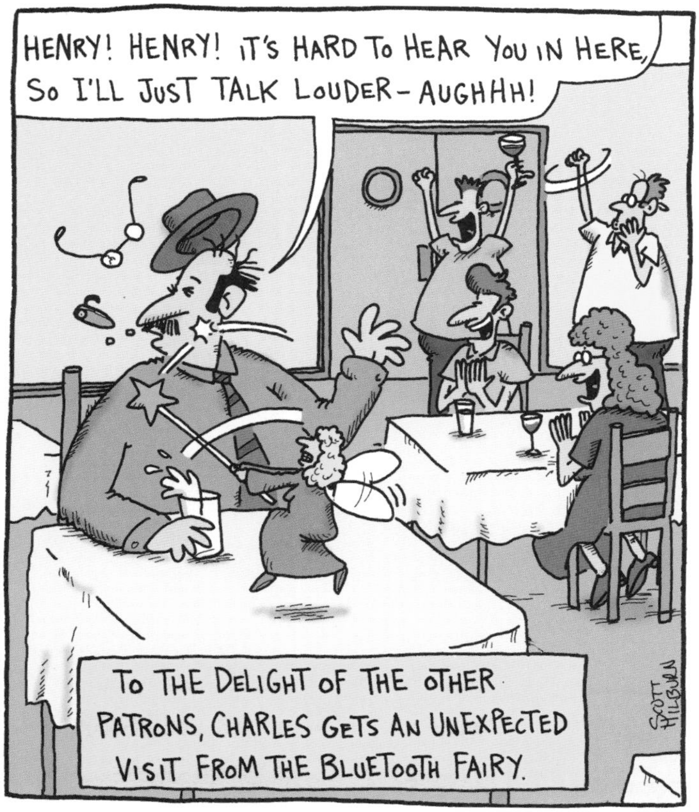
HENRY! HENRY! IT'S HARD TO HEAR YOU IN HERE, SO I'LL JUST TALK LOUDER- AUGHHH!
TO THE DELIGHT OF THE OTHER PATRONS, CHARLES GETS AN UNEXPECTED VISIT FROM THE BLUETOOTH FAIRY.
SCOTT HILBURN

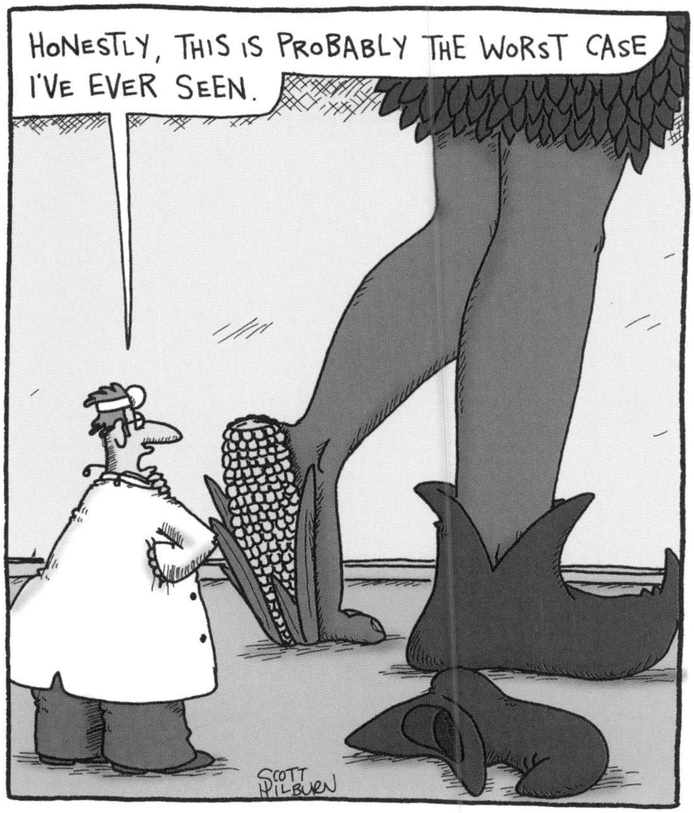
HONESTLY, THIS IS PROBABLY THE WORST CASE I'VE EVER SEEN.
SCOTT HILBURN

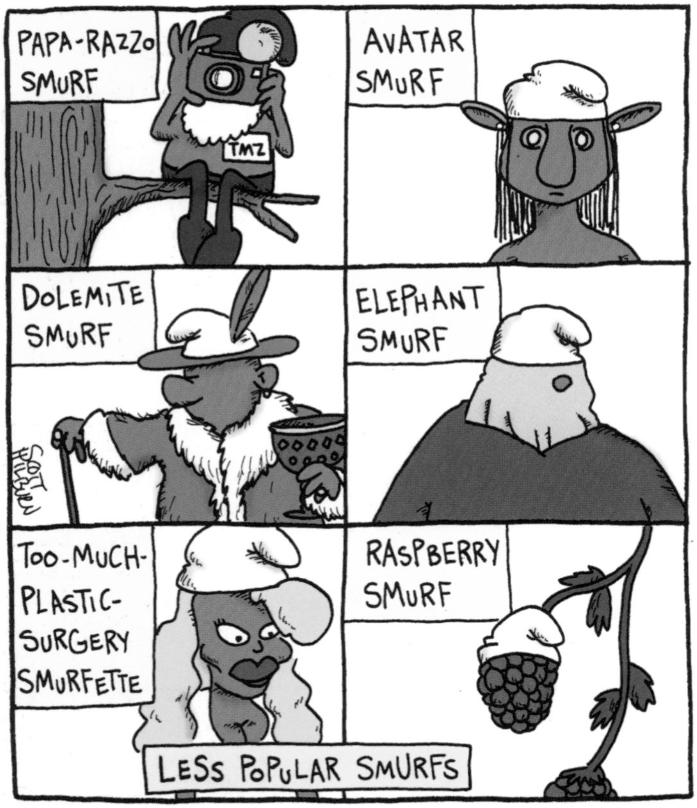
PAPA-RAZZO SMURF
TMZ
AVATAR SMURF
DOLEMITE SMURF
ELEPHANT SMURF
TOO-MUCH-PLASTIC-SURGERY SMURFETTE
RASPBERRY SMURF
LESS POPULAR SMURFS
SCOTT HILBURN

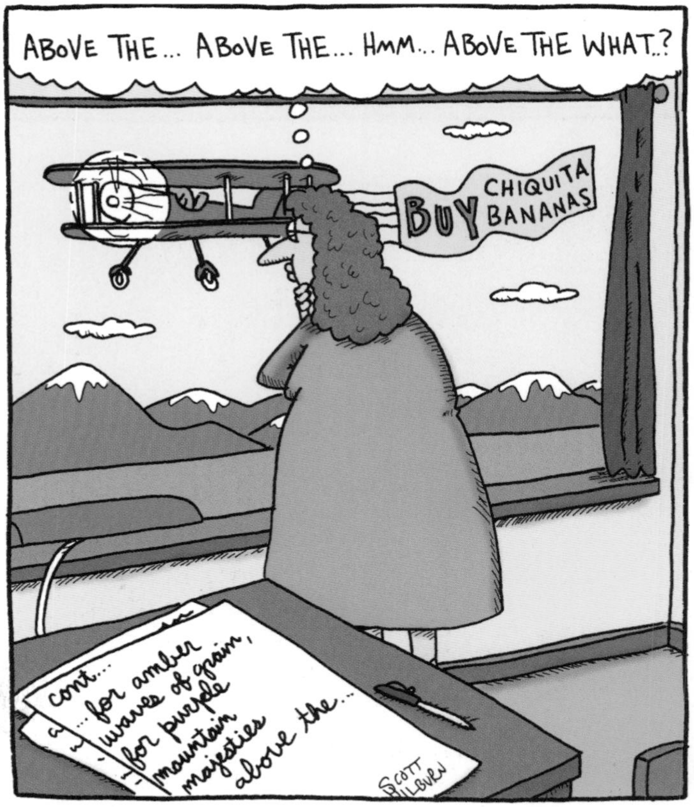
ABOVE THE... ABOVE THE... HMM... ABOVE THE WHAT..?
BUY CHIQUITA BANANAS
cont.... ...for amber waves of grain, for purple mountain majesties above the...
SCOTT HILBURN

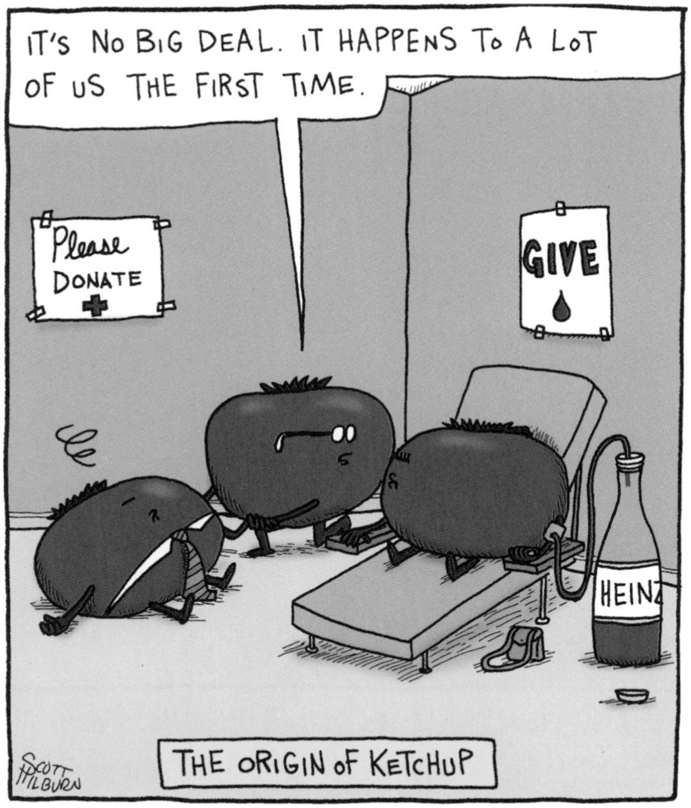
IT'S NO BIG DEAL. IT HAPPENS TO A LOT OF US THE FIRST TIME.
Please DONATE
GIVE
HEINZ
THE ORIGIN OF KETCHUP
SCOTT HILBURN

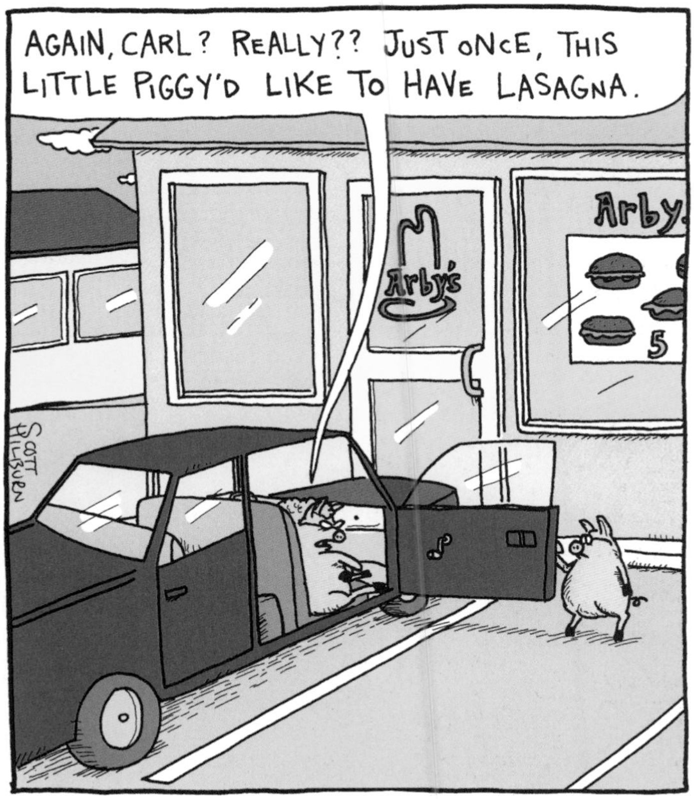
AGAIN, CARL? REALLY?? JUST ONCE, THIS LITTLE PIGGY'D LIKE TO HAVE LASAGNA.
Arby's
Arby
5
SCOTT HILBURN

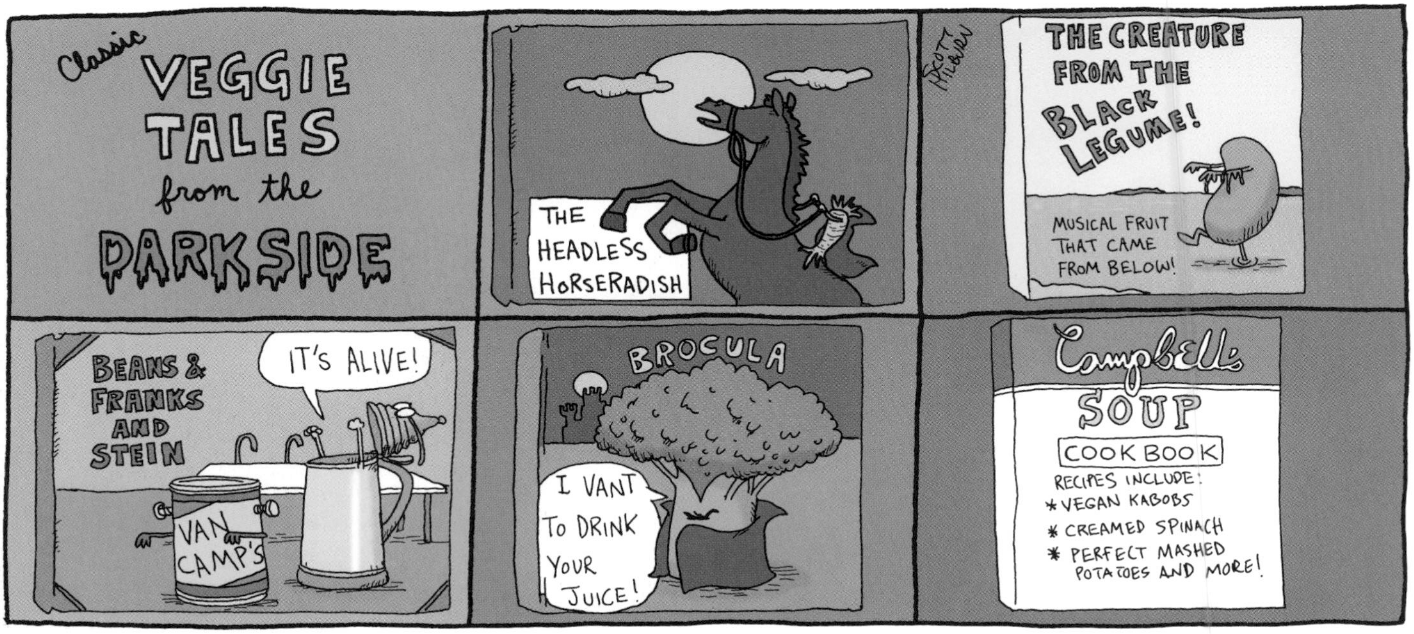
Classic VEGGIE TALES from the DARKSIDE
THE HEADLESS HORSERADISH
SCOTT HILBURN
THE CREATURE FROM THE BLACK LEGUME!
MUSICAL FRUIT THAT CAME FROM BELOW!
BEANS & FRANKS AND STEIN
IT'S ALIVE!
VAN CAMP'S
BROCULA
I VANT TO DRINK YOUR JUICE!
Campbell's
SOUP
COOKBOOK
RECIPES INCLUDE:
* VEGAN KABOBS
* CREAMED SPINACH
* PERFECT MASHED POTATOES AND MORE!

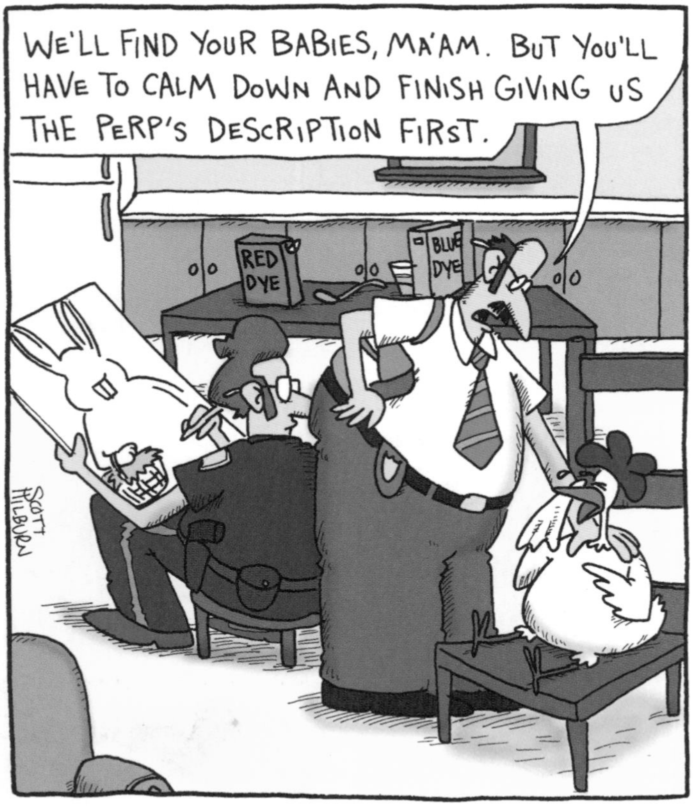
WE'LL FIND YOUR BABIES, MA'AM. BUT YOU'LL HAVE TO CALM DOWN AND FINISH GIVING US THE PERP'S DESCRIPTION FIRST.
RED DYE
BLUE DYE
SCOTT HILBURN

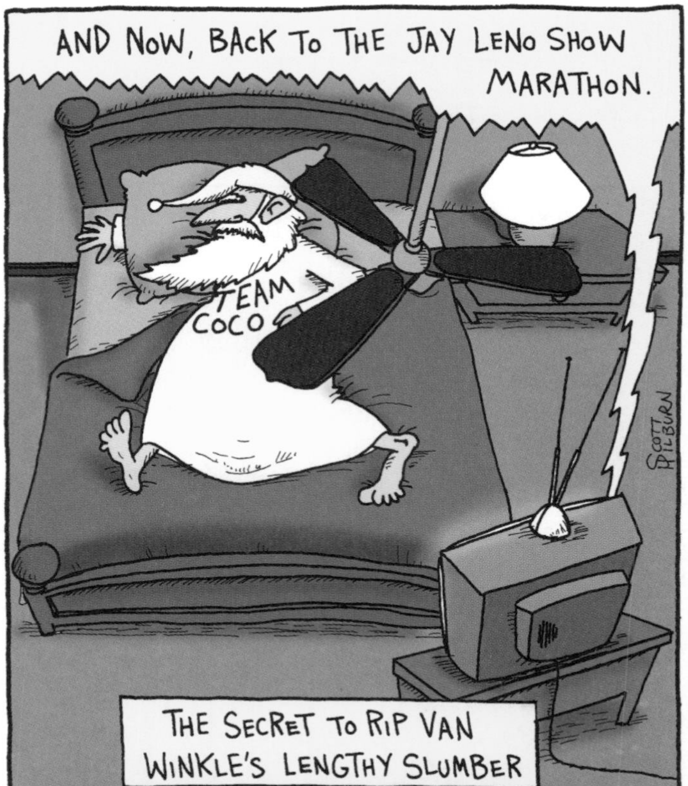
AND NOW, BACK TO THE JAY LENO SHOW MARATHON.
TEAM COCO
SCOTT HILBURN

THE SECRET TO RIP VAN WINKLE'S LENGTHY SLUMBER

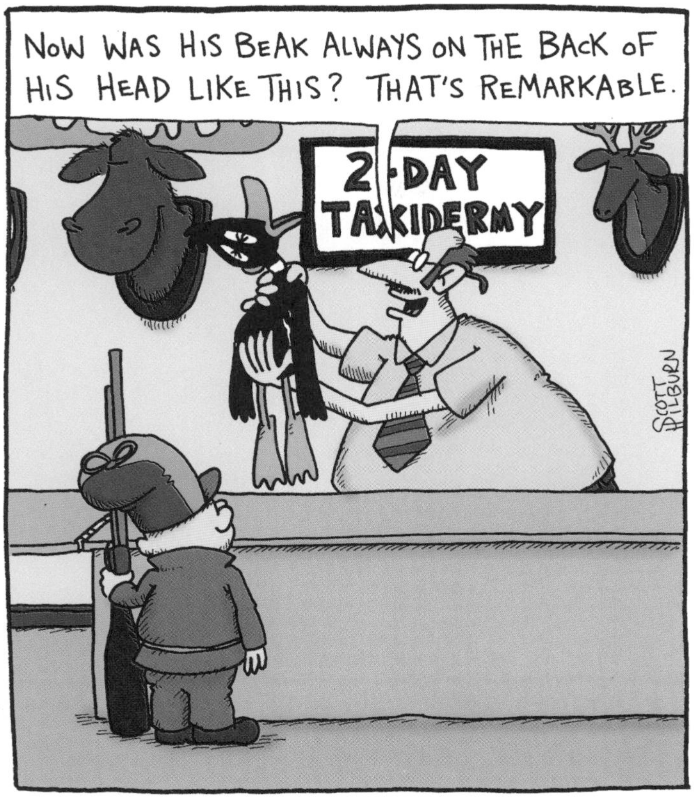
NOW WAS HIS BEAK ALWAYS ON THE BACK OF HIS HEAD LIKE THIS? THAT'S REMARKABLE.
2-DAY TAXIDERMY
SCOTT HILBURN

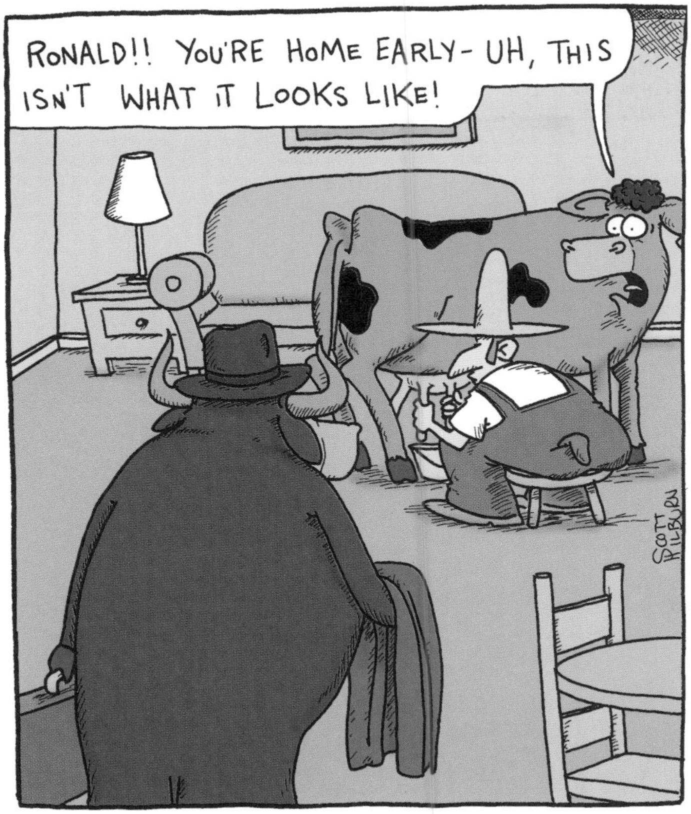
RONALD!! YOU'RE HOME EARLY- UH, THIS ISN'T WHAT IT LOOKS LIKE!
SCOTT HILBURN

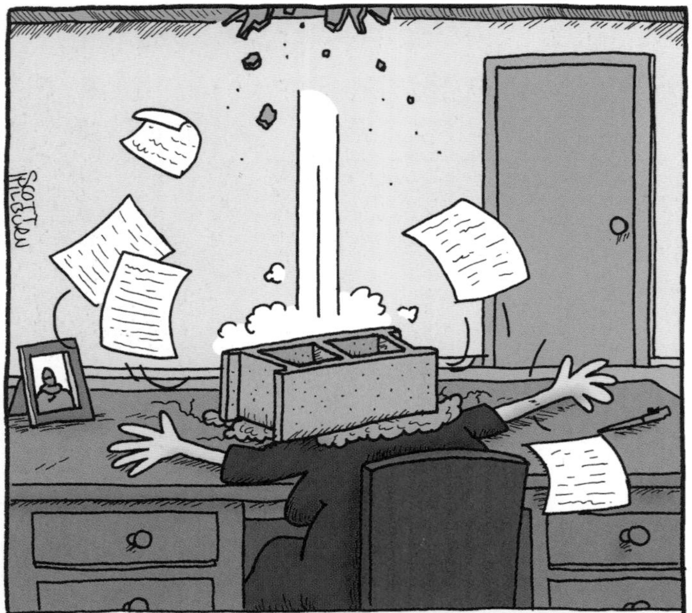
SCOTT HILBURN

AN EXPERIENCED AUTHOR, GIGI DEVAULT WAS NO STRANGER TO WRITER'S BLOCK. THIS WAS, HOWEVER, HER FIRST ENCOUNTER WITH THE EQUALLY DISRUPTIVE CINDER BLOCK.

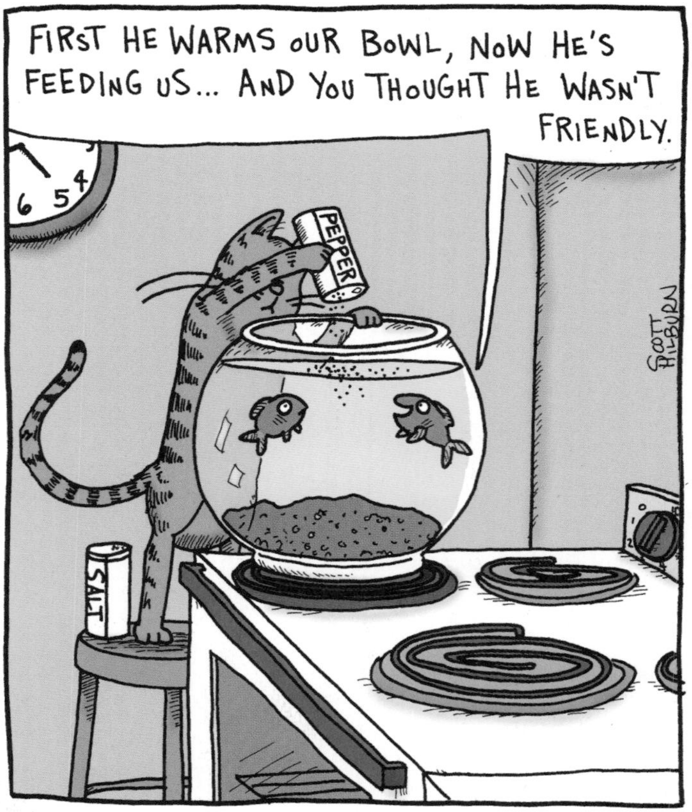
FIRST HE WARMS OUR BOWL, NOW HE'S FEEDING US... AND YOU THOUGHT HE WASN'T FRIENDLY.
PEPPER
SALT
SCOTT HILBURN

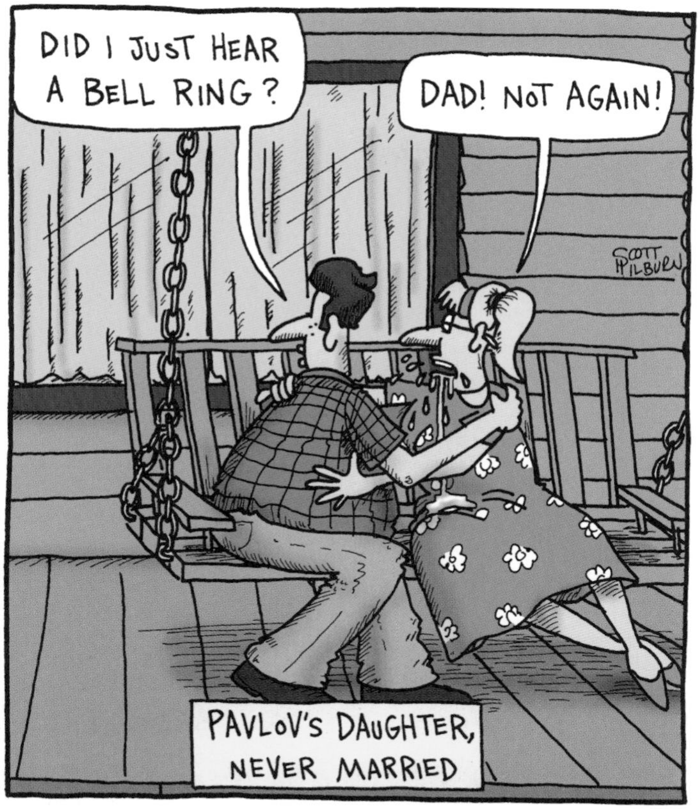
DID I JUST HEAR A BELL RING?
DAD! NOT AGAIN!
SCOTT HILBURN

PAVLOV'S DAUGHTER, NEVER MARRIED

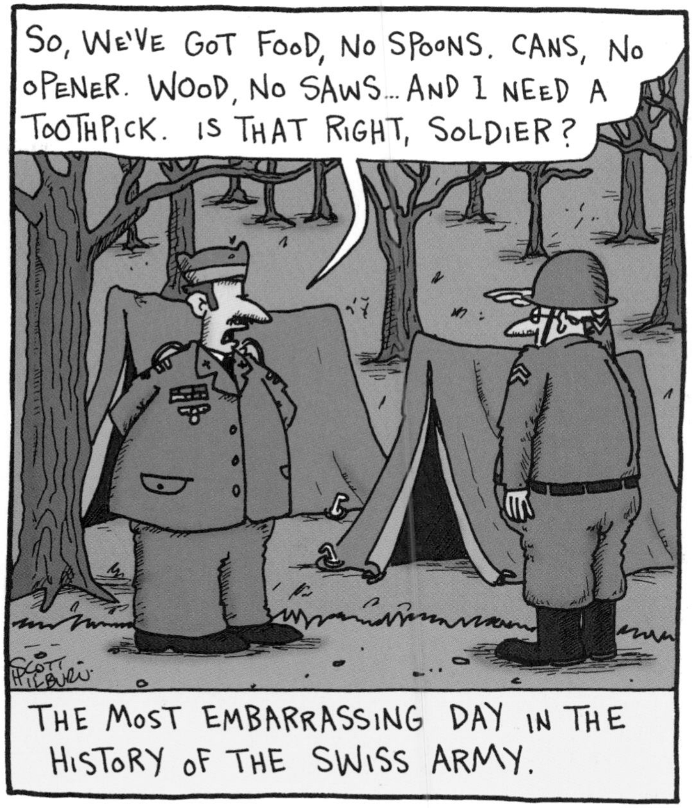
SO, WE'VE GOT FOOD, NO SPOONS. CANS, NO OPENER. WOOD, NO SAWS... AND I NEED A TOOTHPICK. IS THAT RIGHT, SOLDIER?
SCOTT HILBURN

THE MOST EMBARRASSING DAY IN THE HISTORY OF THE SWISS ARMY.

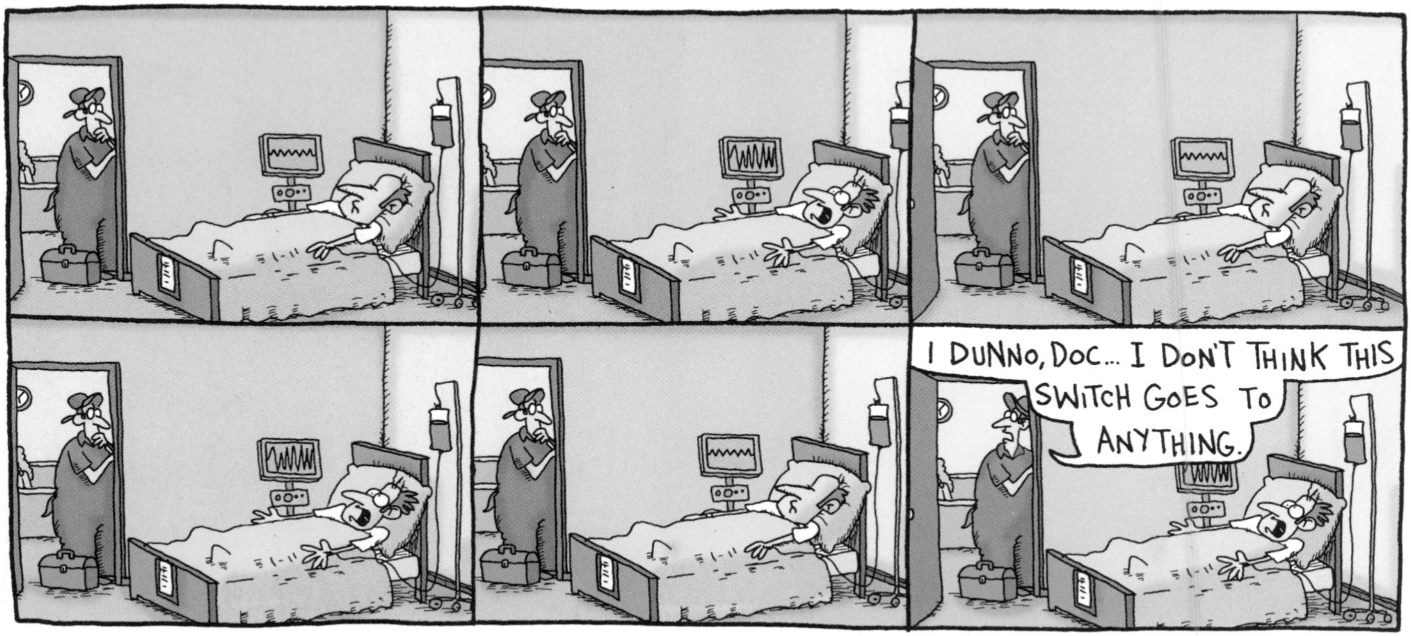
I DUNNO, DOC... I DON'T THINK THIS SWITCH GOES TO ANYTHING.

PAPYRUS BEATS ROCK?? WHAT THE SPHYNX ARE YOU TALKING ABOUT? DO YOU EVEN **KNOW** HOW IT'S MADE??
SCOTT HILBURN

ALL RIGHT, YOU'RE ON... DON'T BREAK A LEG.
SCOTT HILBURN

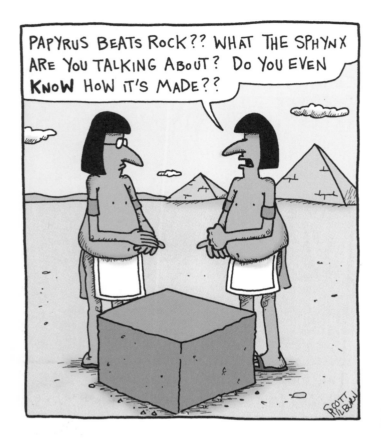

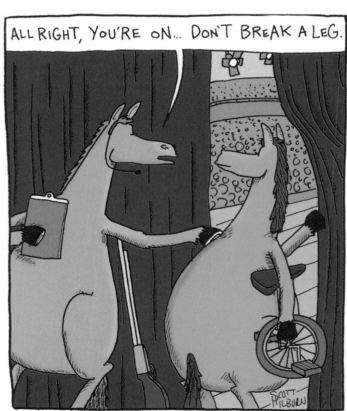

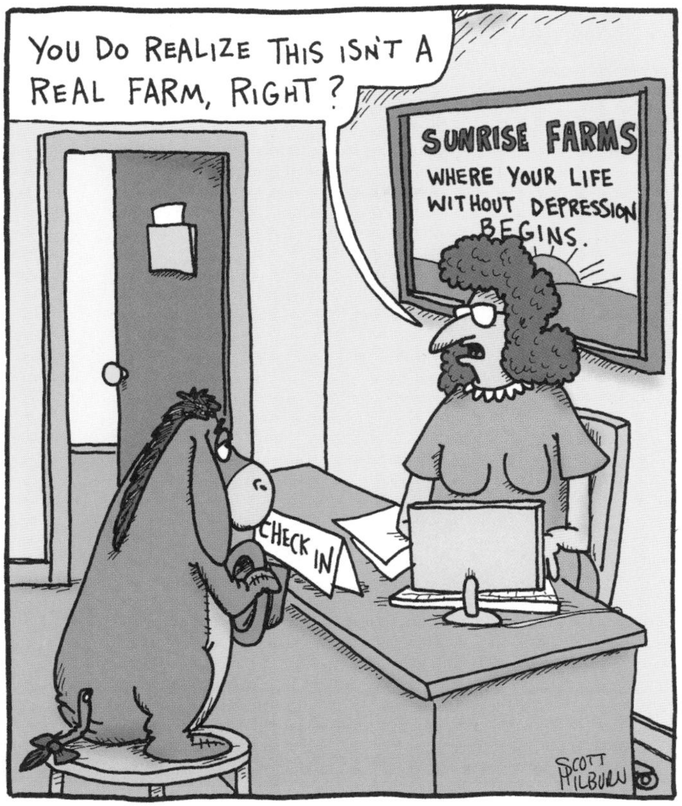
YOU DO REALIZE THIS ISN'T A REAL FARM, RIGHT?
SUNRISE FARMS
WHERE YOUR LIFE WITHOUT DEPRESSION BEGINS.
CHECK IN
SCOTT HILBURN

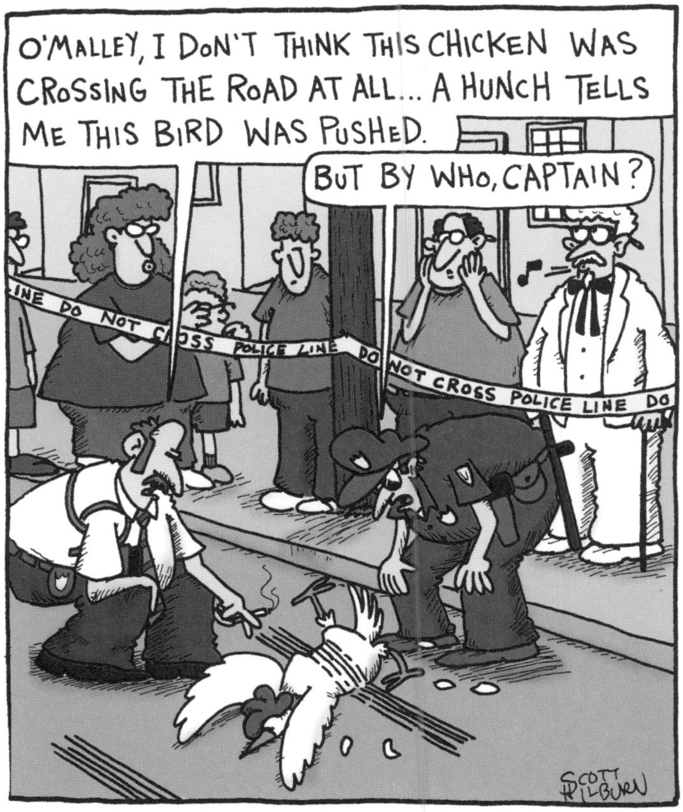
O'MALLEY, I DON'T THINK THIS CHICKEN WAS CROSSING THE ROAD AT ALL... A HUNCH TELLS ME THIS BIRD WAS PUSHED.
BUT BY WHO, CAPTAIN?
LINE DO NOT CROSS POLICE LINE DO NOT CROSS POLICE LINE DO
SCOTT HILBURN

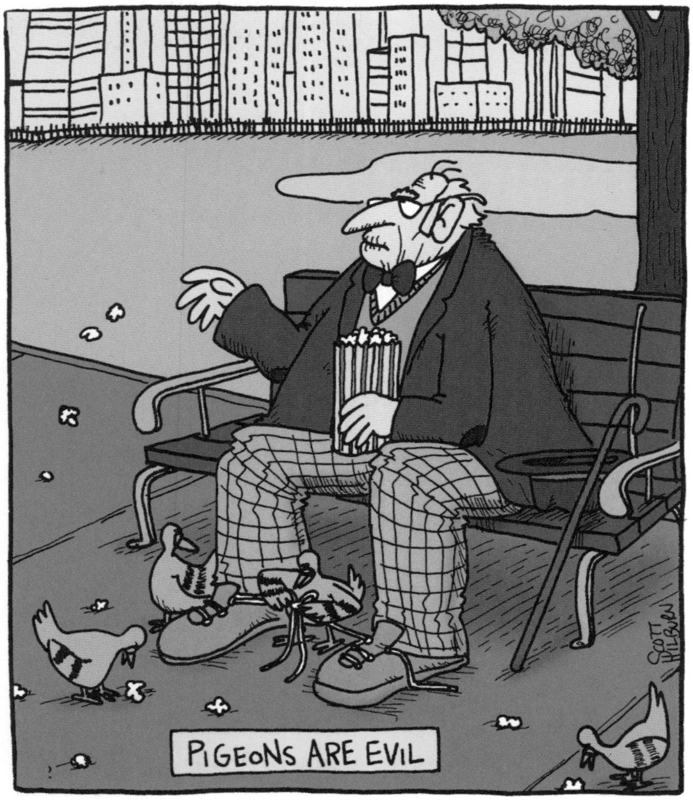
SCOTT HILBURN
PIGEONS ARE EVIL

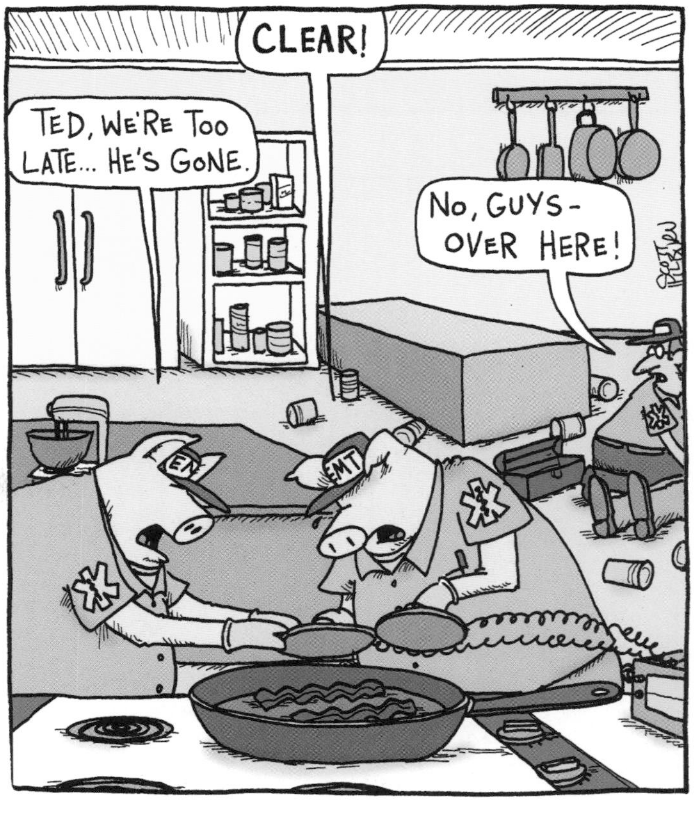
CLEAR!
TED, WE'RE TOO LATE... HE'S GONE.
NO, GUYS - OVER HERE!
EMT
EMT

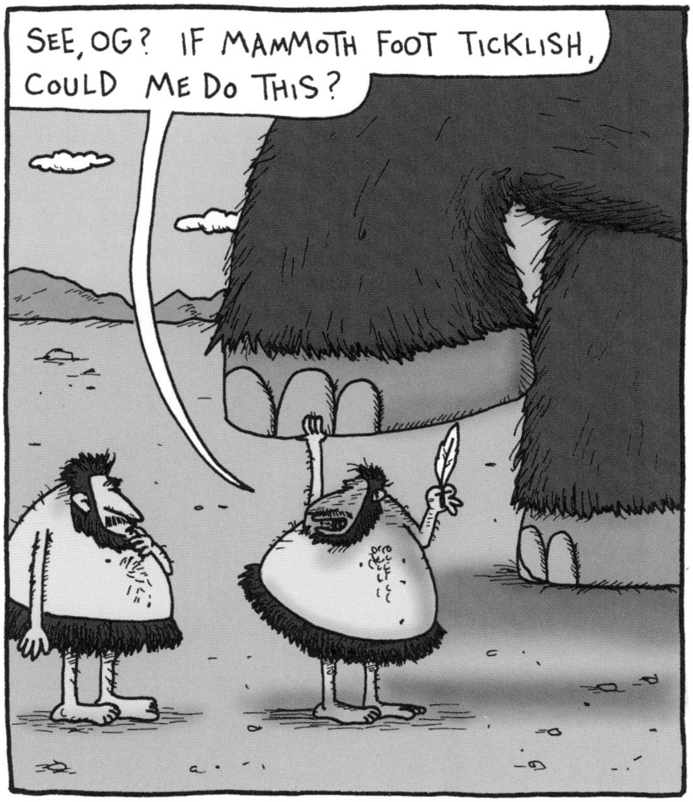
SEE, OG? IF MAMMOTH FOOT TICKLISH, COULD ME DO THIS?

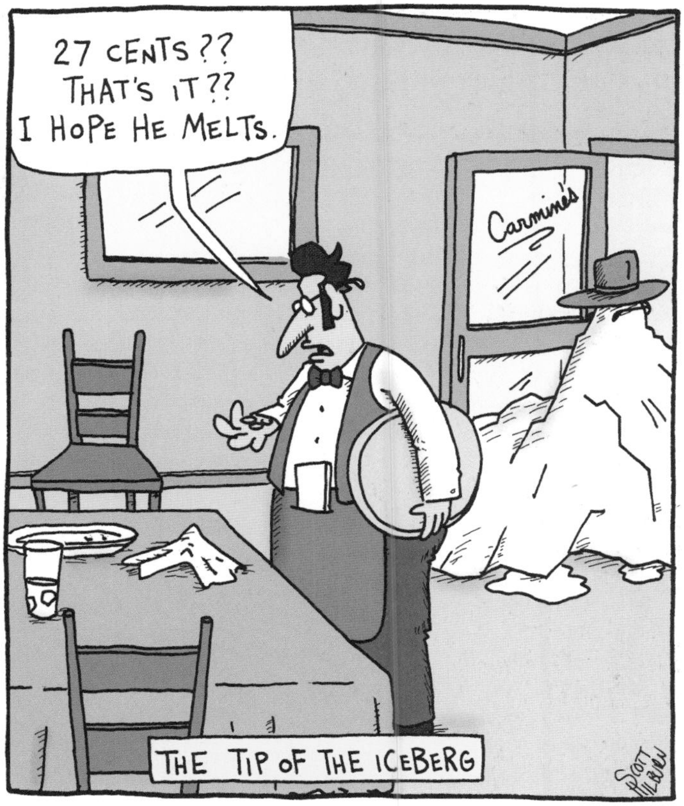
27 CENTS?? THAT'S IT?? I HOPE HE MELTS.
Carmine's
THE TIP OF THE ICEBERG
SCOTT HILBURN

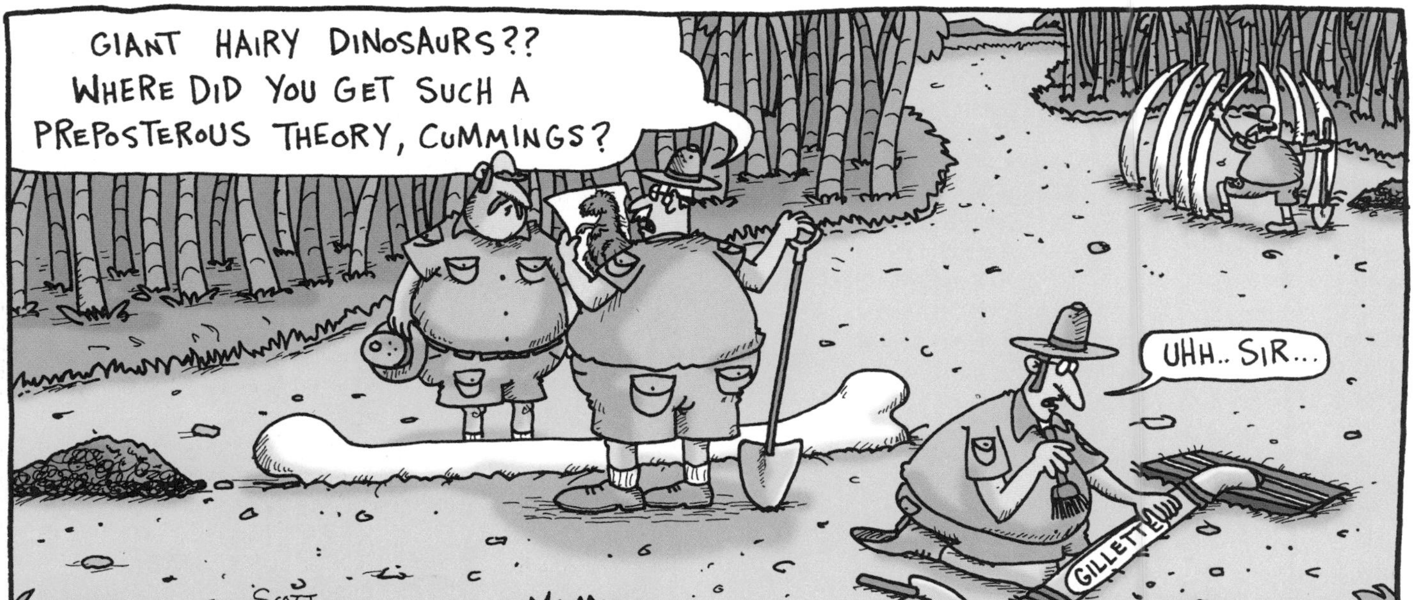
GIANT HAIRY DINOSAURS?? WHERE DID YOU GET SUCH A PREPOSTEROUS THEORY, CUMMINGS?
UHH.. SIR...
GILLETTE
SCOTT HILBURN

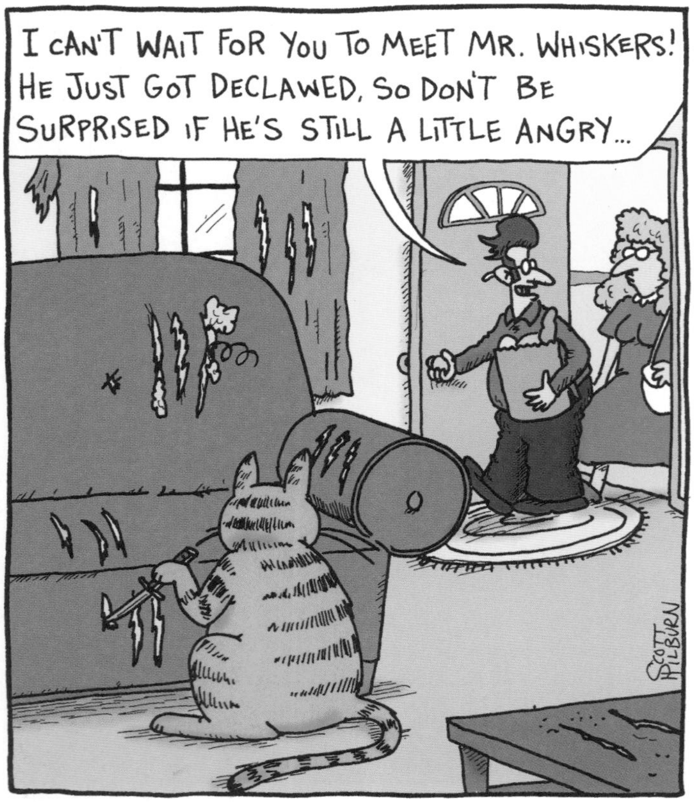
I CAN'T WAIT FOR YOU TO MEET MR. WHISKERS! HE JUST GOT DECLAWED, SO DON'T BE SURPRISED IF HE'S STILL A LITTLE ANGRY...
SCOTT HILBURN

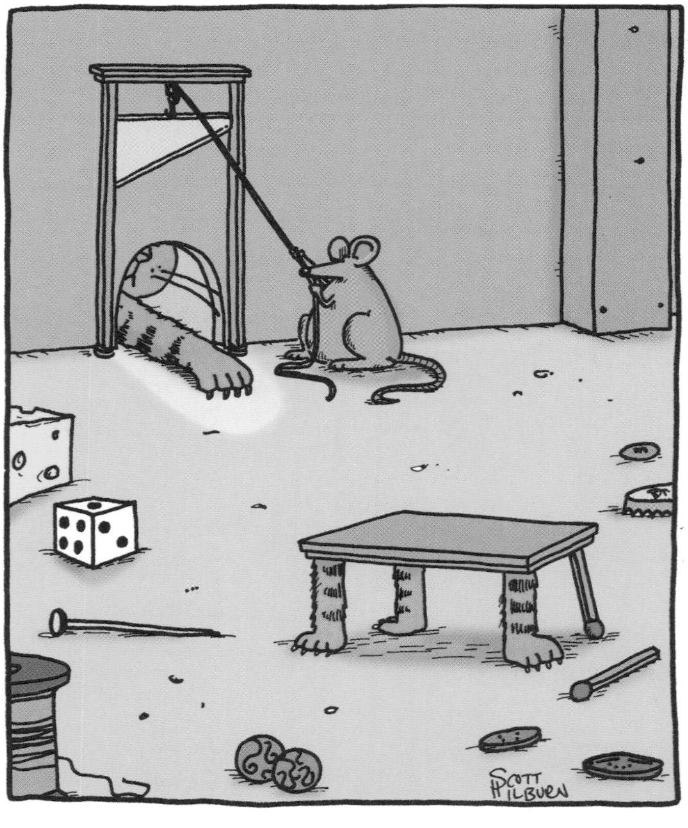
SCOTT HILBURN

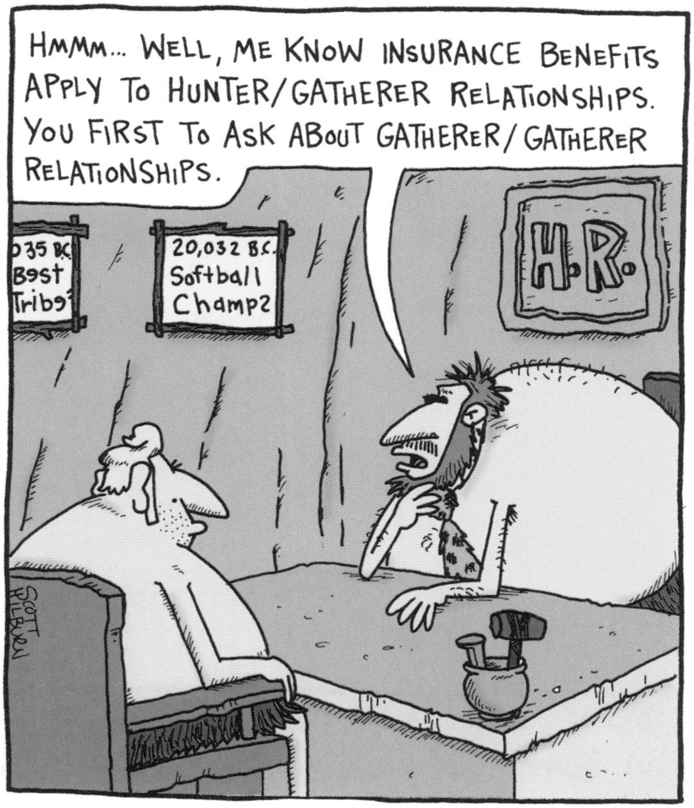
HMMM... WELL, ME KNOW INSURANCE BENEFITS APPLY TO HUNTER/GATHERER RELATIONSHIPS. YOU FIRST TO ASK ABOUT GATHERER/GATHERER RELATIONSHIPS.
20,032 B.C. Softball Champs
H.R.
SCOTT HILBURN

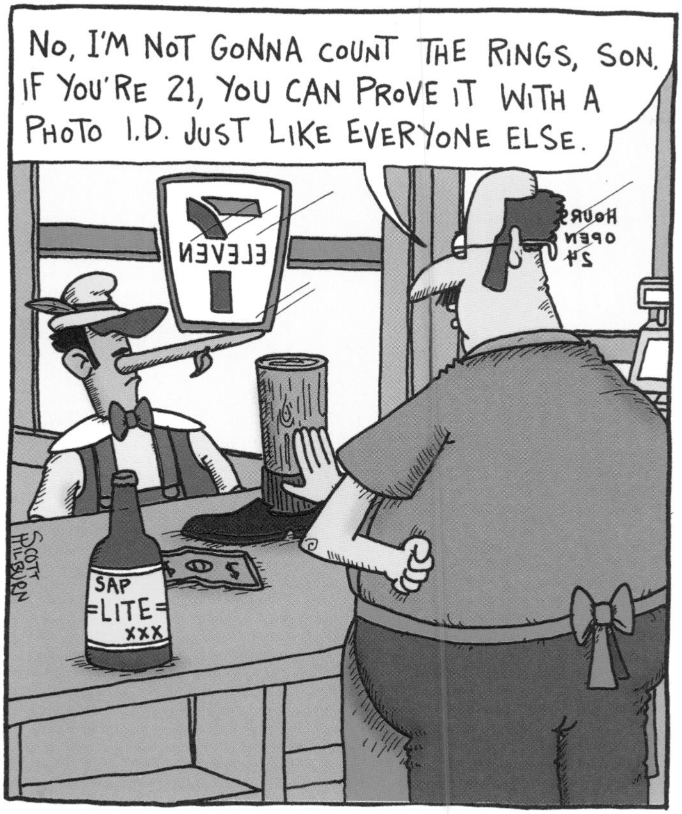
NO, I'M NOT GONNA COUNT THE RINGS, SON. IF YOU'RE 21, YOU CAN PROVE IT WITH A PHOTO I.D. JUST LIKE EVERYONE ELSE.
ELEVEN
SAP LITE XXX
SCOTT HILBURN

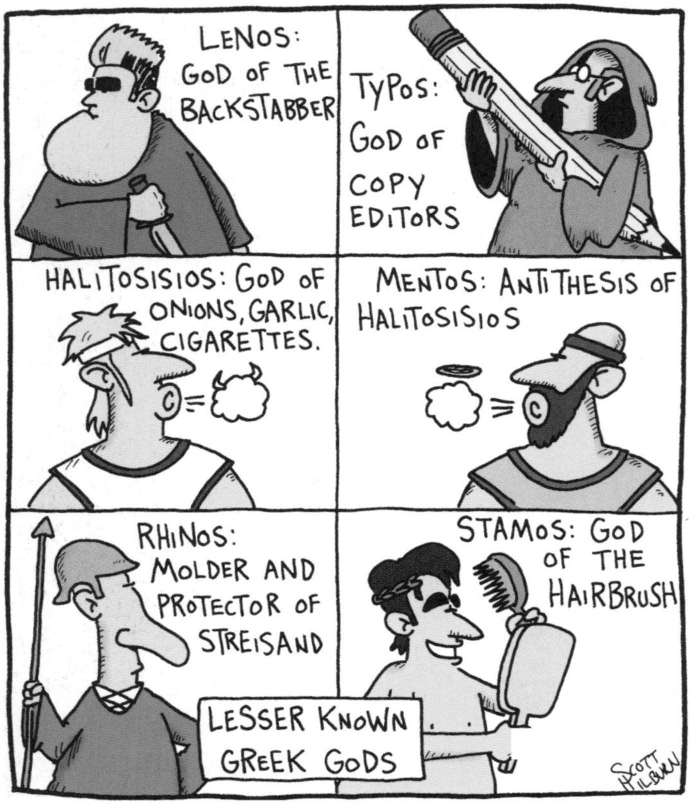
LENOS: GOD OF THE BACKSTABBER
TYPOS: GOD OF COPY EDITORS
HALITOSISIOS: GOD OF ONIONS, GARLIC, CIGARETTES.
MENTOS: ANTITHESIS OF HALITOSISIOS
RHINOS: MOLDER AND PROTECTOR OF STREISAND
STAMOS: GOD OF THE HAIRBRUSH
LESSER KNOWN GREEK GODS
SCOTT HILBURN

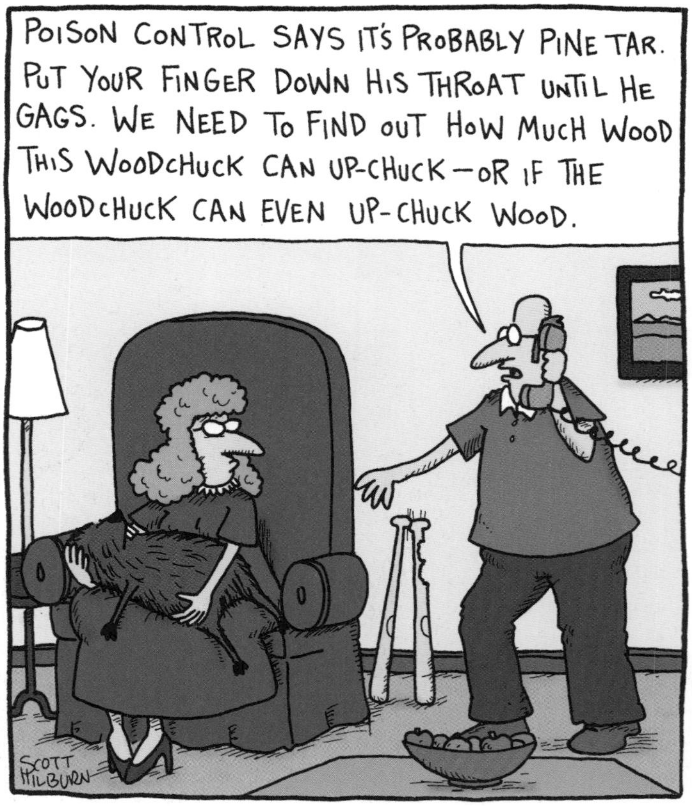
POISON CONTROL SAYS IT'S PROBABLY PINE TAR. PUT YOUR FINGER DOWN HIS THROAT UNTIL HE GAGS. WE NEED TO FIND OUT HOW MUCH WOOD THIS WOODCHUCK CAN UP-CHUCK—OR IF THE WOODCHUCK CAN EVEN UP-CHUCK WOOD.
SCOTT HILBURN

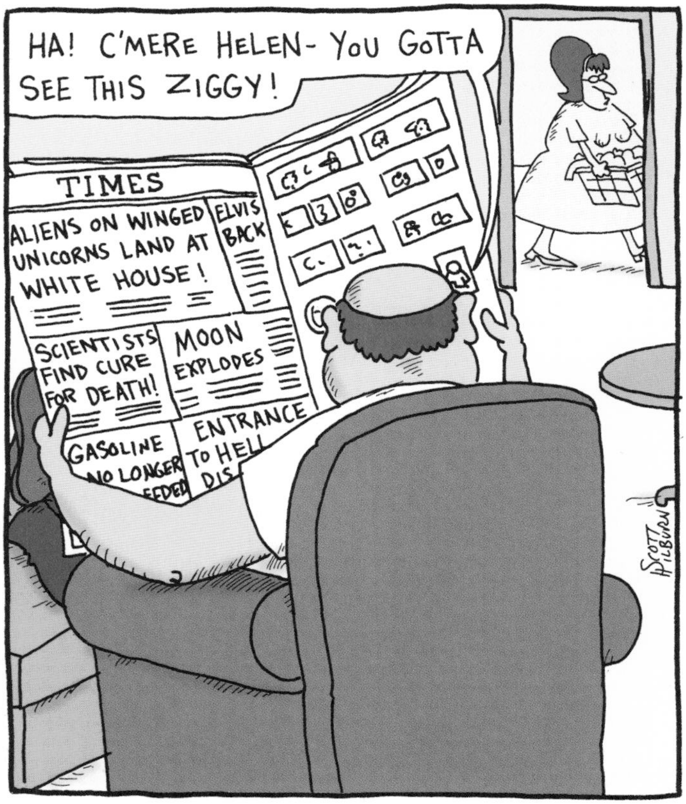
HA! C'MERE HELEN- YOU GOTTA SEE THIS ZIGGY!
TIMES
ALIENS ON WINGED UNICORNS LAND AT WHITE HOUSE!
ELVIS BACK
SCIENTISTS FIND CURE FOR DEATH!
MOON EXPLODES
GASOLINE NO LONGER NEEDED
ENTRANCE TO HELL DIS
SCOTT HILBURN

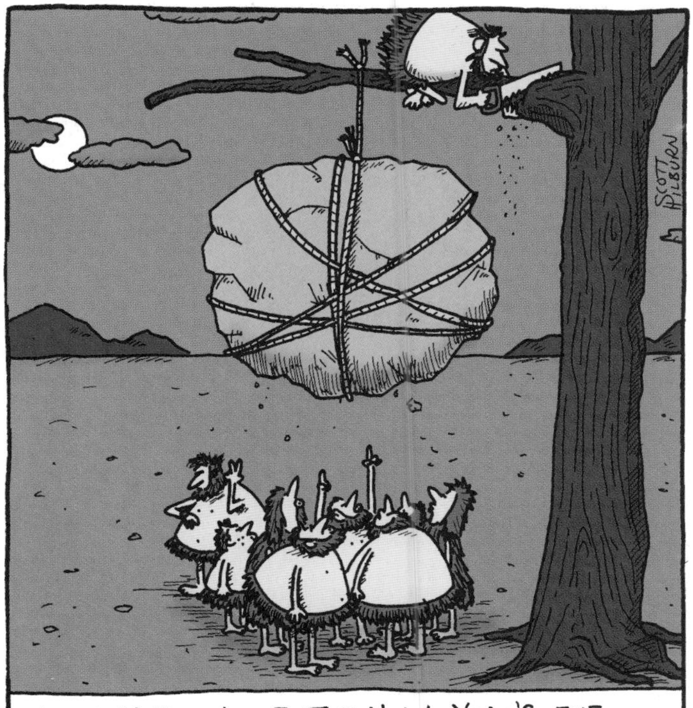
SCOTT HILBURN

EARLY VERSIONS OF THE NEW YEAR'S EVE BALL DROP PROVED LESS POPULAR AMONG REVELERS.

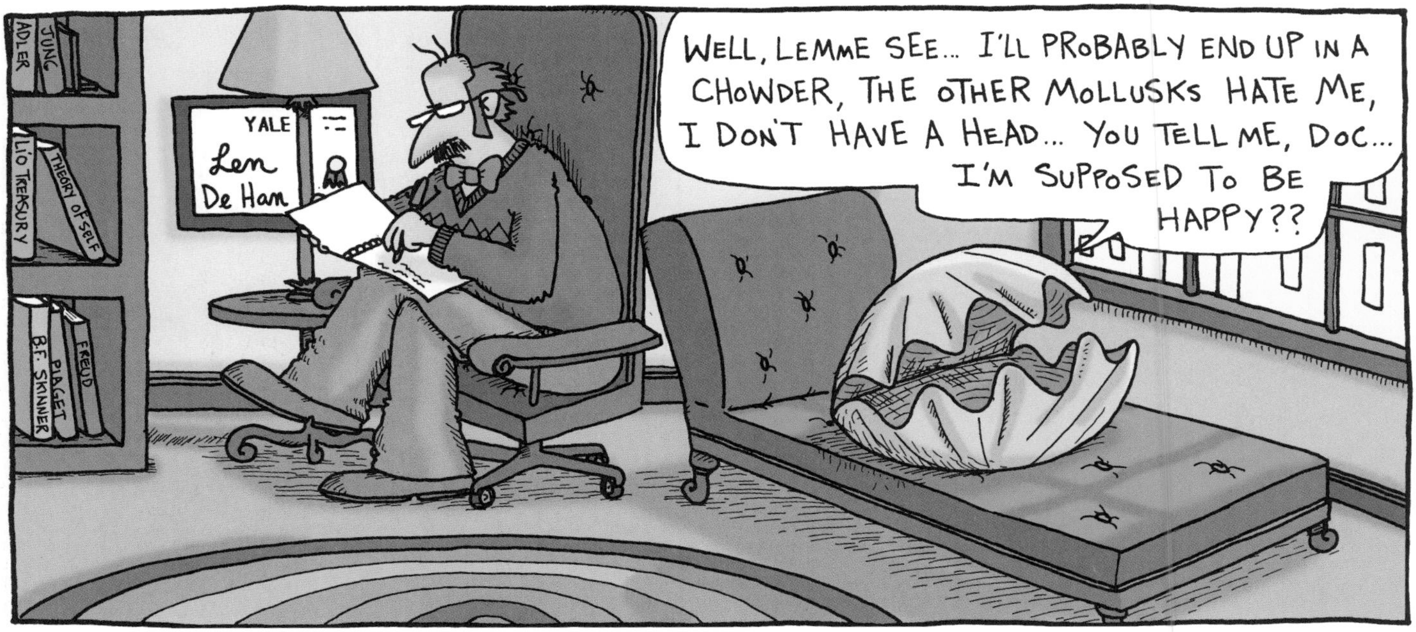
WELL, LEMME SEE... I'LL PROBABLY END UP IN A CHOWDER, THE OTHER MOLLUSKS HATE ME, I DON'T HAVE A HEAD... YOU TELL ME, DOC... I'M SUPPOSED TO BE HAPPY??
ADLER
JUNG
LIO TREASURY
THEORY OF SELF
B.F. SKINNER
PIAGET
FREUD
YALE
Len De Ham

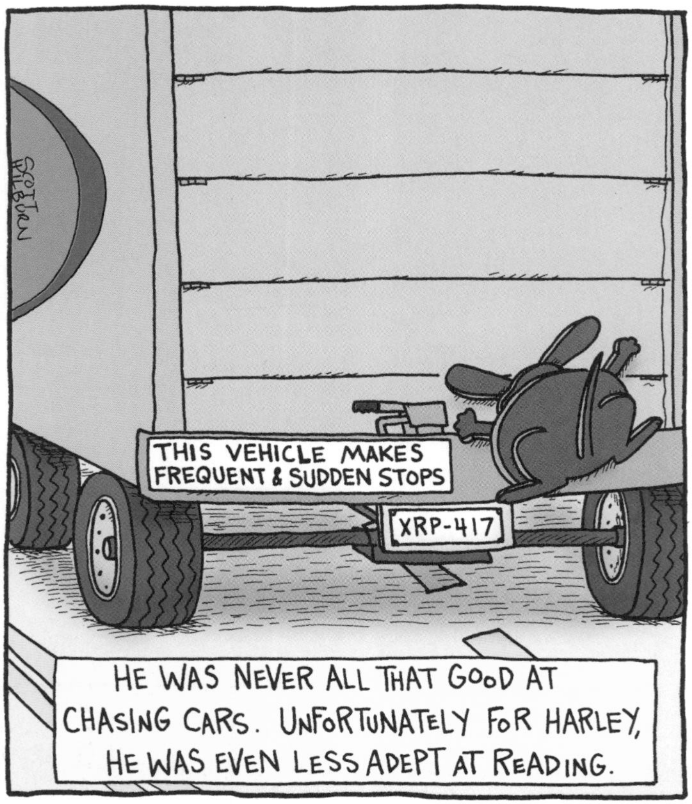
THIS VEHICLE MAKES FREQUENT & SUDDEN STOPS
XRP-417
HE WAS NEVER ALL THAT GOOD AT CHASING CARS. UNFORTUNATELY FOR HARLEY, HE WAS EVEN LESS ADEPT AT READING.

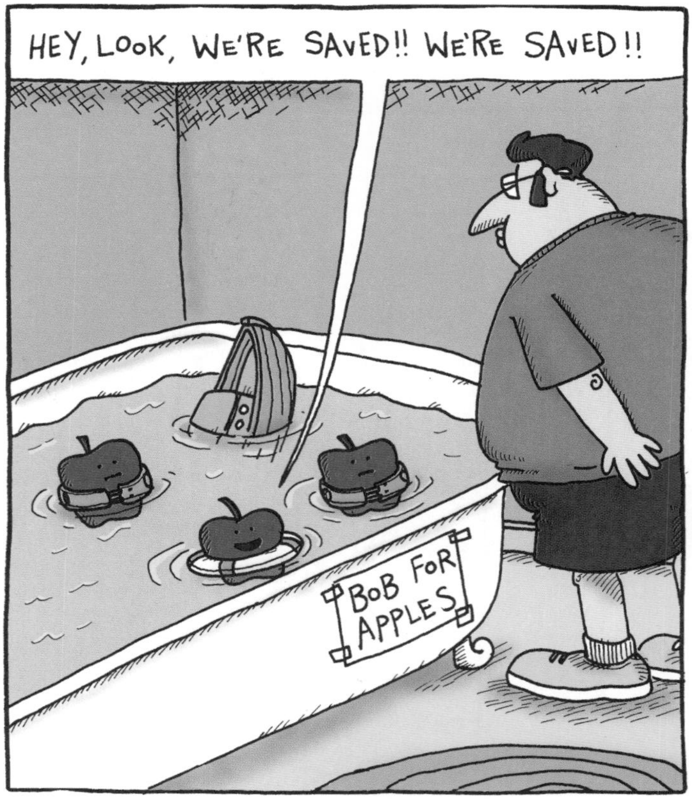
HEY, LOOK, WE'RE SAVED!! WE'RE SAVED!!
BOB FOR APPLES

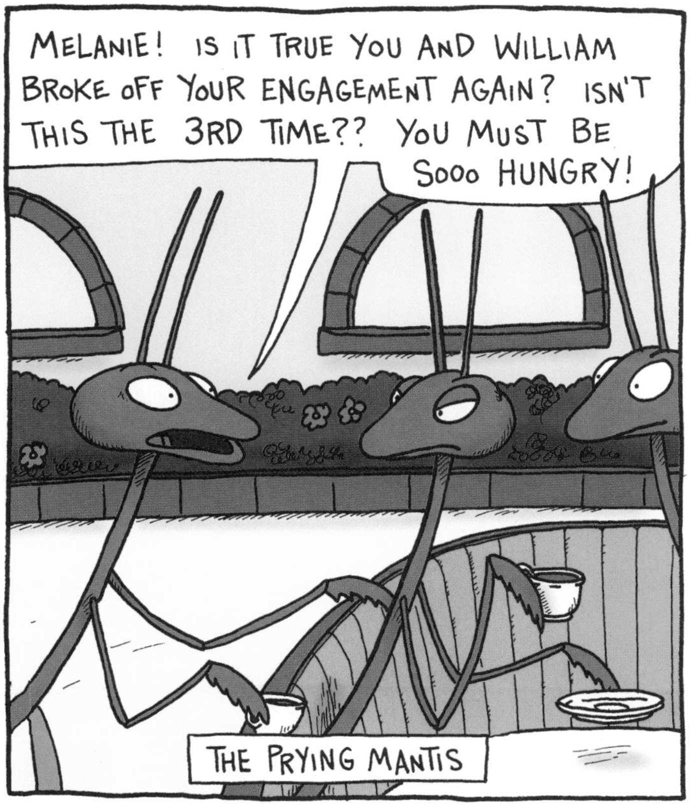
MELANIE! IS IT TRUE YOU AND WILLIAM BROKE OFF YOUR ENGAGEMENT AGAIN? ISN'T THIS THE 3RD TIME?? YOU MUST BE SOOO HUNGRY!

THE PRYING MANTIS

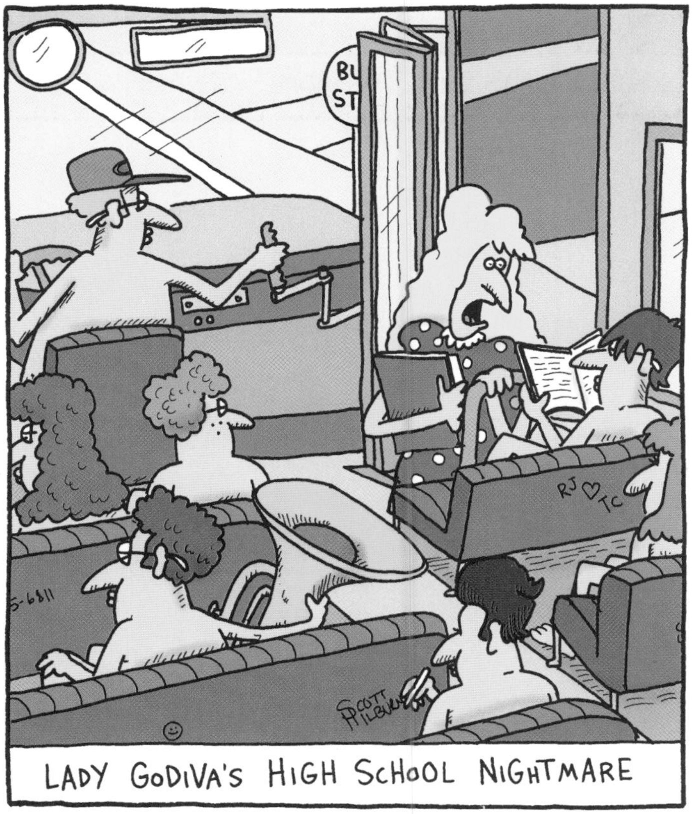
RJ ♡ TC
SCOTT HILBURN

LADY GODIVA'S HIGH SCHOOL NIGHTMARE

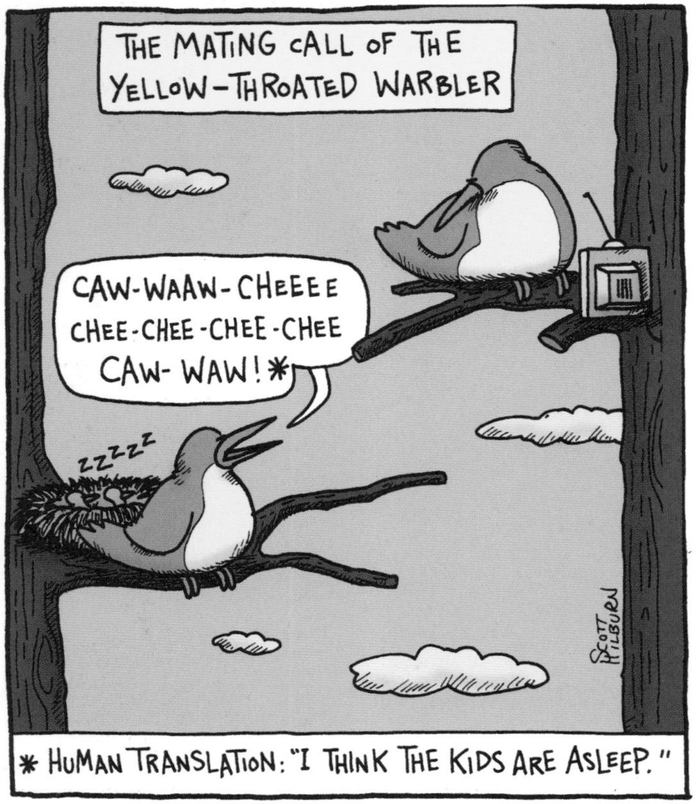
THE MATING CALL OF THE YELLOW-THROATED WARBLER
CAW-WAAW-CHEEEE CHEE-CHEE-CHEE-CHEE CAW-WAW!*
ZZZZZ
SCOTT HILBURN
* HUMAN TRANSLATION: "I THINK THE KIDS ARE ASLEEP."

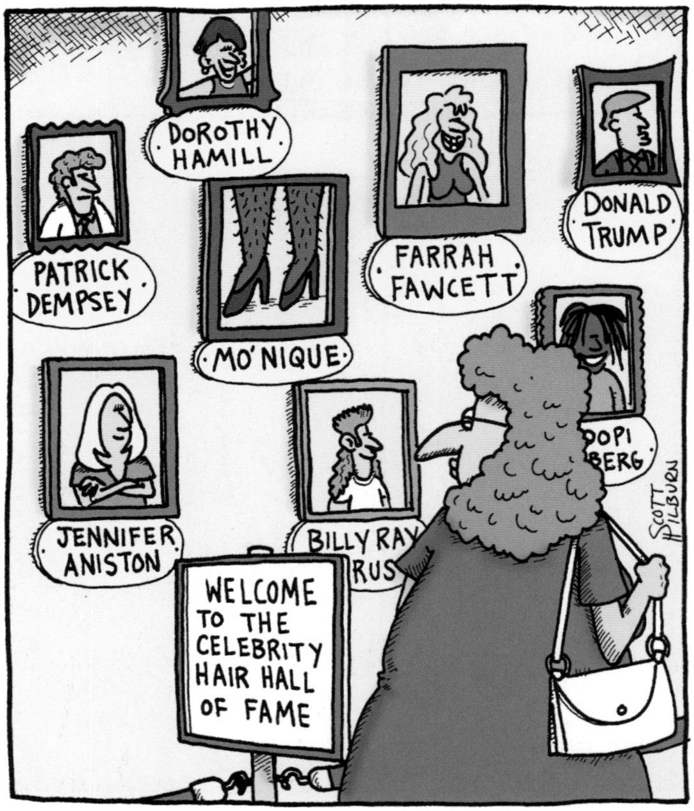
DOROTHY HAMILL
PATRICK DEMPSEY
FARRAH FAWCETT
DONALD TRUMP
MO'NIQUE
JENNIFER ANISTON
BILLY RAY
WELCOME TO THE CELEBRITY HAIR HALL OF FAME
SCOTT HILBURN

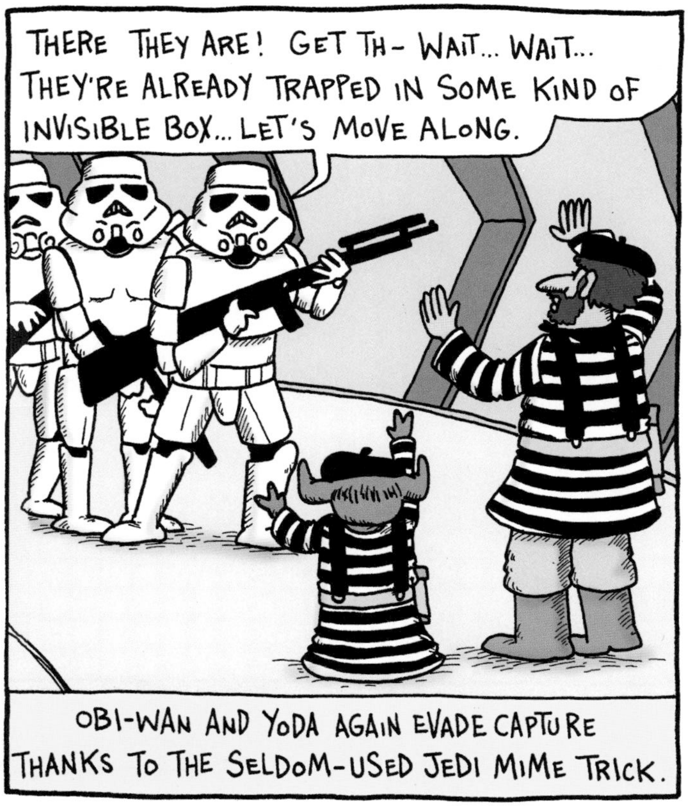
THERE THEY ARE! GET TH- WAIT... WAIT... THEY'RE ALREADY TRAPPED IN SOME KIND OF INVISIBLE BOX... LET'S MOVE ALONG.

OBI-WAN AND YODA AGAIN EVADE CAPTURE THANKS TO THE SELDOM-USED JEDI MIME TRICK.

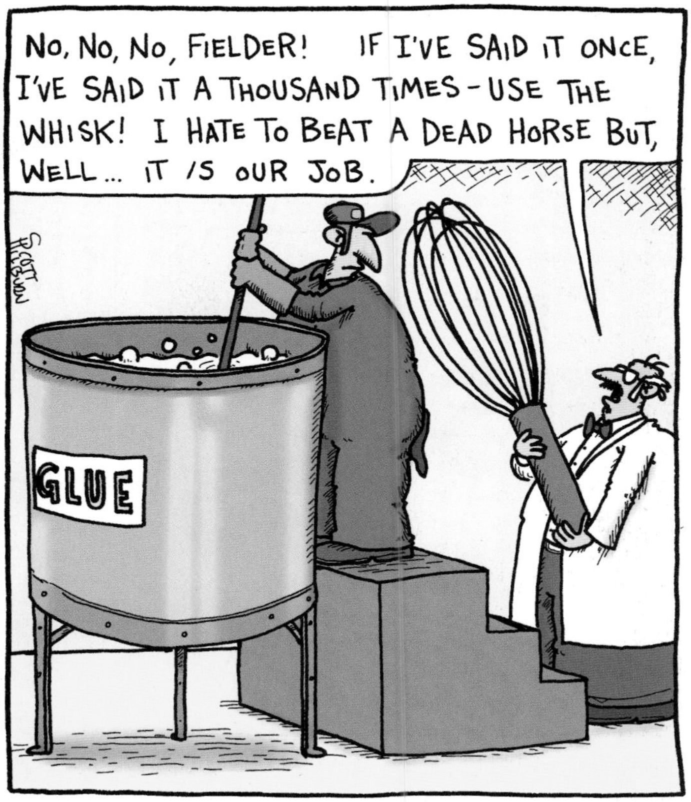
NO, NO, NO, FIELDER! IF I'VE SAID IT ONCE, I'VE SAID IT A THOUSAND TIMES - USE THE WHISK! I HATE TO BEAT A DEAD HORSE BUT, WELL... IT IS OUR JOB.
GLUE

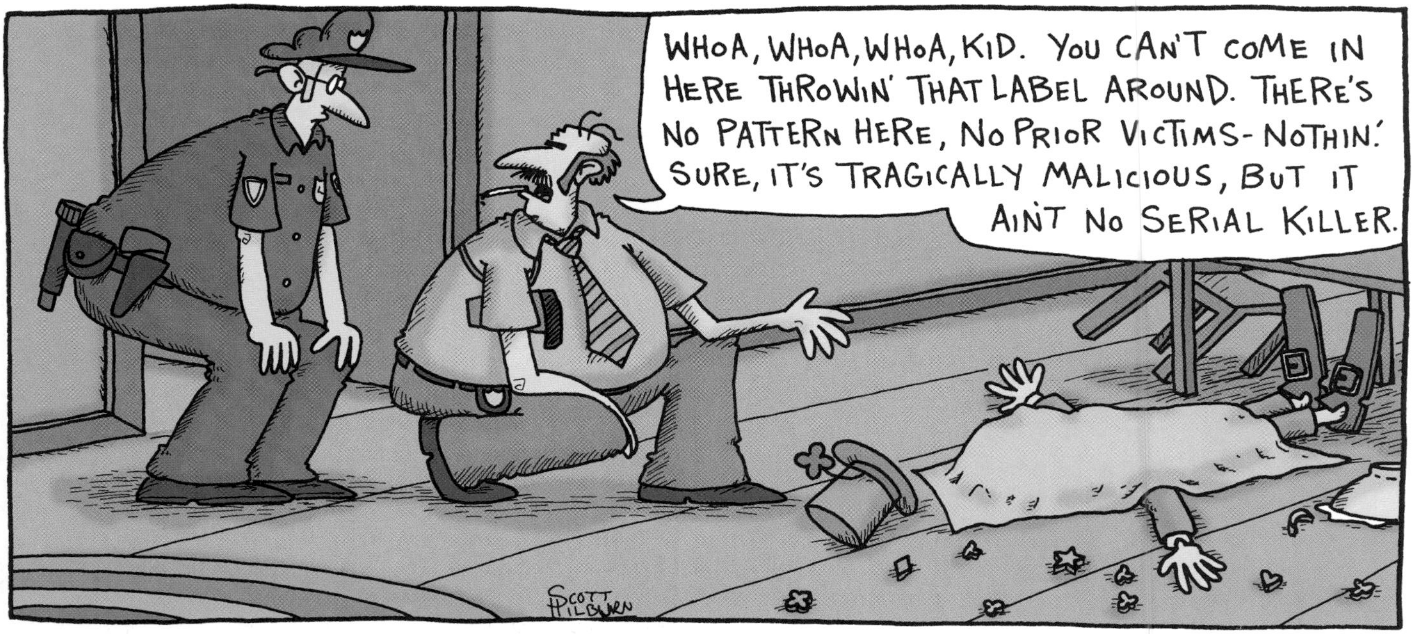
WHOA, WHOA, WHOA, KID. YOU CAN'T COME IN HERE THROWIN' THAT LABEL AROUND. THERE'S NO PATTERN HERE, NO PRIOR VICTIMS - NOTHIN'. SURE, IT'S TRAGICALLY MALICIOUS, BUT IT AIN'T NO SERIAL KILLER.

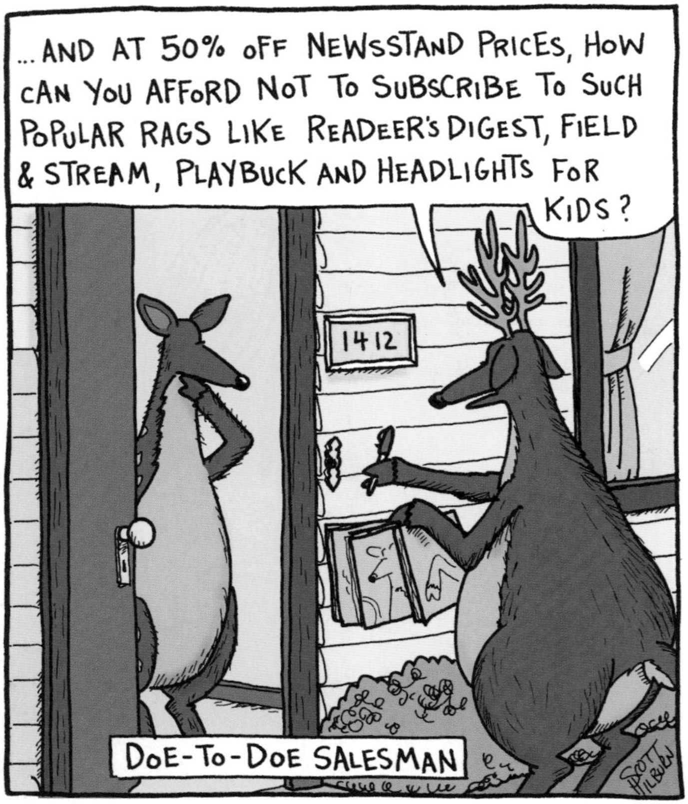
...AND AT 50% OFF NEWSSTAND PRICES, HOW CAN YOU AFFORD NOT TO SUBSCRIBE TO SUCH POPULAR RAGS LIKE READEER'S DIGEST, FIELD & STREAM, PLAYBUCK AND HEADLIGHTS FOR KIDS?
1412
DOE-TO-DOE SALESMAN
SCOTT HILBURN

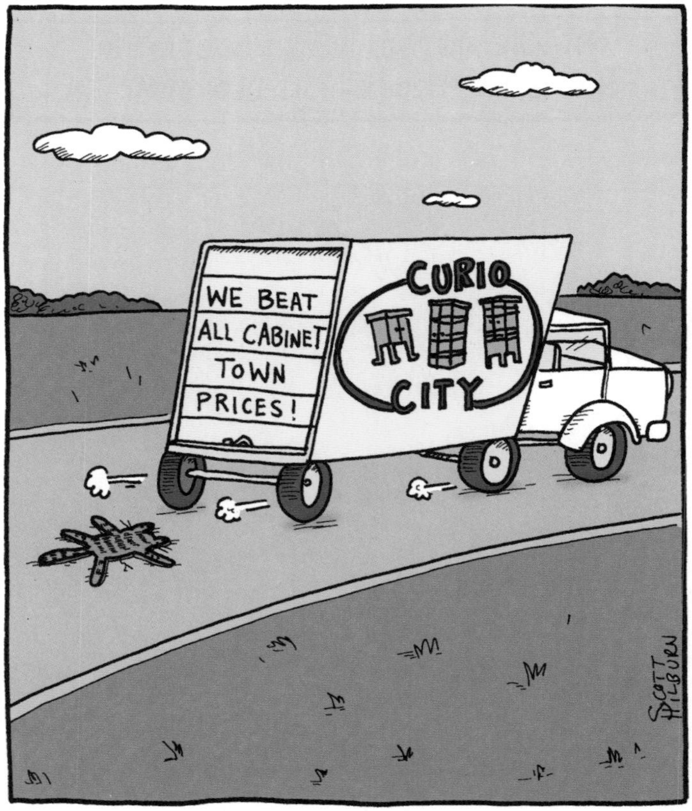
WE BEAT ALL CABINET TOWN PRICES!
CURIO CITY
SCOTT HILBURN

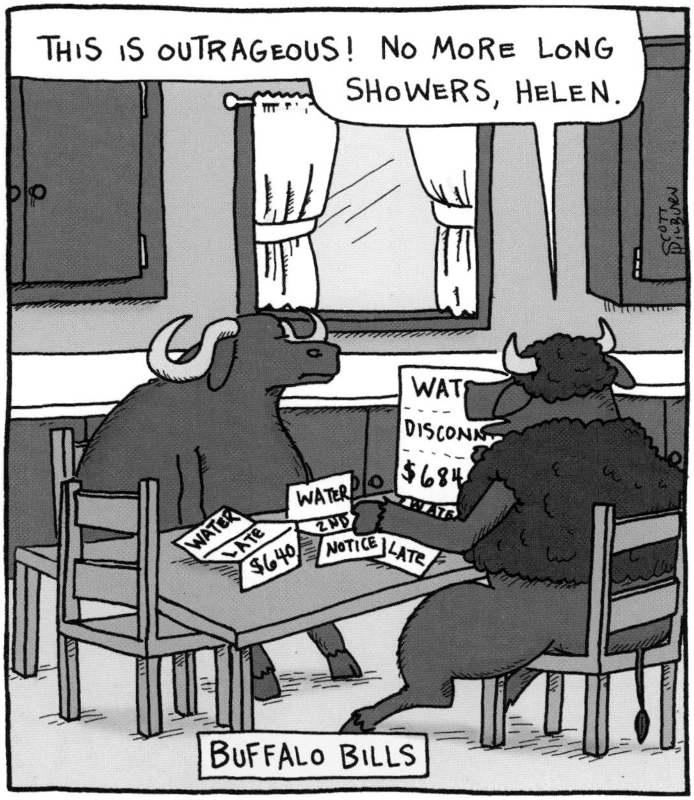
THIS IS OUTRAGEOUS! NO MORE LONG SHOWERS, HELEN.
WAT
DISCONN
$684
WATER
2ND
NOTICE
WATER
LATE
$640
LATE
BUFFALO BILLS

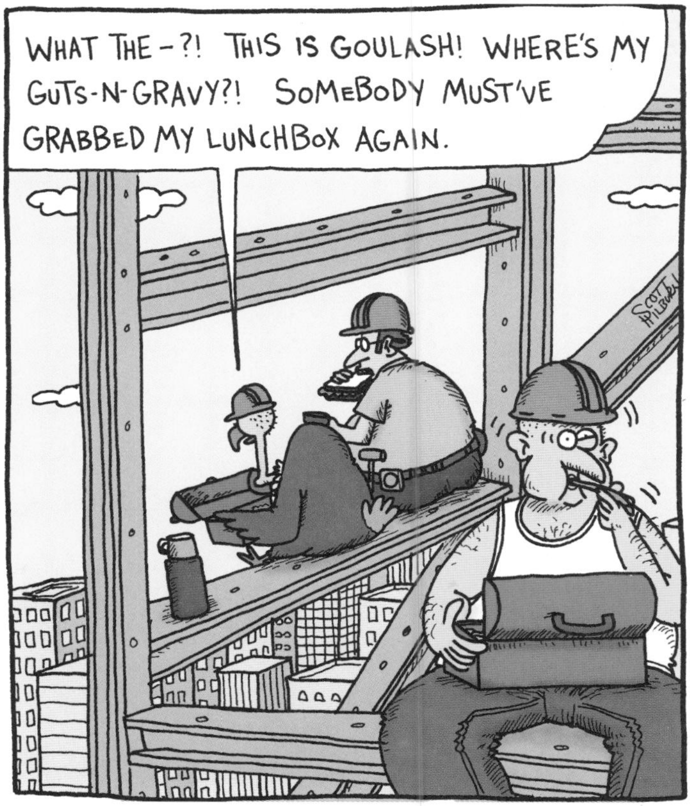
WHAT THE-?! THIS IS GOULASH! WHERE'S MY GUTS-N-GRAVY?! SOMEBODY MUST'VE GRABBED MY LUNCHBOX AGAIN.

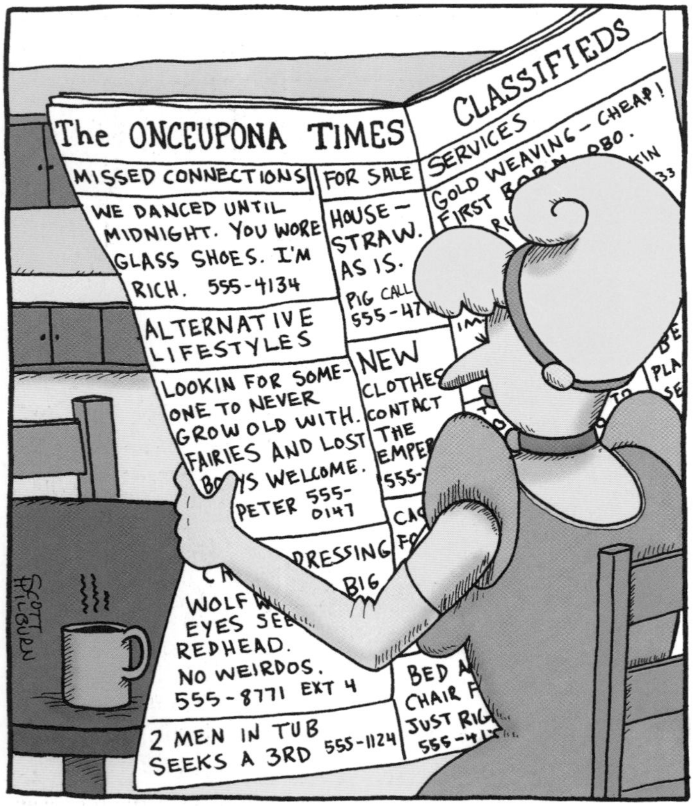
The ONCEUPONA TIMES
CLASSIFIEDS
MISSED CONNECTIONS
WE DANCED UNTIL MIDNIGHT. YOU WORE GLASS SHOES. I'M RICH. 555-4134
ALTERNATIVE LIFESTYLES
LOOKIN FOR SOME-ONE TO NEVER GROW OLD WITH. FAIRIES AND LOST BOYS WELCOME. PETER 555-0147
REDHEAD. NO WEIRDOS. 555-8771 EXT 4
2 MEN IN TUB SEEKS A 3RD 555-1124
FOR SALE
HOUSE— STRAW. AS IS.
NEW CLOTHES CONTACT THE
SERVICES
GOLD WEAVING - CHEAP!
SCOTT HILBURN

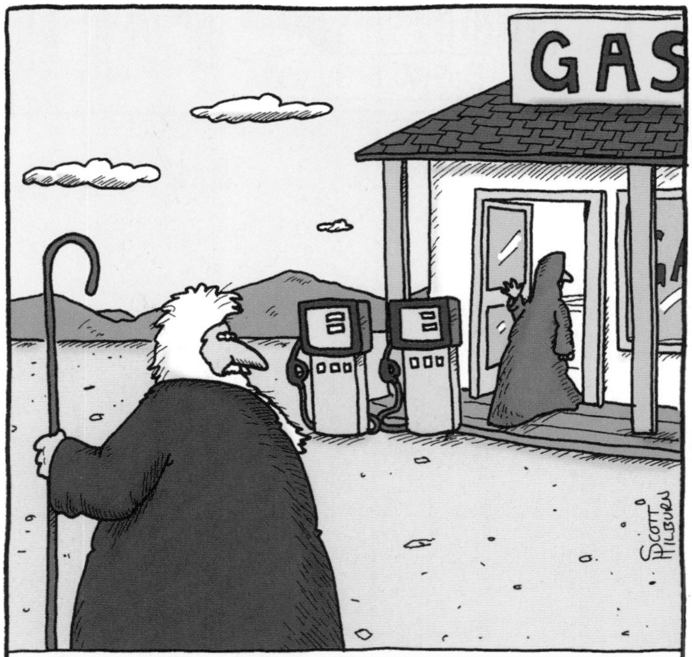
GAS
SCOTT HILBURN

AFTER 39 YEARS AND 11 MONTHS OF STUBBORNLY WANDERING THE DESERT, MOSES' WIFE DECIDES TO ASK FOR DIRECTIONS TO THE PROMISED LAND.

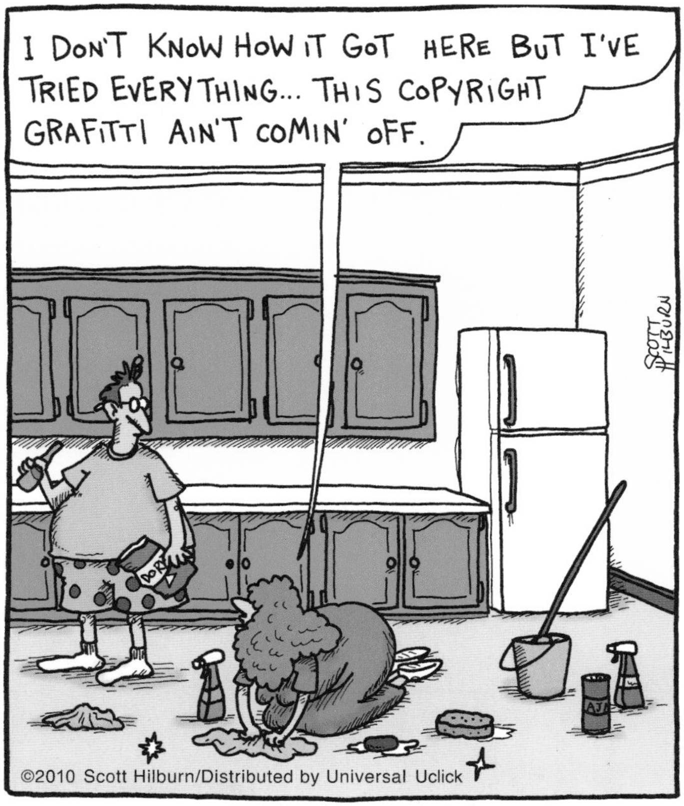
I DON'T KNOW HOW IT GOT HERE BUT I'VE TRIED EVERYTHING... THIS COPYRIGHT GRAFITTI AIN'T COMIN' OFF.
SCOTT HILBURN
©2010 Scott Hilburn/Distributed by Universal Uclick

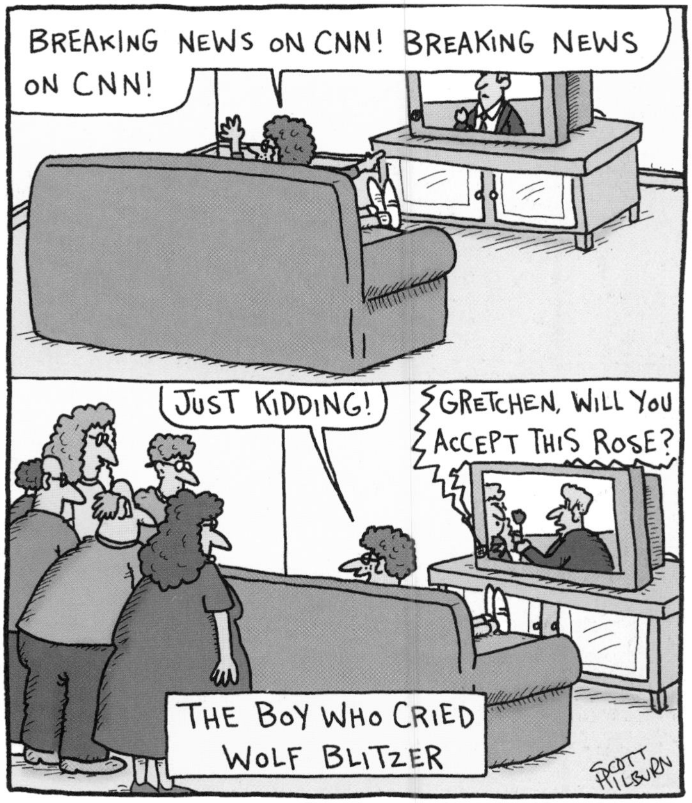
BREAKING NEWS ON CNN! BREAKING NEWS ON CNN!
JUST KIDDING!
GRETCHEN, WILL YOU ACCEPT THIS ROSE?
THE BOY WHO CRIED WOLF BLITZER
SCOTT HILBURN

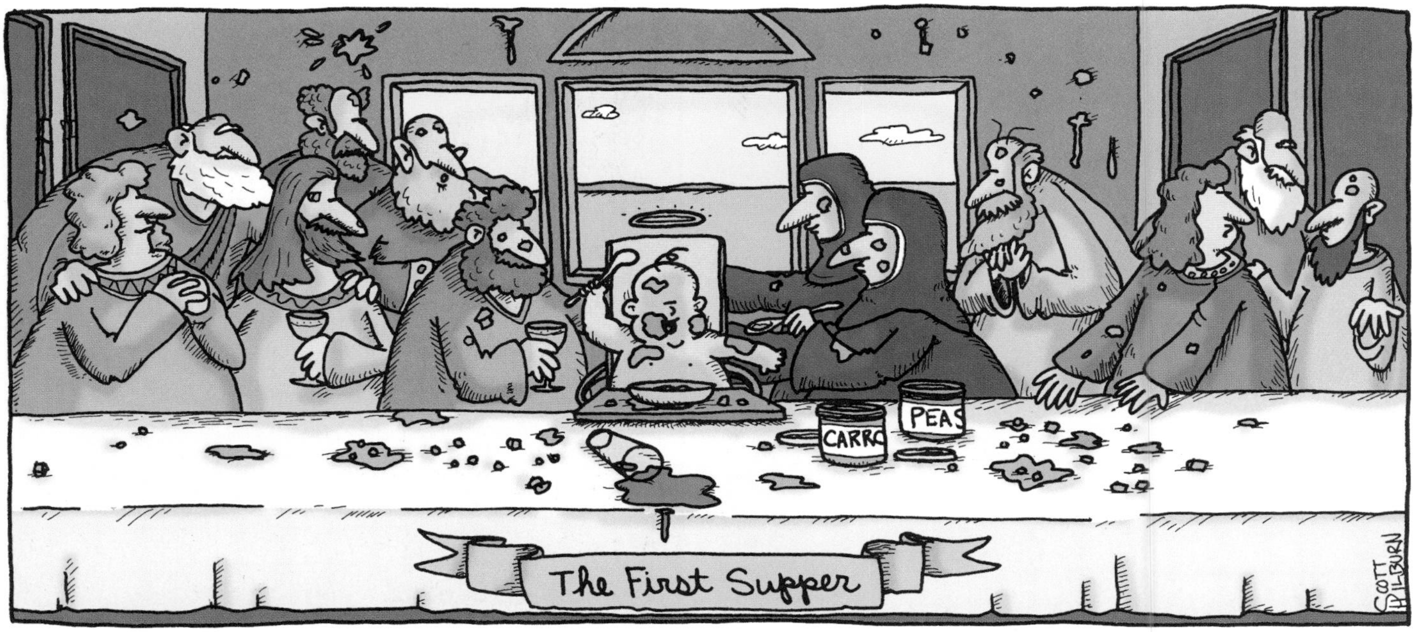
PEAS
CARRO
The First Supper
SCOTT HILBURN

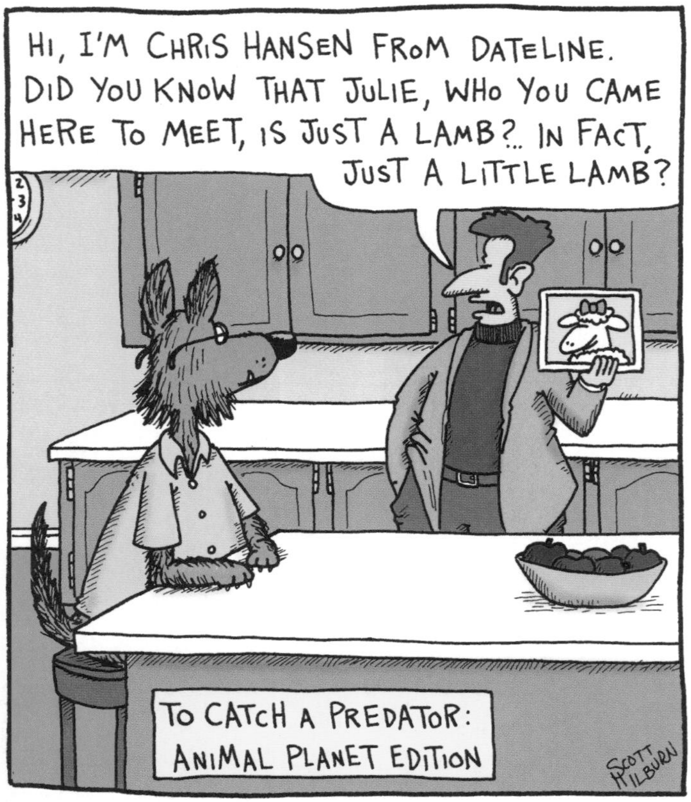
HI, I'M CHRIS HANSEN FROM DATELINE. DID YOU KNOW THAT JULIE, WHO YOU CAME HERE TO MEET, IS JUST A LAMB?... IN FACT, JUST A LITTLE LAMB?
SCOTT HILBURN
TO CATCH A PREDATOR: ANIMAL PLANET EDITION

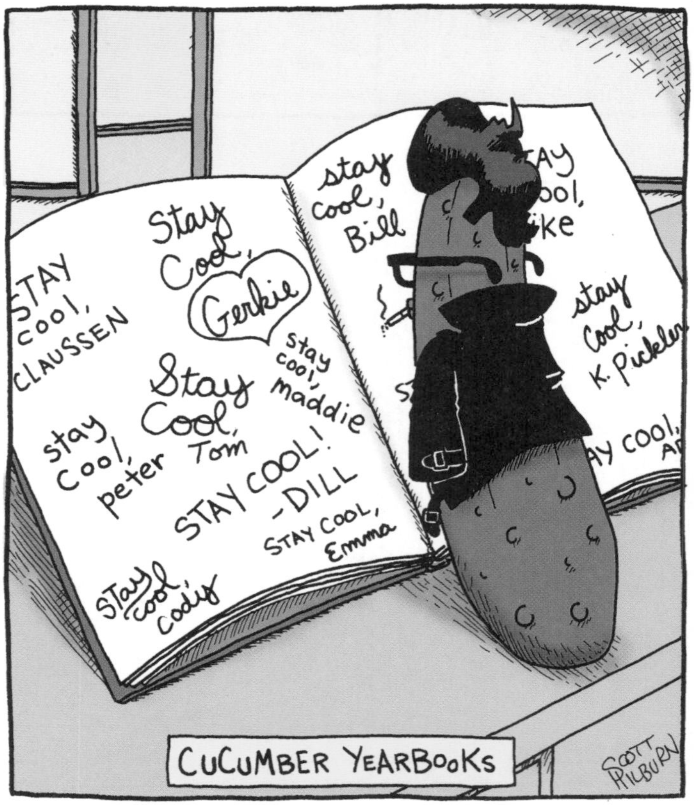
stay cool, Bill
STAY cool, CLAUSSEN
Stay Cool, Gerkie
stay cool, maddie
Stay Cool, Tom
stay cool, peter
STAY COOL! -DILL
STAY COOL, Emma
Stay cool cody
stay cool,
SCOTT HILBURN
CUCUMBER YEARBOOKS

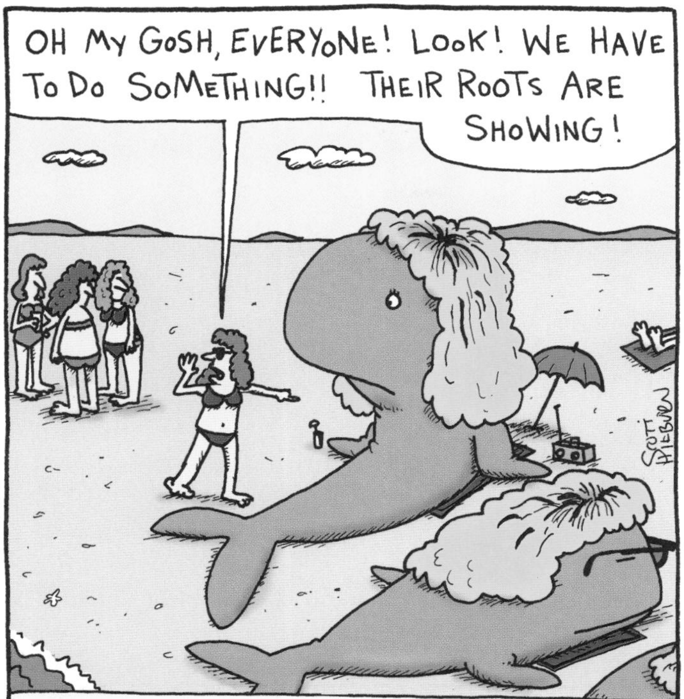
OH MY GOSH, EVERYONE! LOOK! WE HAVE TO DO SOMETHING!! THEIR ROOTS ARE SHOWING!
SCOTT HILBURN
DURING SPRING BREAK, GAIL AND HER COSMETOLOGY CLASSMATES HAPPEN UPON A POD OF BLEACHED WHALES.

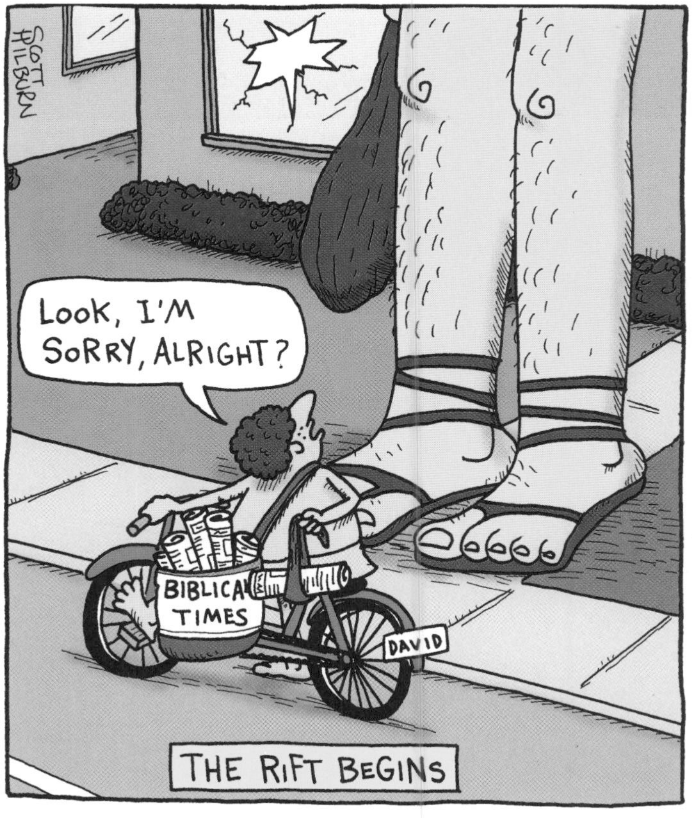
SCOTT HILBURN
LOOK, I'M SORRY, ALRIGHT?
BIBLICAL TIMES
DAVID
THE RIFT BEGINS

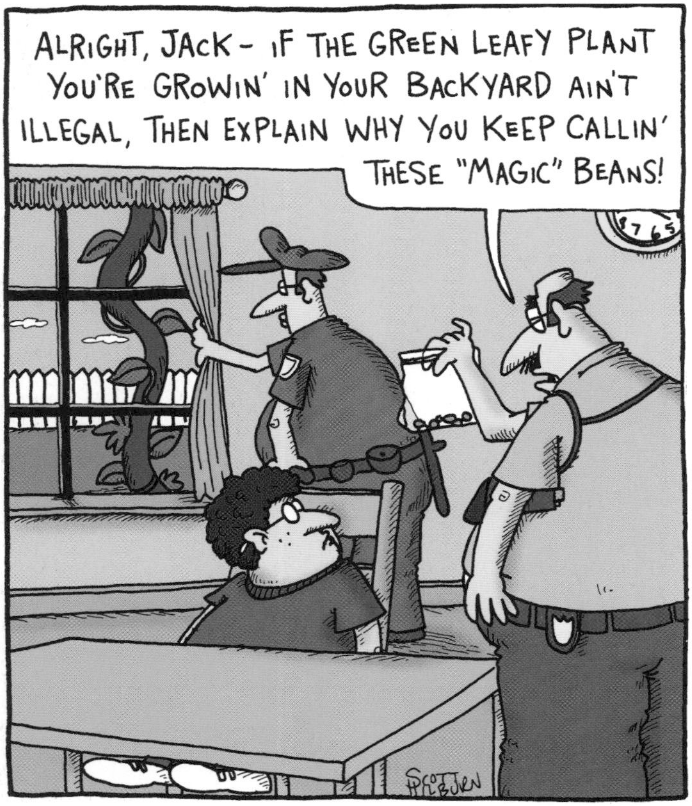
ALRIGHT, JACK - IF THE GREEN LEAFY PLANT YOU'RE GROWIN' IN YOUR BACKYARD AIN'T ILLEGAL, THEN EXPLAIN WHY YOU KEEP CALLIN' THESE "MAGIC" BEANS!
SCOTT HILBURN

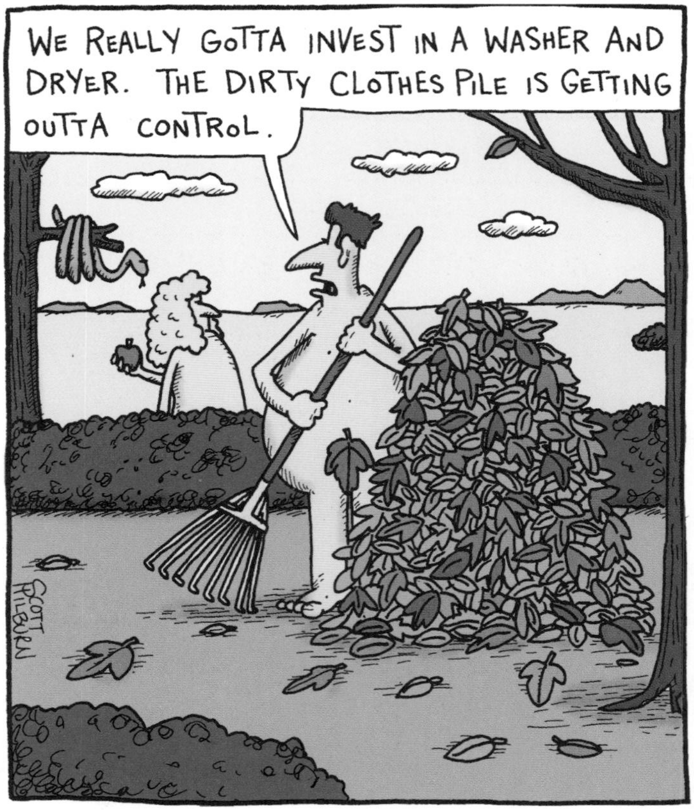
WE REALLY GOTTA INVEST IN A WASHER AND DRYER. THE DIRTY CLOTHES PILE IS GETTING OUTTA CONTROL.
SCOTT HILBURN

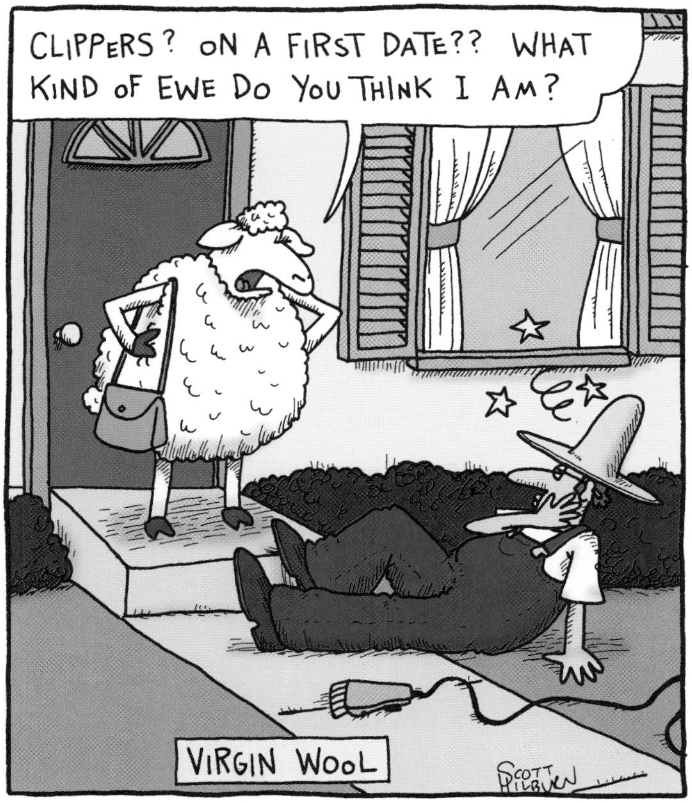
CLIPPERS? ON A FIRST DATE?? WHAT KIND OF EWE DO YOU THINK I AM?
VIRGIN WOOL
SCOTT HILBURN

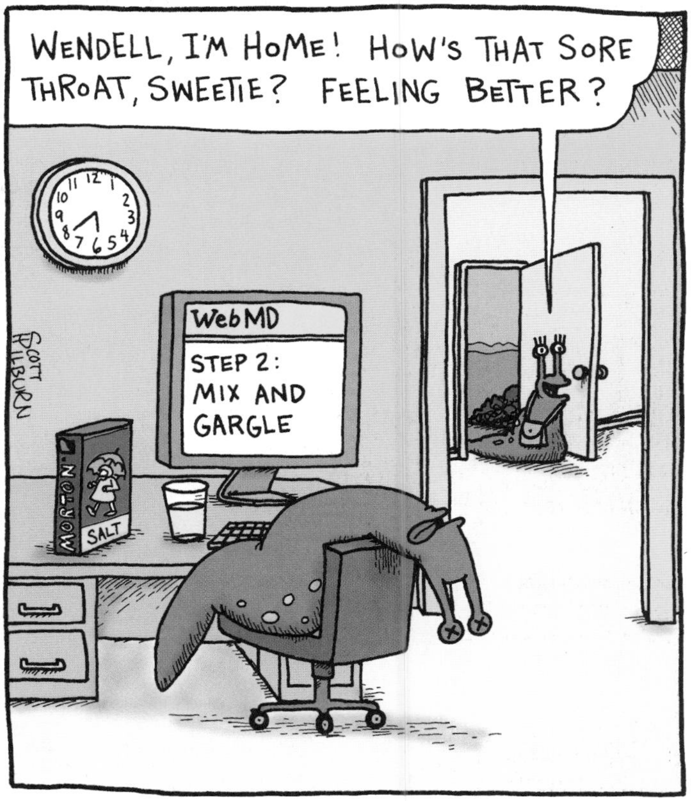
WENDELL, I'M HOME! HOW'S THAT SORE THROAT, SWEETIE? FEELING BETTER?
WebMD
STEP 2: MIX AND GARGLE
MORTON
SALT
SCOTT HILBURN

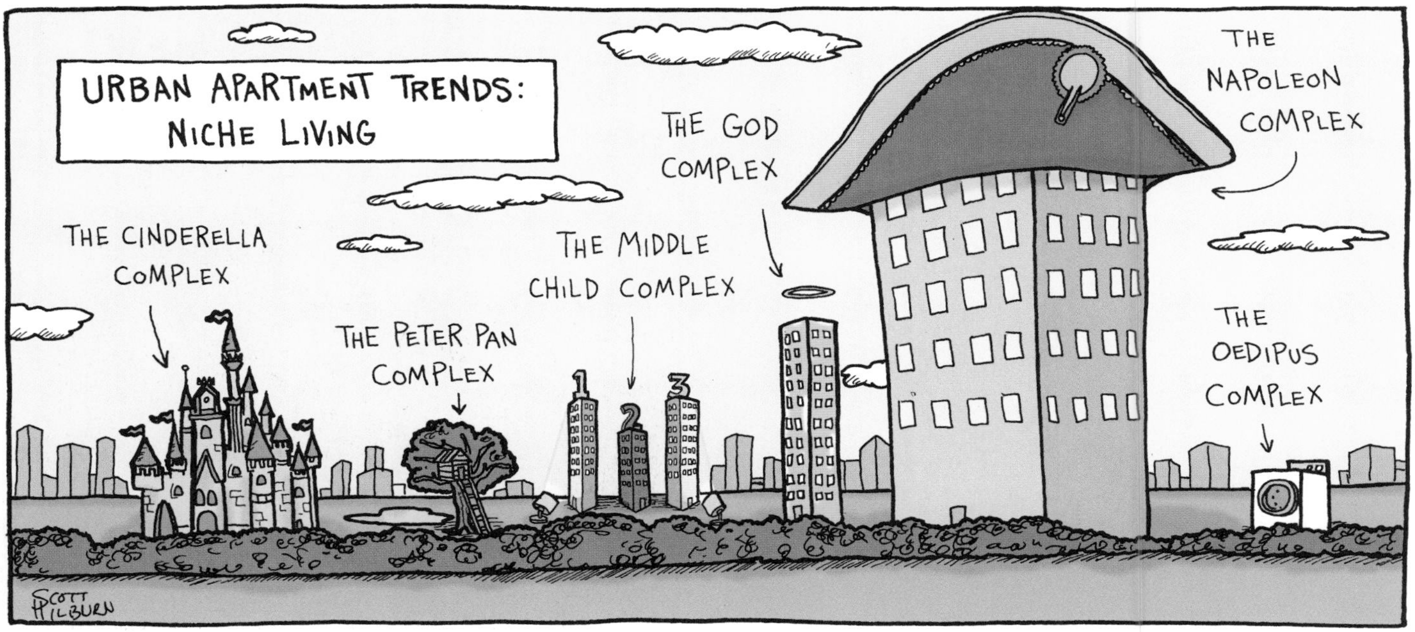
URBAN APARTMENT TRENDS: NICHE LIVING
THE CINDERELLA COMPLEX
THE PETER PAN COMPLEX
THE MIDDLE CHILD COMPLEX
1
2
3
THE GOD COMPLEX
THE NAPOLEON COMPLEX
THE OEDIPUS COMPLEX
SCOTT HILBURN

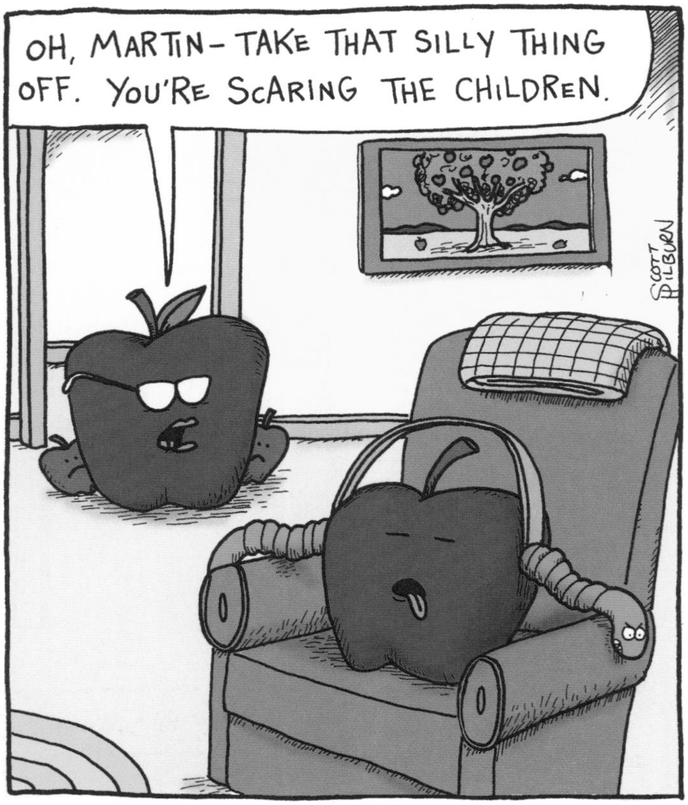
OH, MARTIN- TAKE THAT SILLY THING OFF. YOU'RE SCARING THE CHILDREN.
SCOTT HILBURN

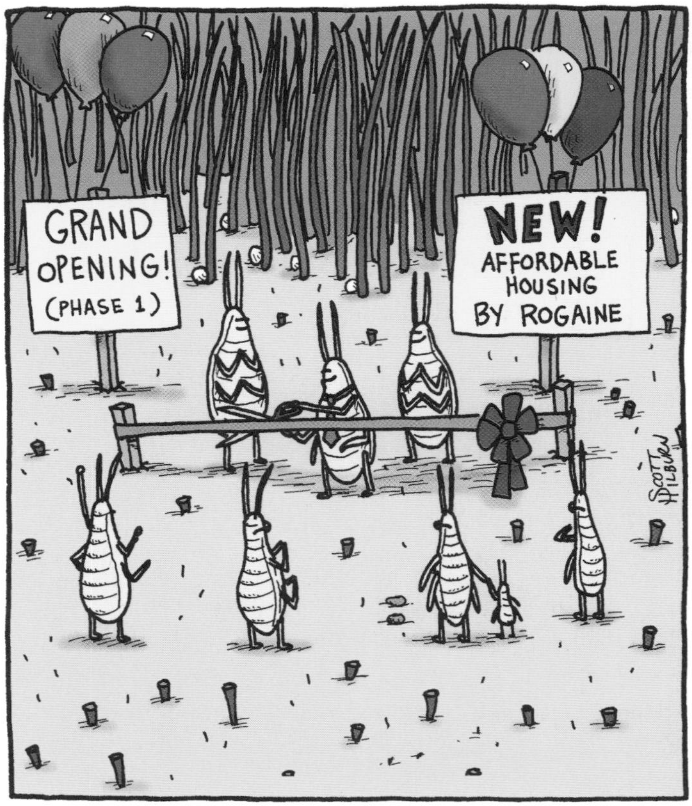
GRAND OPENING! (PHASE 1)
NEW! AFFORDABLE HOUSING BY ROGAINE
SCOTT HILBURN

TRUEMAN DeWAYNE LAFAYETTE: COLLECTOR OF THE IMAGINARY

DANCES WITH WOLVES' LESSER-KNOWN SIBLINGS

BOOGIES WITH ELK

FLIRTS WITH COUGARS

FERTILIZES WITH BEARS

RUNS WITH ELEPHANTS

LEAPFROGS WITH UNICORNS

STAN

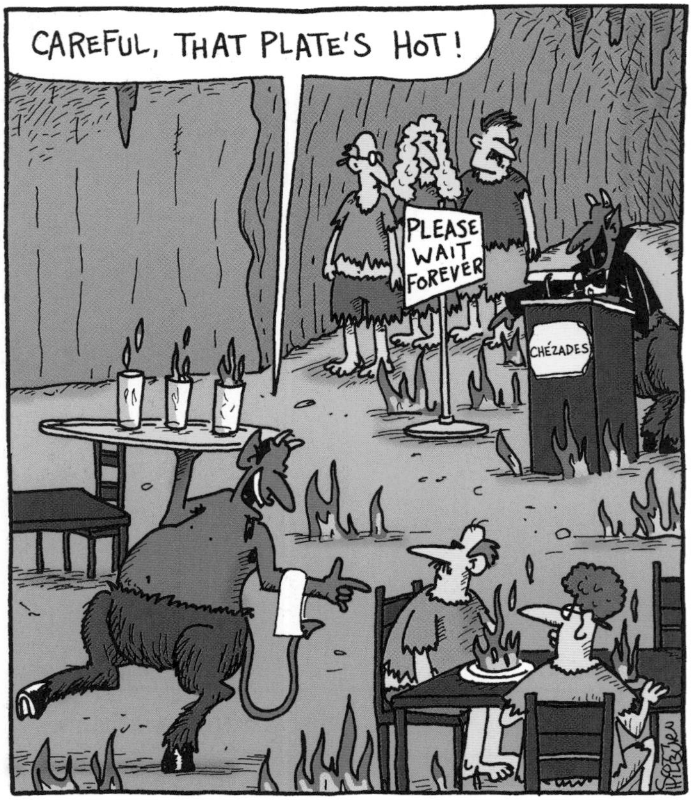
CAREFUL, THAT PLATE'S HOT!
PLEASE WAIT FOREVER
CHÉZADES

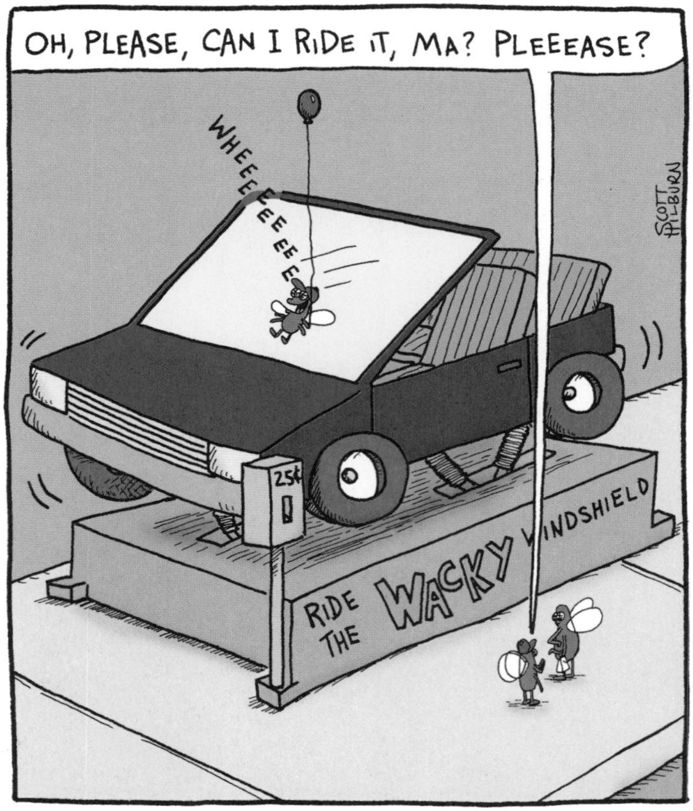
OH, PLEASE, CAN I RIDE IT, MA? PLEEEASE?
WHEEEEEEEEE
25¢
RIDE THE WACKY WINDSHIELD
SCOTT HILBURN

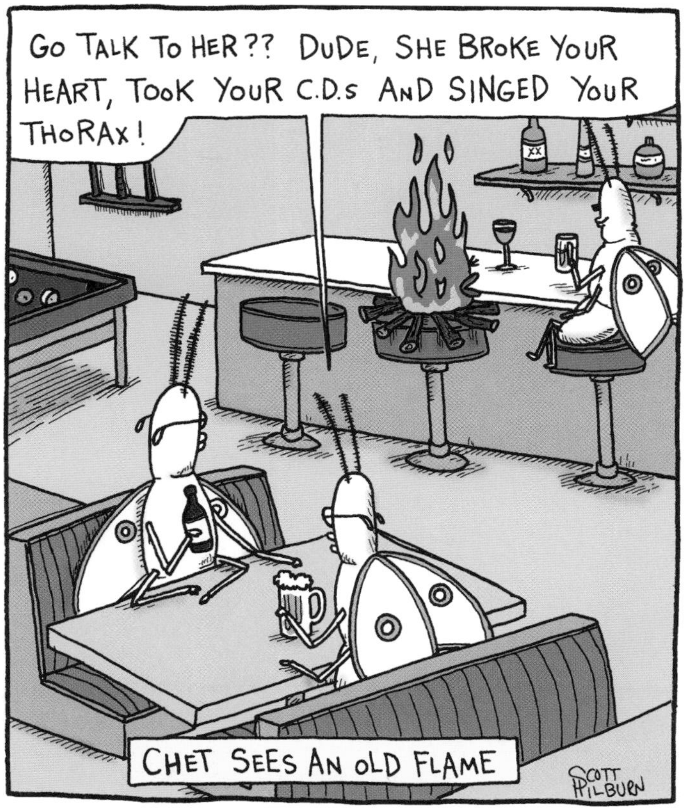
GO TALK TO HER?? DUDE, SHE BROKE YOUR HEART, TOOK YOUR C.D.s AND SINGED YOUR THORAX!
CHET SEES AN OLD FLAME
SCOTT HILBURN

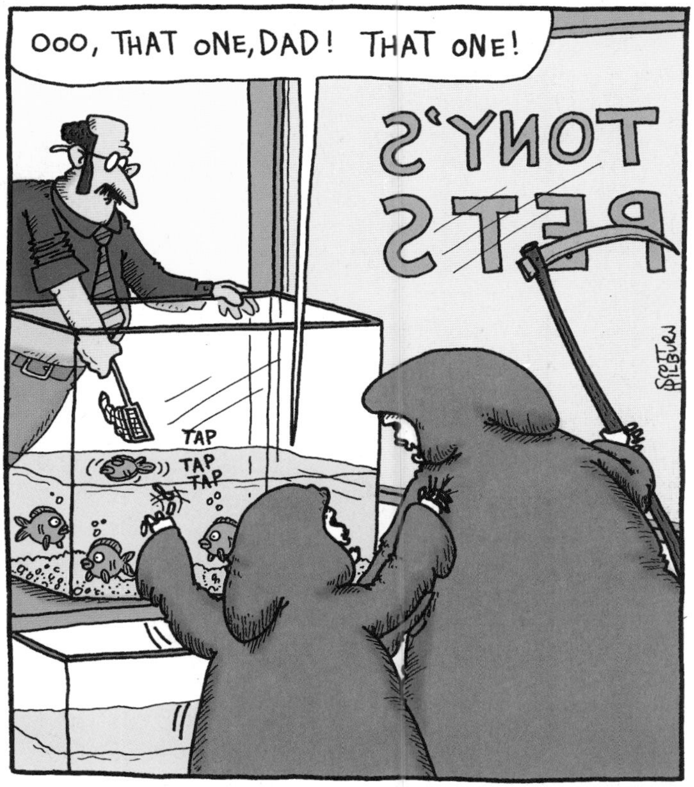
OOO, THAT ONE, DAD! THAT ONE!
TONY'S PETS
TAP
TAP
TAP
SCOTT HILBURN

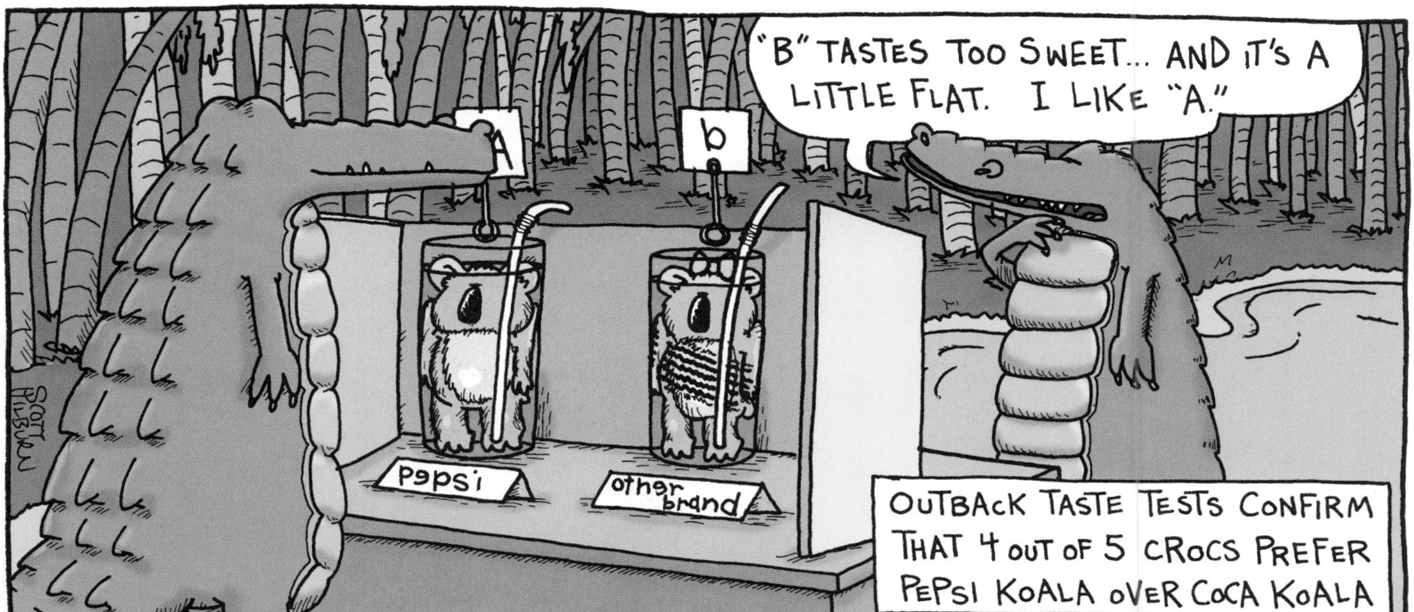
"B" TASTES TOO SWEET... AND IT'S A LITTLE FLAT. I LIKE "A."
A
b
pepsi
other brand
SCOTT HILBURN
OUTBACK TASTE TESTS CONFIRM THAT 4 OUT OF 5 CROCS PREFER PEPSI KOALA OVER COCA KOALA

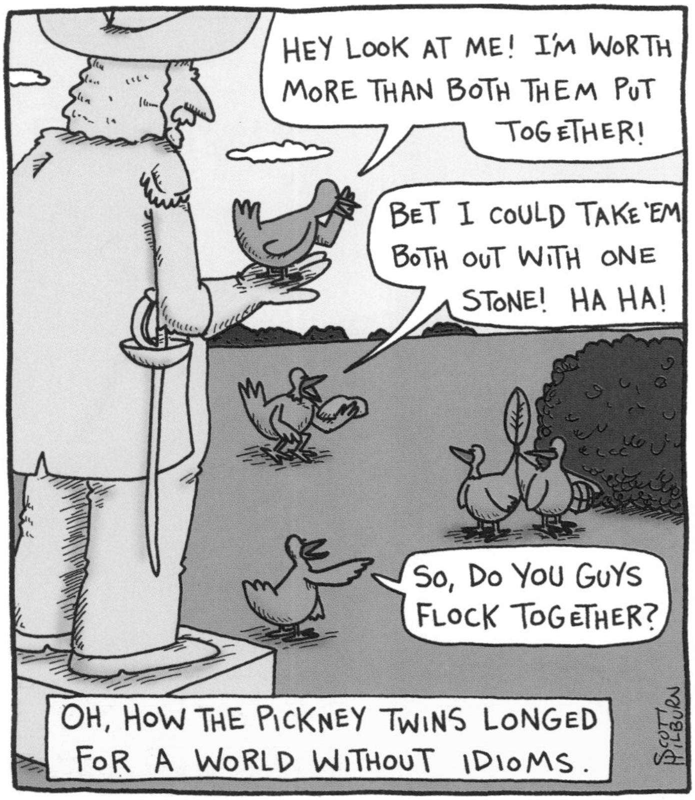
HEY LOOK AT ME! I'M WORTH MORE THAN BOTH THEM PUT TOGETHER!
BET I COULD TAKE 'EM BOTH OUT WITH ONE STONE! HA HA!
SO, DO YOU GUYS FLOCK TOGETHER?
SCOTT HILBURN
OH, HOW THE PICKNEY TWINS LONGED FOR A WORLD WITHOUT IDIOMS.

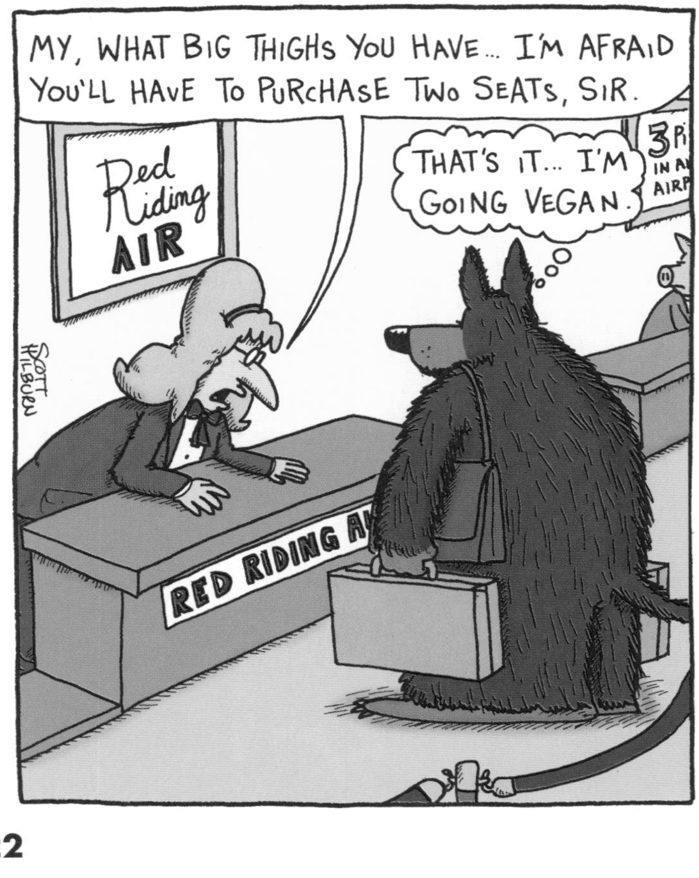
MY, WHAT BIG THIGHS YOU HAVE... I'M AFRAID YOU'LL HAVE TO PURCHASE TWO SEATS, SIR.
Red Riding AIR
THAT'S IT... I'M GOING VEGAN.
SCOTT HILBURN

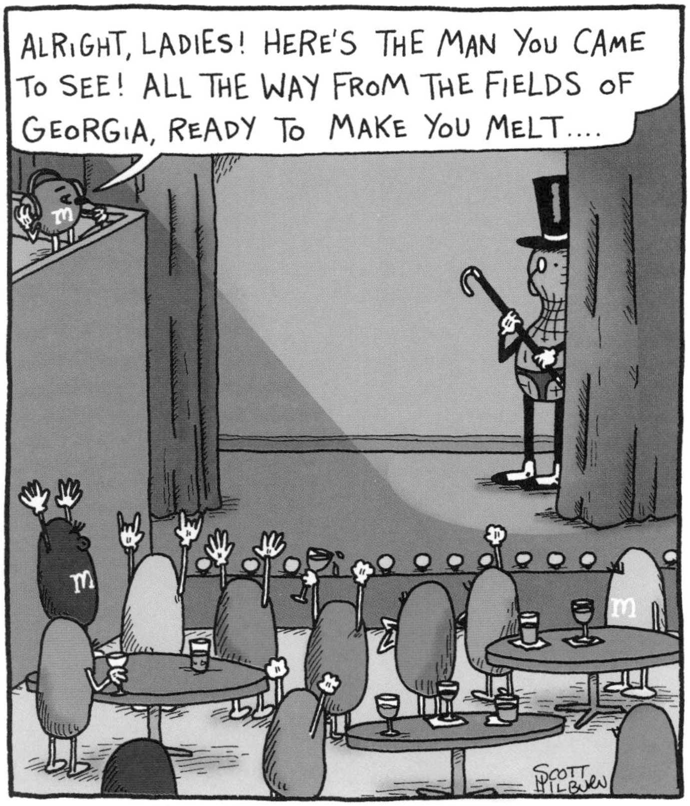
ALRiGHT, LADIES! HERE'S THE MAN YOU CAME TO SEE! ALL THE WAY FROM THE FIELDS OF GEORGIA, READY TO MAKE YOU MELT....
SCOTT HILBURN

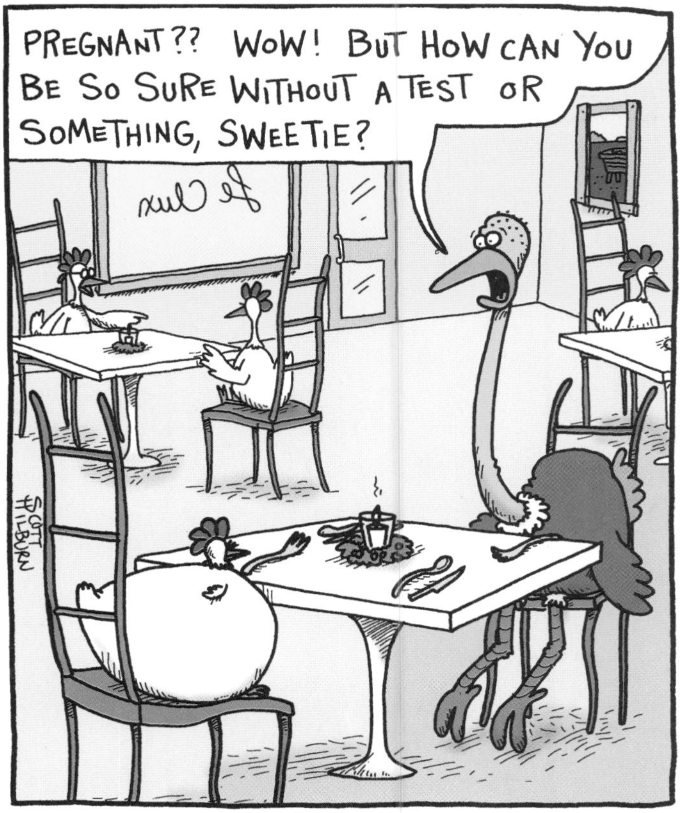
PREGNANT?? WOW! BUT HOW CAN YOU BE SO SURE WITHOUT A TEST OR SOMETHING, SWEETIE?
SCOTT HILBURN

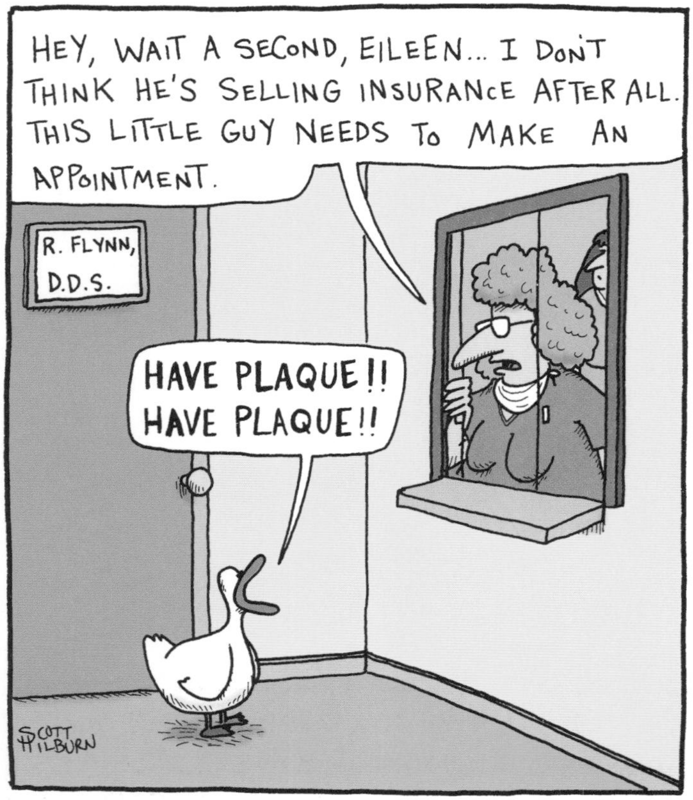
HEY, WAIT A SECOND, EILEEN... I DON'T THINK HE'S SELLING INSURANCE AFTER ALL. THIS LITTLE GUY NEEDS TO MAKE AN APPOINTMENT.
R. FLYNN, D.D.S.
HAVE PLAQUE!! HAVE PLAQUE!!
SCOTT HILBURN

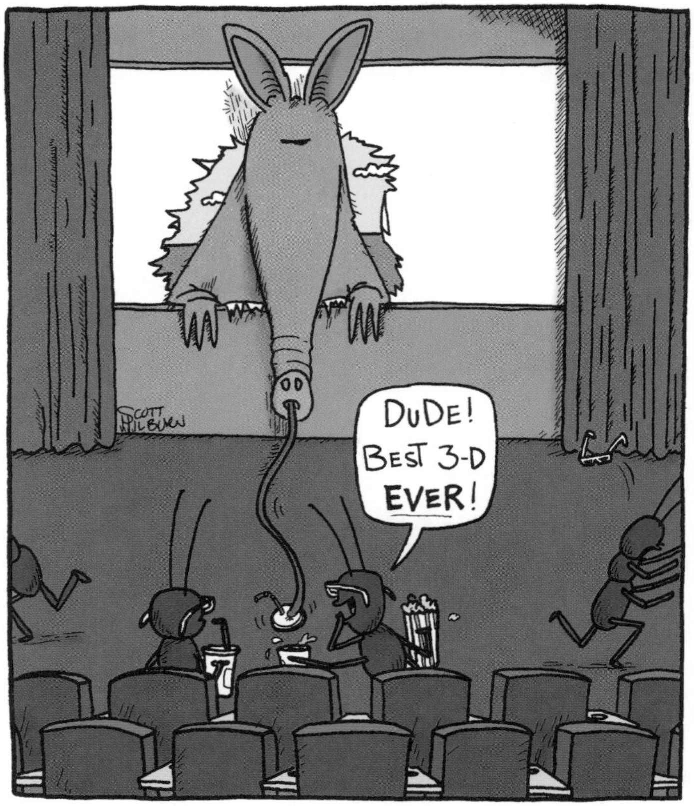
DUDE! BEST 3-D EVER!
SCOTT HILBURN

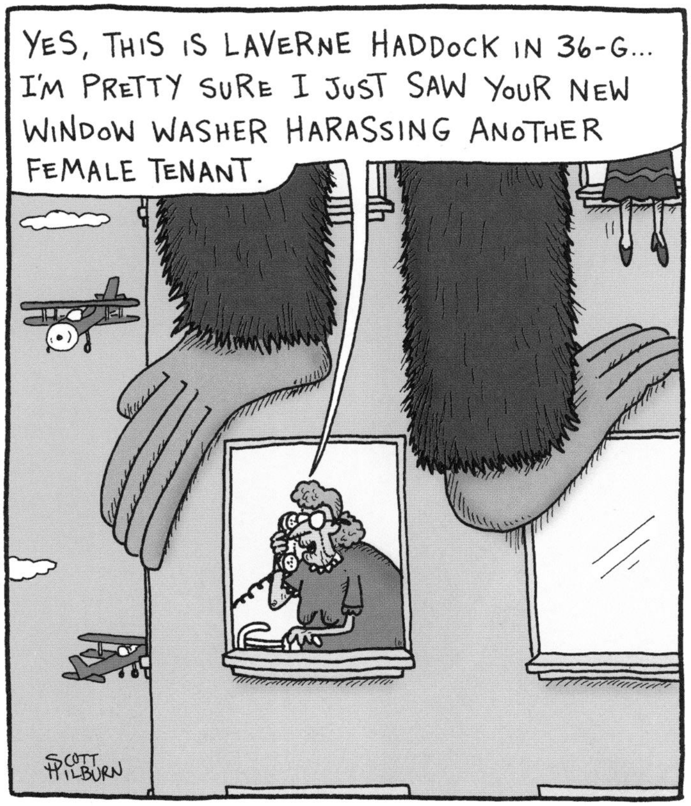
YES, THIS IS LAVERNE HADDOCK IN 36-G... I'M PRETTY SURE I JUST SAW YOUR NEW WINDOW WASHER HARASSING ANOTHER FEMALE TENANT.
SCOTT HILBURN

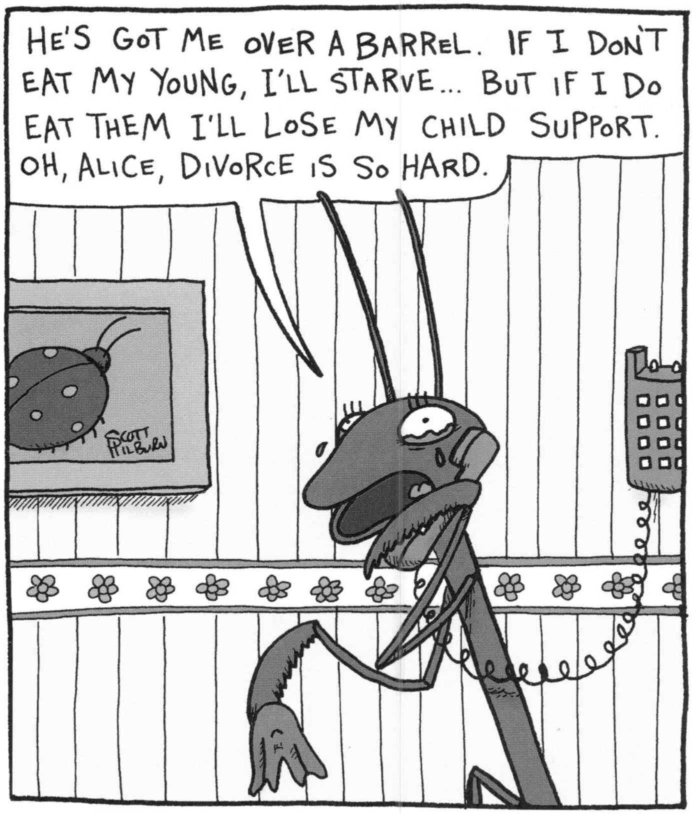
HE'S GOT ME OVER A BARREL. IF I DON'T EAT MY YOUNG, I'LL STARVE... BUT IF I DO EAT THEM I'LL LOSE MY CHILD SUPPORT. OH, ALICE, DIVORCE IS SO HARD.
SCOTT HILBURN

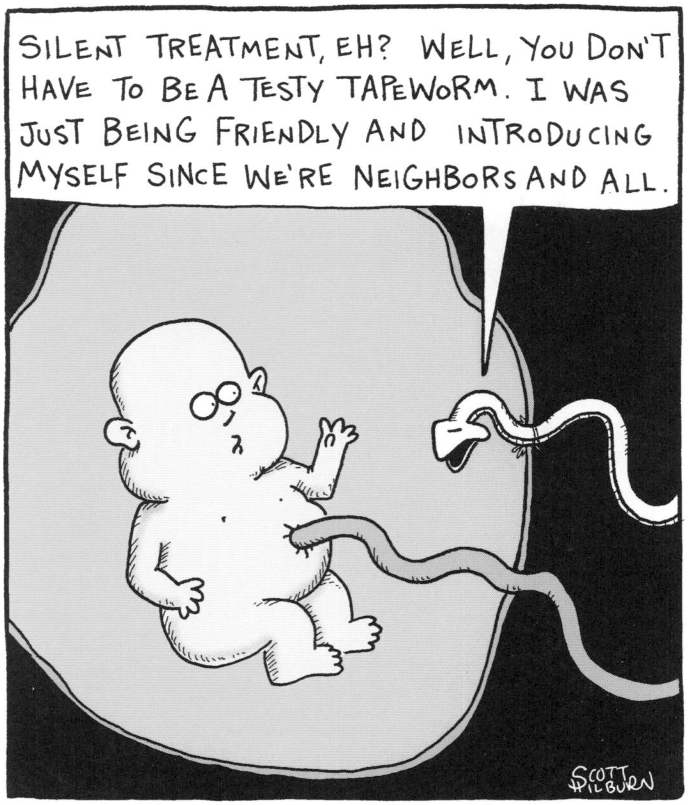
SILENT TREATMENT, EH? WELL, YOU DON'T HAVE TO BE A TESTY TAPEWORM. I WAS JUST BEING FRIENDLY AND INTRODUCING MYSELF SINCE WE'RE NEIGHBORS AND ALL.
SCOTT HILBURN

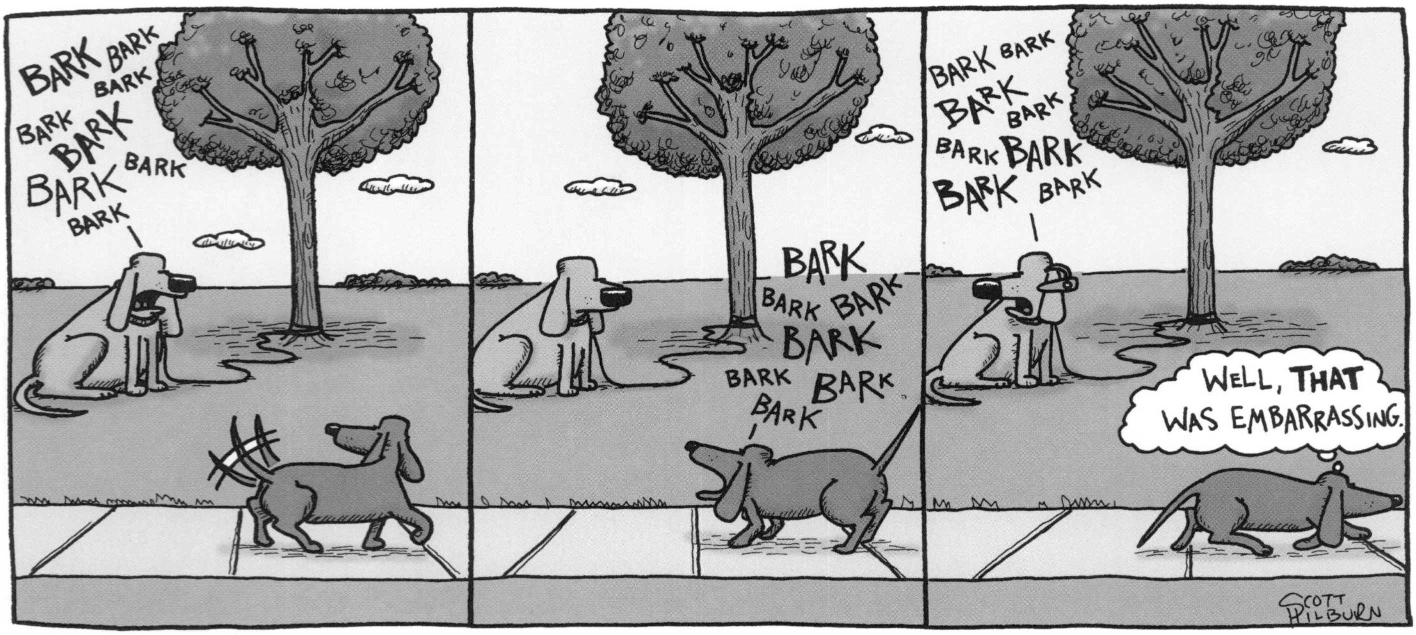
BARK BARK BARK BARK BARK BARK BARK BARK
BARK BARK BARK BARK BARK BARK BARK
BARK BARK BARK BARK BARK BARK BARK BARK
WELL, THAT WAS EMBARRASSING.
SCOTT HILBURN